How to Be a Tudor

How to Be a Tudor

A Dawn-to-Dusk Guide to Tudor Life

RUTH GOODMAN

LIVERIGHT PUBLISHING CORPORATION
A Division of W. W. Norton & Company
Independent Publishers Since 1923
New York • London

For information about permission to reproduce selections from this book, write to
Permissions, Liveright Publishing Corporation, a division of W. W. Norton & Company, Inc.,
500 Fifth Avenue, New York, NY 10110

For information about special discounts for bulk purchases, please contact
W. W. Norton Special Sales at specialsales@wwnorton.com or 800-233-4830

Manufacturing by Quad Graphics Fairfield

ISBN 978-1-63149-139-9

Liveright Publishing Corporation, 500 Fifth Avenue, New York, N.Y. 10110
www.wwnorton.com
W. W. Norton & Company Ltd., Castle House, 75/76 Wells Street, London W1T 3QT

1 2 3 4 5 6 7 8 9 0

To Claire and Geoff Steeley,
who taught me to truly look at the world around me

Contents

Introduction

Trying to understand the trials and tribulations of ordinary Tudor life has been my passion for the last twenty-five years. There are other periods of history that I have an interest in, but in truth my heart lies somewhere in the middle of Elizabeth I's reign. I am both constantly delighted with the 'otherness' of Tudor thinking and beguiled by the echoes that have slipped through into modern life, from the belief that redheads have hot tempers to the order in which we eat our meals, with starters, mains and desserts to follow. To get the chance to write some of it down and share my love for all things sixteenth-century has therefore been a delight, rather like being let loose in the sweet shop.

The Tudor era is a long and complicated one, encompassing some of the greatest changes in our history, and no book can hope to tell the truth about all the lives lived throughout it. This, then, is necessarily a series of snapshots of the daily realities of some of the people, some of the time, but for all its incompleteness it is still a heartfelt attempt to understand the practicalities, thoughts and difficulties of our forebears.

To set the scene, in 1485 when Henry Tudor seized the throne, there were under two million people in England and perhaps another half a million in Wales (figures for Scotland and Ireland are almost entirely conjectural). By the time his granddaughter Elizabeth I died in 1603, the population of England and Wales combined had doubled to around four million. More than 90 per cent of the population lived in rural areas. London boasted a population of no more than 50,000 at the start of the period but quadrupled in size to 200,000 by the end, and at all times it contained around half of the entire urban population. This small but energetic population was to become a cultural powerhouse whose ideas and way of life were to influence the subsequent history not just of Britain but of the world.

Throughout this book I have used the term 'Britain' as a loose cultural concept, not a political reality. Scotland was an independent nation; Wales was controlled by England throughout the period but the two nations only became legally united in 1536; and English control over Ireland was distant, patchy and fraught. Politically it makes more sense to speak only of England and Wales as an effective power bloc, and when you start to search through the surviving evidence there is a temptation to speak only of England, and southern England at that, where the vast bulk of available information is concentrated. Yet I feel that in much of Wales and at least in some parts of Ireland and indeed Scotland cultural connections and shared ways of life were present, and to write only of England would be quite misleading.

The rural majority were socially organized according to land holdings. The aristocracy at the top of the tree – limited to those holding titles as peers of the realm – owned several large estates, maintained households of up to 150 people and moved periodically between their houses on each estate and a town house in London. Theirs was a very public life of politics and power. Beneath them sat the gentry, whose land holdings were generally smaller and more concentrated geographically. Officially a gentleman was someone who had the right to a coat of arms, but in practice a gentleman was anyone who lived according to generally accepted standards, engaging in no productive labour, owning and renting out land for others to work, maintaining a suitable-sized house, wearing suitable clothing, and entertaining on a suitable scale. Those who were called gentlemen by their neighbours boasted homes of six or more rooms, had several servants whose main focus was personal and domestic service, dressed in the best woollen broadcloths trimmed with silks and furs, sat down to three or four dishes of meat at dinner, and expected to lead local society and hold public office.

Far more numerous were the yeomen. Their land was often rented from those above them, though many owned portions as well, and they farmed it all themselves. In terms of pure wealth, some were richer than some of the gentlemen, but theirs was a life of active involvement on the land. Most of their servants were not of a personal or domestic nature, but farm servants helping to till the soil and care for livestock. Some did hold junior public positions such as churchwarden or constable, but essentially they were prosperous farmers with four- or five-room houses, good wool clothing and simple but hearty dinners.

Next came the husbandmen, farming their rented lands on a much smaller scale. Their homes were generally two-room affairs and most of the labour came purely from within the family. They were the most numerous of all the groups and their lives held precious few luxuries.

Below them were the labourers who held no land at all but had to hire themselves out to their socially superior neighbours for a daily wage. As our period moves forward, their numbers gradually grew as husbandmen increasingly struggled to maintain an independent hold on the land and joined their ranks. It was a precarious life and one generally lived in single-room dwellings with a diet dominated by bread and little else.

For our tiny urban population the hierarchy was a little different, with international merchants occupying the top spots, serving as mayors, living in large, well-furnished and well-staffed town houses, occasionally hobnobbing with the landed elite. Other merchants formed the next layer down, employing apprentices and servants and living a life that was a little more comfortable, but of a similar social level to that of yeomen.

Craftsmen occupied the next slot, aided by their apprentices and family, with typically one or two rooms in addition to a workshop. And, just as in the countryside, the bottom of the pile consisted of labourers paid by the day.

The Tudor economy was essentially a money economy, barter being no more common than in our own times, but what it could buy was fundamentally different. Within a twenty-first-century household, food costs consume typically around 17 per cent of the total income, but within a Tudor context food dominated most people's expenses, taking around 80 per cent. To understand what money meant to a craftsman contemplating a new coat, it is necessary to think more in terms of disposable income, what was left once the family were fed and the rent paid. For a husbandman's wife, the decision whether to buy in ale, make it herself or let the family make do with water was one that required weighing one set of monetary needs against another, with the margins tipping the balance. At the start of our period a skilled man could command a wage of 4d a day when he was in work, and women could bring in about half that. By the end of the era a skilled wage was more usually 6d. These figures represented the basic survival level for a small family in regular work, enough to eat a plain, cheap diet, but not much more. It is against this subsistence level of financial resources that prices and resources can be gauged.

This then was the structure within which people had to negotiate a livelihood and find a sense of self.

There are many books and studies based on the lives of the Tudor elite, upon the powerful and well-documented, but my interest has always been bound up with the more humble sections of society. As a fairly ordinary person myself who needs to eat, sleep and change the occasional nappy, I wanted from the beginning to know how people coped day to day, to know what resources they really had at their disposal, what skills they needed to acquire and what it all felt like. Twenty-five years ago I could find no book to tell me, and even now when social history receives far more academic attention than before, information is still thin on the ground. So I set out to try and work it out for myself: hunting up period recipes and trying them out; learning to manage fires and skin rabbits; standing on one foot with a dance manual in one hand, trying to make sense of where my next move should be. The more I experimented, the more information I began to find within the period texts that I was looking at. Things that I had just skimmed past in the reading became quite critical in practice, prompting more questions and very much more intense research. Many repeated statements about Tudor life, quoted in very respectable works, turned out to be pure fantasy.

Take for example the assertion that Tudor food was all highly spiced in order to disguise the taste of bad meat. It has thankfully now faded from view as a commonly repeated 'fact', but for many years appeared in materials for school use and even within the preambles of some of our most respected historians' works. A little practical thought quickly points out that nothing disguises the taste of bad meat, that spices were considerably more expensive than a new fresh piece of meat, and that rotten meat makes you sick regardless of its taste. If received wisdom was wrong and food was not highly spiced for disguising taste, was it highly spiced at all? Such thoughts sent me back to look at the import records to see how much spice was entering the country, and at the few surviving household accounts to see how much was bought; and to look again at prices and wages, and to begin to treat the recipe books as well as oft-repeated 'truths' with a pinch of salt. These were clearly not records of diet but rather aspirational documents, concentrating upon all that was most luxurious, desirable and fashionable. If I wanted to know about what people ate, how they cooked it and what it tasted like, I was going to have to look a lot further than the recipes.

I found myself increasingly drawn into the web of life, the way everything connected, the interplay between the physical world, ideas, beliefs and practice. Why on earth, for example, would someone believe that tying herrings to the soles of the feet would cure insomnia? Would they really do it and could it possibly work? I found that it was the whole lifestyle that interested me, which is why this book is a broad gallop through a typical day, touching upon the different threads that made up the Tudor way of life, a taste of the ordinary that seems to us so extraordinary.

Wills and probate inventories have been invaluable in hunting out the commonplace. While they have their shortcomings as historical sources, rarely including those at the bottom and seriously underrepresenting women, they do give a feel for what resources were usual and point out the contrasts in the lives of different social groups and geographical locations. Sometimes they even give us a glimpse of a person's thoughts, feelings and family relationships, such as the baker John Abelson of Olney, Buckinghamshire, who made provision for his wife and his six children, from mention of a grown-up son now in London to his daughter Elizabeth 'being an innocent'. The phrase 'being an innocent' points to her as being mentally handicapped, and another of her brothers is left a substantial holding on condition that he gives her a permanent home. Court records meanwhile contain snapshots of lives at crisis point, when people's beliefs and assumptions as well as their behaviour come under the spotlight. Testimony can often record their very words. Coroners' records talk of the accidents and personal conflicts that beset daily life. Books, pamphlets and ballad sheets give us an insight into the thought processes of the more educated and masculine portion of society, and their moans and diatribes hint at the differing values and experiences of others. Even tax records have their place in outlining daily habits, such as the prevalence of cheap combs and the scarcity of pepper.

I have attempted many aspects of the Tudor life, often repeatedly as I try to hone my skills and experiment with different interpretations of the evidence that I am seeking to understand. I don't claim to have cracked it, but I do have a very much fuller idea of Tudor realities now than I did when I started all those years ago. It's an ongoing journey and one that I would love to share with you.

1.   At Cock's Crow

First in a mornyng whan thou arte waken and purpose to ryse, lyfte up thy hande and blesse the, and make a sygne of the holy crosse, In nomine patris et filii et spiritus sancti, Amen. In the name of the father, the sonne, and the holy gooste. And if thou say a pater noster, an Ave and a crede, and remember thy maker, thou shalt spede moch the better.

John Fitzherbert, *The Boke of Husbandry* (1533)

Just before dawn the cockerels began their morning chorus and people clambered out of bed. Few were far from a farmyard alarm clock. The vast majority of people lived a rural life. Towns were generally small and interspersed with agricultural spaces, and huge numbers of urban dwellers still kept their own chickens and pigs in the yard out the back. Cattle and sheep grazed on town commons, and a cockerel and his hens could pick a free living on every dungheap, whether it was in the stable yard of an inn or on the edge of the weekly livestock market. Only London and perhaps Norwich and Bristol could truly claim to have a population undisturbed by the morning crowing of farmyard cocks.

Cockerels like to begin their labours at the very first hint of a lightening in the sky, long before the first rays break over the horizon. Those people who waited for the initial beams of light were known as 'slugabeds', and likely to find their livestock restless and loudly complaining by the time they got to them. Most people rose as the sky paled, to the sounds of birds and animals stirring. Summer days began at 4 a.m. therefore, while deep in the depths of winter there was little point in rising in the pitch black of night, delaying the business of the day to the much later hour of 7 a.m.

Window glass was still a luxury product, the preserve of the gentry and the richer sorts of merchants, so for the majority of the population the first grey of predawn would have made its way in through an oiled cloth shutter that kept the rain and the worst of the wind out while letting some light through. Some people had wooden shutters, however, which were more secure and kept all but the thinnest fingers of light out.

Yet if window glass was uncommon, curtains at the window were even rarer. Curtains were not for windows, they were for beds. The owner of a curtained bed was lucky indeed. A room within a room – warm, dark and private – a four-poster, curtained and canopied bed was one of the most sought after and highly prized household items in Tudor times. After bequests of landholdings and cash, beds were often the very first thing upon the minds of those making their wills. Shakespeare's famous bequest of his second-best bed to his wife, Anne, is sometimes seen as a slight, a symbol of a broken relationship, but I doubt that Anne or anyone else in the family saw it like that. Although his best bed went to his married daughter, he made sure that his wife would be warm and comfortable in her later years.

Many people have spent a night in a four-poster bed at a hotel, and some may have one at home, but they are unlikely to have got the full benefit from it within a modern building. Think instead of a Tudor room, which would have been draughty even if there was glass in the window frame. Tudor houses rarely had corridors, and access to rooms was generally through other rooms, so people would wander through now and again, and servants and children would be asleep on other beds within the same room. Even within larger, wealthier homes, few people had a room to themselves. With no separate servants' quarters (that was a later architectural development), some of the largest houses had the most crowded bedrooms. A house's occupants were more likely to be divided according to sex rather than social class, with male children and servants in one room and female children and servants in another. You, meanwhile, are tucked up inside your own private tent of thick, usually woollen, curtains, which muffle the sounds of other people's snores, allow a fug of warmth to build overnight, and keep away prying eyes and ears.

Beds came in a range of shapes, sizes and materials, and I have slept in them all: simple piles of straw on earthen floors; sacks of straw on raised sleeping platforms; pieces of rush matting; wooden box beds; rope-strung truckle beds (small bedsteads on wheels that could be moved out of the way during the day, beneath larger bedsteads); hay mattresses, flock or wool mattresses and feather beds. Some had just blankets, while others had sheets, pillows, bolsters and coverlets. Some of the four-posters came with wooden ceilings (generally called 'testers'), and some with cloth tops. I have used such beds at all times of year, in temperatures ranging from twenty-eight degrees Centigrade to minus ten, in the snow and frost as well as the height of summer, alone and in company. I can confidently state that I understand why so many Tudor people gave beds a central position in their thoughts.

The more elaborate the bed, the more expensive it was, and beds belonging to the nobility – with four-post testers, silken hangings, multiple mattresses, fine linen sheets and ample sumptuous coverings – could be worth more than a small-scale farmer's entire holding. Yeomen and husbandmen living and working upon the land generally made do with a wooden bedstead and a flock or wool mattress, while their labourers and servants were lucky to be up off the floor. A simple loose pile of straw formed the bedding of many of the landless, especially at the beginning of the period.

Sleeping in a loose pile of straw upon an earthen floor in your clothes is fine when the straw is clean and well fluffed up, and there is plenty of it, at least for a night or two. But it is not a good long-term solution. Mice and rats were common, and loose straw can work its way between every layer of clothing. After a few days the straw begins to break into short lengths and splinters, which irritate the skin far more. The dust can cause problems for many people, and it is hard to keep yourself clean. Simply putting the straw into a closely woven sack, and sleeping on that, works much better so long as you give the sack a really good shake each day. If you fail to look after your bed, it can quickly become compacted and lumpy.

The word 'bed' in Tudor England meant something close to what we today mean by the word 'mattress', so this straw-filled sack was known as a straw bed in its own right. A wooden frame to raise it off the floor was an additional refinement, listed in inventories and wills as a bedstead. Hay-filled beds are far more comfortable than straw beds, as hay is a softer, finer material, and there are even differences between types of straw. Barley straw is more comfortable than wheat straw, for example.

Many people carefully selected not just the main bulk of the straw, but also additional stuffing from the straw of particular plants to aid a good night's sleep. A whole family of plants has the common name 'bedstraw' for precisely this reason. Lady's bedstraw, or *Galium verum*, was considered to be the finest. Not only is it very soft to sleep on, but it smells of freshly mown hay even when dry and old, and it helps to deter insects, in particular fleas and body lice. If such insects were a major problem and lady's bedstraw was simply not powerful enough to ensure nocturnal safety, then small amounts of dried wormwood were effective, if smelly. Changing the bed regularly – emptying out the old straw and refilling with fresh – also helped with both comfort and hygiene. According to the medical theory of the time (and something that is also believed today), lavender was good at promoting sleep, so a handful of dried lavender among the straw at the head end of the bed was also a good idea.

At the beginning of the Tudor period many people didn't even have a straw bed of their own but simply lay down upon the floor. This is not quite as grim as it sounds, however. Many homes still used loose rushes in a deep layer as a floor covering, which removed the necessity for furniture. In addition, domestic buildings were mostly heated by open hearths in the very centre of the room, which allowed the smoke of the fire to make its own way up and out. These central hearths were good at heating the indoor space, with none of the energy being lost up a chimney (chimneys had yet to make much impact on ordinary life, and in 1500 were still largely confined to stone-built castles and monasteries). Hearths were also convenient for cooking upon, allowing 360-degree access. However, the smoke did tend to hang in the air. The higher up you were, the more smoke there was. Spend time in such a building with the fire lit and you'll soon notice that there is a distinct smoke horizon below which the air is clear and breathable and above which it is not. Life, then, must be lived beneath the smoke layer. Furniture that raises you up is not helpful; you are better off living on the floor, so that floor needs to be warm, dry and comfortable to sit and sleep upon.

There are plenty of references to the strewing of rushes upon floors, from Thomas Tusser's *A Hundreth Good Pointes of Husbandrie* (1557) back to thirteenth-century poems and on to the plays of Shakespeare. In 1515 the Dutch humanist Desiderius Erasmus wrote in a letter that the floors of English houses 'are, in general, laid with white clay, and are covered with rushes, occasionally renewed, but so imperfectly that the bottom layer is left undisturbed, sometimes for twenty years, harbouring expectoration, vomiting, the leakage of dogs and men, ale droppings, scraps of fish and other abominations not fit to be mentioned'. If you can accept that this is a man ranting about foreign customs – he goes on to make a huge fuss about the disgusting, unhealthy damp air in England – then it sounds much like a description of modern fitted carpets. The top surface is regularly cleaned, but drinks do get spilled, accidents from pets and children do happen, and the carpet itself carries on getting nastier and nastier at its base. But exactly how well (or poorly) strewn rushes work in practice is something that I have learnt a lot about from experimentation. The earliest trial I was involved in was at the Globe Theatre. There are accounts from Tudor times of the London stages being strewn with rushes. Inspired by these records, we bought fresh rushes, at considerable cost, and scattered them upon the wooden stage. It soon became clear that the rushes were problematic, however: the long stems became caught up in the skirts of the men playing female characters. The rushes were then cut into shorter lengths, which did help, but the actors still found the surface difficult to move around on. We talked about whether the rushes were spread too thinly, and if there needed to be an edge, rather like a kerb, to contain them, but budgets did not allow us to experiment any further.

My chance to try again with rushes came during the making of a programme about castle building. I had a one-room, timber-framed house to work with, an earthen floor, a central hearth, and a nearby marshy area where rushes grew. I found that they performed best when laid in bundles rather than as individual stems, and that the layer needed to be a minimum of two inches thick if the rushes were to stay put and form a consolidated surface. With walls all around, the rushes were contained and much more stable than they were on the theatre stage; I never had any problem with them becoming caught up in my skirts. Left to dry, the rushes turned straw yellow and eventually began to fray and break down into dusty, splintery pieces, but if they were occasionally dampened they kept their suppleness, their pale green colour and their fresh, cucumberish smell. This had the added advantage of ensuring that they didn't catch light when sparks from the fire landed on them. Since we were sitting and lying on the rushes, I never wet them enough to make them soggy, but just sprayed them lightly from a watering can every few days.

When I laid them at six inches thick I had a floor that was genuinely comfortable to sleep on. The rushes are good insulators, so none of the chill of the ground reached me and the depth gave me a springy and soft bed. A couple of blankets provided all the additional bedding I needed. It certainly makes sense of the sleeping arrangements that one finds detailed in medieval and early Tudor sources. When people talk of the majority of the household sleeping on the floor in the Great Hall, this is how it worked. If you imagine beds or even bed rolls that are put up and down daily, you also have to wonder where they were stored during the day. With a rush floor there is no difficulty. One chest could store the blankets for six or seven people, and converting the space from daytime to night-time use becomes extremely easy.

At the end of my six months of castle building I had a look at the state of the rushes. Not all of us had been sleeping on them every night, but they had most certainly been heavily used by my colleagues and me, both on and off screen, for sitting, walking, standing and working on. Much food had been cooked in there, much drink drunk, and all the spillages that you might expect had certainly happened. A hen had moved in and raised a brood of chicks among us on the rush floor – we didn't have the heart to evict her – and they of course had been rather messy; there was also a mouse that kept trying to raid the grain ark. But there was no sign whatsoever of any of this activity. That the surface remained clean was no great surprise: stuff simply fell down between the rushes, out of sight, smell and mind. We never noticed any odour or muck the whole time we were there. But when I came to clean it all out at the end I had expected there to be gunge at the bottom. There wasn't. It was clean and sweet-smelling, free of both insects and evidence of rodents. The earth was clean and smelt only of itself, while the bottom layer of rushes had broken down a little into a dryish, fibrous sort of compost. There was no mould, mildew, slime or gunge of any sort. What it would be like after twenty years I don't know, but as Erasmus himself implies it was only in the occasional home that the bottom layer was left undisturbed for that long. It is clear to me that it is possible to manage a floor with strewn rushes cleanly and comfortably without too much effort.

As the sixteenth century rolled on, however, fewer and fewer people lay down at night upon the floor. In a wave of home improvements that swept the nation, open hearths become less and less common and chimneys begin to dominate the skyline. As chimneys were installed and homes were divided up into more rooms, there were far worse draughts at floor level. Chimneys draw the smoke up and out, and in doing so pull in cold air at ground level. A bed frame to raise you up off the floor and out of the draught becomes a much more desirable thing, and with the smoke now channelled away up the chimney, the additional height is not going to cause you breathing difficulties.

Many people took some rushes up on to the raised bed frames with them. A wooden box bed, or a frame with a solid wooden base, worked very well with the same laid rushes that had been on the floor; a rope-strung bed worked better with a rush mat. Rope-strung beds gradually took over, probably because they were cheaper to produce. An open frame was made and holes drilled all along the four sides of it, then a rope was strung back and forth lengthways. The same rope, or a separate one, was then strung widthways, between the lengthways rope. This created a square, net-like pattern with a bit of bounce to it. If the ropes loosened, the whole bed would sag in the middle, which would give one dreadful backache, so it was important to 'sleep tight' with the ropes under tension. Many surviving beds come with a wooden peg to help retighten the rope. Loose rushes upon this surface would simply fall through, but a woven mat not only lies firmly in place but spreads the load evenly over the whole structure so that you cannot feel the ropes digging into you. On top of the mat you could lay more loose rushes if you wished or perhaps a straw bed. Almost as a postscript, it is worth mentioning that with wooden furniture raising people up off the floor there was now very little reason to bother strewing rushes down there, and by the end of the Tudor era the practice was rapidly dying out.

A flock bed, which was found in abundance among yeomen and husbandmen, was a major step up from a straw bed. Once again it was just a tightly woven sack, but this time stuffed with sheep's wool rather than straw. Although you can simply shove a couple of fleeces into the sack, this will quickly become lumpy and hard. Unlike a straw bed, a flock bed won't regain its softness and open structure with just a good shake: the wool tends to felt together quite quickly. It is well worth, therefore, taking a little time to make a proper flock bed. To do this, lay out a piece of stout, tightly woven hemp or linen cloth on a table and begin to lay equal-sized, well-combed locks of wool evenly and thickly all over it, with the fibres pointing in one direction. Then add a second layer with all the fibres pointing at ninety degrees to the first. The more thoroughly combed the wool, the better. You don't want any bits of twig, grass or even tangles causing hard lumps in the finished bed. Take a second equal-sized piece of fabric and lay it on top. Sew all the way through the layers with two or three tight stitches at about two-inch intervals, trapping the wool in place. A long strip of cloth three or four inches wide can then be attached all the way around the open edge to neaten off the bed. Naturally, fleeces were more expensive than straw, and a flock bed requires more labour to make than a straw one, so most people wanted to look after their flock beds in order to make them last. The best way to do this is to lay a flock bed on top of a straw bed. The straw bed then takes the rubbing against either ropes or boards.

Feather beds sat at the top of the comfort tree and graced the beds of the nobility, gentry and the wealthiest merchants and yeomen. Again they were just filled sacks, but the fabric containing the feathers needed to be especially tightly woven or they would work their way out. Like straw, feathers respond well to vigorous shaking, so there is no need to make a more structured bed. Feather beds are not just the softest beds to sleep on, they are also the warmest. As you sink into them they hold the heat around as well as beneath you. They are most effective when used in conjunction with another bed beneath. And like so many things they vary in quality. How many feathers there are in the bed makes a big difference – the more the better, generally. Small, fluffy, down feathers are better than larger feathers, and the down from eider ducks is the warmest and softest of all; however, as eider ducks are seabirds, eiderdown was hard to get hold of in most of inland Britain.

With all of these various stuffed beds, there is of course nothing to say that you had to sleep *on* them. Each and every one, from straw to feather, would have worked equally well as a sort of duvet on top. It may be that where people had multiple beds they slept between them.

Ideally, then, the very best Tudor bed would have consisted of a wooden frame with posts at all four corners, a substantial wooden headboard, a thick fabric top, and heavy full curtains all around. It would have had tightly pulled ropes across the bottom, upon which would have sat a thick fresh rush mat; a straw bed packed full of lady's bedstraw interspersed with a little lavender would have sat on top of the rush. Next would have come a flock bed, with not one but two feather beds above that, the finer quality one sitting at the very top. A bed so soft, warm and comfortable that even a princess should not feel a pea buried down at the bottom. Sheets of finest linen, with bolsters and pillows of feather encased in more linen, together with blankets and an embroidered coverlet, would have completed the ensemble.

From such a bed it would have been hard indeed to rise at cockcrow. But how many people had such a bed to tempt them? It is hard to be certain. If a bedstead, its hangings and beds were listed in someone's will or inventory, then you know that they had such things at the end of their life, but if they were not listed you cannot be sure that they didn't possess them. Beds may, for example, just have been part of a general category, such as when someone simply mentions 'all of my household goods', and only some people left wills at all.

What we can say is that there are a lot more such beds mentioned at the end of the Tudor period than at the beginning, and that wealthier people were more likely to have had them than those of modest means. In 1587 Thomas and Sarah Taylor, who lived in Stratford-upon-Avon, were a very ordinary urban couple, reasonably well off, but not rich. They had been married for over fourteen years and had five surviving children – Florence, Annis, William, George and Joan – having lost four other children. Thomas made his living in the cloth trade and had a small workshop as part of the house in Sheep Street where he fulled and sheared woven cloth (a finishing process that turned open-textured cloth into something that looked attractively sheer and was much more windproof and waterproof) before it went on to the dyers. Thomas and Sarah had one joined bedstead (with a headboard, posts and curtains), one truckle bed and three other bedsteads. To go on top of the wooden frames they had five flock beds, five coverlets, five bolsters, four pillows, a pair of blankets and two pairs of sheets. It was a comfortable amount then for a family of seven, but not full provision for everyone, and certainly nothing was spare. Presumably Thomas and Sarah shared the joined bedstead with its curtains around, lying upon one of the flock beds and one of the bolsters. They may also have enjoyed one of the pairs of sheets and two of the pillows, with a coverlet over the top. Three of the children could have had a bedstead, flock bed, bolster and coverlet to themselves, but the other two may have had to double up. Since the youngest, Joan, was only just over a year old, it is possible that she had a makeshift crib or shared with her parents, but either way most of the children had to manage without sheets.

Meanwhile, the maidservant of a woman named Katherine Salisbury, who was also from Stratford, was provided with just a flock bed, blanket and covering. The rooms of Katherine's house were inventoried one by one. Her own room contained both a bedstead and a truckle bed, and the guest room had a full standing bed, but the maid's room was conspicuously without a bedstead of any type. Even at the end of the century there were plenty of people who still slept on the floor.

Morning prayer

The prayer at first waking was a personal affair, said alone and privately, though preferably aloud rather than silently. Beginning the day with a prayer was a constant throughout the Tudor era, although the language and content of that prayer would undergo a fundamental change. Christianity was almost entirely unchallenged as an explanation of the universe, but the nature of Christianity was the hottest of all topics and the focus of vast conflict and upheaval: from Catholic to Protestant, back to Catholic and then back to Protestant again, with many variations in both denominations along the way and often at the same time. It was a subject over which people were willing to suffer impoverishment, become social outcasts, or even die.

When the goldsmith John Collan of York died in 1490 he left among his goods a primer – a book of prayers in Latin – that was valued at just six pence, roughly two days' wages for a labouring man at that time. It may have been an old book in very poor condition to be so cheap, or it may have been brand new, straight off the presses of William Caxton, whose first printed primer was produced that same year. Six pence would have been a fair price for one of the new printed prayer books, whether it was Caxton's or one imported from the Continent. With this book John Collan could have followed a basic version of the monastic cycle of prayer, reciting a slightly simplified version of the office of Lauds at dawn. Perhaps he did so in private every morning when he rose, or perhaps he led his household in a more communal act of devotion. In either case he would have read the Latin words aloud. Such familiar words may well have needed only occasional prompting from the written text.

As the fifteenth century slipped into the sixteenth, such relatively inexpensive primers became more available. New editions were being produced by Wynkyn de Worde here in Britain, and on the Continent some were being specifically designed for the English market and printed mainly in Paris and the Low Countries. For the gentry and for wealthy merchants, these new printed books offered a form of morning prayer that had previously been the preserve of the clergy and the aristocracy. For everyone else, morning prayer meant the recitation of a stock of prayers learnt by rote.

John Fitzherbert's advice at the beginning of this chapter was entirely conventional at the time. Written just before the Reformation, it recommends the recitation out loud of the most well-known blessing in Latin, 'In nomine patris et filii et spiritus sancti, Amen', while making the traditional gesture of a cross over the chest, and also suggests the optional addition of the paternoster (the Lord's Prayer) and the Ave Maria prayer, along with the Creed (a list of the core Christian beliefs). The ubiquity of this beginning to the day is hinted at by the context of Fitzherbert's advice. This was not an extract from a devotional book, nor was it part of the educational literature aimed at the training up of wealthy children: this was advice to housewives in a book about agricultural practice and farming techniques.

After Henry VIII broke away from Rome, morning prayer began to undergo a series of changes. Initially they were slight, but by 1545 there was an official primer, with all references to the Pope and to Thomas à Becket and the word 'purgatory' removed, and with much less focus upon the Virgin Mary; no other primer was to be used. Surviving older primers often have offending references dutifully rubbed or crossed out. Pressure too was beginning to build in favour of the rote-learnt prayers being recited in English rather than Latin. During Edward VI's reign the Lord's Prayer in English came to dominate the approved list of rote devotions, and the official primer began to resemble the later Book of Common Prayer. Latin and something akin to the 1545 primer returned under Mary I, but as Elizabeth I's reign began to settle down it is clear that the recitation of fixed prayers, whether learnt by rote or read from a primer, was beginning to lose its centrality in the daily practice of morning prayer. Religious literature instead began to resemble extended essays or sermons, where people extemporized upon a theme.

By 1577 the educationalist Hugh Rhodes was telling children in his *Boke of Nurture*:

At five of the clocke, without delay,
Use commonly to ryse:
And give God thanks for thy good rest
When thou openest thyne eyes.
Pray him also to prosper thee,
And thyne affayres in deede
The better shalte thou speede.

The idea of morning prayer holds strong, but there is no approved list of words to be used. The recitation of doctrinally screened forms of words could encourage orthodox behaviour and belief, but the Protestant reformers were keen to promote a more personal and direct approach to God, and many had come to see rote-learnt prayers as a barrier to emotional and intellectual engagement with the Christian message. Better, they thought, for people to search their own hearts and come up with their own words, words that had significance and meaning to them. Free-form prayer, they believed, could offer a deeper spiritual experience.

Many people, of course, were keen to have some guidance about the nature of this more free-form, unscripted prayer. *A Handfull of Holesome (though Homelie) Hearbs*, written by Anne Wheathill in 1584, is unusual only in having been written by a woman. It offered a series of prayers for different situations that a person could read and think upon. Carefully conventional and well within the doctrines of the Church of England, it begins with a prayer for the morning. It is one of the shorter of her prayers and could easily be read through in five minutes, ending with the plea 'here me deare Father and send thy holie Ghost to direct me in all my doings. To thee O glorious and blessed Trinity, the Father, the Sonne, and the holie Ghost, be given all honour and praise, now and for ever more, Amen.' Protestant, English and free-form it may be, but the echoes of the old traditional Catholic form of morning prayer are very audible.

2. To Wash or Not to Wash

A first thy Poet, never let him lacke
A comely cleanly Shirt unto his backe.
Cleane Linnen, is my Mistris, and my Theme

   John Taylor, *In Praise of Cleane Linen* (1624)

With prayers said, it was time to prepare the body for the day. With no separate bathrooms, people cleaned themselves in their chambers, spaces which, as we have noted before, could be far from private. Ideally, hair, skin and teeth would all receive attention before the day's clothes were donned.

Washing the body with hot soapy water was obviously a stupid and dangerous thing to do in a world wherein disease entered the body through the open pores of the skin. Only a fool would expose himself or herself to the evil miasmas that carried plague, sweating sickness and smallpox from person to person. The physician Thomas Moulton, in his *This is the Myrrour or Glasse of Helth* of 1545, spelt it out: 'Also use no baths or stoves; nor swet too much, for all openeth the pores of a manne's body and maketh the venomous ayre to enter and for to infecte the bloode.' The medical advice of the era was clear: avoid places where the air was stagnant, or where vapours rose from marshes, pools, tanyards and muck heaps; keep the air about you fresh and sweet-smelling; keep the pores of your skin tightly sealed, and cover the body as fully as possible. Hands and face were to be rinsed regularly, both when rising in the morning and before every meal, but it was to be done in clean cold water that would wash off surface dirt, or with perfumed cold washing waters produced within the home.

While sickness was generally viewed as an imbalance within the body, infection was seen as an outside agency that arose from places of putrefaction and drifted in the air like seeds or spores. If such airs penetrated the body, they could engender that corruption within, pushing your body out of its natural balance and making you sick. There were several ways that the more noxious fumes could enter the body. The mouth and nose were understandably the main infection route, requiring vigilance over food and drink and the avoidance of bad-smelling or stagnant places. The pores of the skin were a secondary route but one that could at least be guarded against by the adoption of a sensible personal hygiene routine, one that maintained the skin as a solid barrier. In addition to the dirt and disease of the outside world, the body was seen to produce its own filth, which needed to be removed as quickly and fully as possible since holding that dirt next to the skin opened up the possibility of reabsorption. Soiled clothing that hung on to the effluvia that passed out of the body through the skin was to be avoided. Clean clothes were therefore essential for health, in particular the layer that touched the skin. Ideally no wool, leather or silk would be in direct contact with your body, as these were difficult to clean. Linen shirts, smocks, under-breeches, hose, ruffs, cuffs, bands, coifs (skull-caps) and caps could be combined by the two sexes to give total coverage in a form that permitted regular vigorous laundry. Each time you changed or 'shifted' this linen layer, you would remove the dirt, grease and sweat that had accumulated. The more regularly you changed your underwear, the healthier and cleaner you would be. Linen was considered to be especially effective at this job as it was absorbent, so it actively drew the grease and sweat away from the skin into the weave of the cloth, like a sponge soaking up a spillage. A change of underwear therefore not only removed the build-up of potentially danger-ous waste products but could actively draw more out from the body, thereby improving the natural circulation of materials through the system, toughening up the constitution, restoring balance within and promoting health.

In John Taylor's seventeenth-century mock-heroic poem *In Praise of Cleane Linen*, dedicated to the laundress Mrs Martha Legge, it is not the healthiness of clean linen that is highlighted but its ability to provide socially acceptable hygiene levels:

> Remember that your laundress paines is great,
> When labours only keep you sweet and neat . . .
> By her thy linnen's sweet and clenely drest,
> Else thou would'st stink above ground like a beast.

Stinking like a beast was not socially acceptable, either for young lawyers (she washed the clothes of those studying at Middle Temple, part of the Inns of Court) or indeed for anyone with a pretension to a decent, respectable life. People ideally smelt 'sweet', and body odour was to be combated wherever possible; clean underwear was a major weapon in most people's arsenal against the pong.

In addition to providing clean clothes, linen could also be employed to cleanse the body actively. In Sir Thomas Elyot's book *The Castel of Helth* (1534), he recommends that the morning routine should include a session whereby a man was to 'rubbe the body with a course lynnen clothe, first softely and easilye, and after to increase more and more, to a harde and swyfte rubbynge, untyll the fleshe do swelle, and be somewhat ruddy, and that not only downe ryghte, but also overthwart and round'. This would ensure that 'his body is clensed'. This vigorous rubbing, especially if done after exercise, was intended to help draw out the body's toxins through the open pores, with the unwanted bodily matter then being carried away by the coarse linen cloth.

'Rubbing cloths' or 'body cloths', despite their very low financial value, occasionally turn up in inventories of people's goods.

Most people seem to have owned only two or three sets of underwear. Many people bequeathed some of their clothes in their wills, and others turn up in probate inventories. The more expensive tailored garments are the ones that are generally mentioned, the 'best gown' or 'my good black doublet'. But sometimes the extent of the bequest is rather fuller. In his will of 1588, William Lane of Chadwell, Essex, listed two lockram shirts (coarse, heavyweight), one 'holland' shirt (fine weight and bleached white) and his 'marrying shirt', which presumably was of the best quality and loaded with sentimental significance. He was a fairly wealthy yeoman farmer, so would have been much better provided for than most. His stock of shirts would have allowed him to have one on, one in the wash and a clean best shirt available for Sundays and other special occasions. We don't know if he had any other shirts unlisted – perhaps not good enough to be left as a bequest – but we can be certain he had at least these four.

Aristocrats and wealthy gentlemen sometimes had several dozen shirts and changed at least once a day, with additional changes if they had been engaged in strenuous exercise. Henry Bridgewater, on the other hand, was only a servant in 1570 and still a young man. All he owned at this stage in his life were the wages due to him, two chests, a bow and set of arrows and a stock of clothes. We can be fairly sure that he bequeathed his entire wardrobe because he describes several items as those he is currently wearing: 'a leather doublet on my back, a pair of hose on my legs'. In this list he enumerates three canvas shirts – two new and one old. Canvas shirts were frequently given to servants to wear by masters whose duty it was to clothe their live-in staff. Of good quality, these shirts were not the cheapest on the market but they washed well and coped with heavy labour. Such provision often meant that servants were better dressed than independent labouring people. Again, Henry had the chance to be wearing one shirt while another one was being washed. A weekly change seems highly likely; he may well have put on a fresh shirt every Sunday morning and then worn it through the rest of the week. The laundry bills of Edward, 3rd Duke of Buckingham, upon a sojourn to London in 1501, reflect the same pattern. The duke presumably arrived with a stock of clean clothing, but then had sixteen shirts laundered along with six headkerchiefs and five pairs of linen sheets seven weeks later. His two serving men, however, had a joint bill for laundering just eleven shirts over an eight-week period. The duke was changing much more frequently than the serving men, who were changing weekly.

Charitable institutions also found it necessary to provide underwear for their inmates. St Bartholomew's Hospital in Smithfield, London, provided shirts for men and smocks for women when it was 'needful either at their coming in or departure', highlighting perhaps the woeful state, or even complete lack, of decent underwear among some of the poor and sick who sought out their help. Since St Bartholomew's was a medical hospital treating the sick, the perceived therapeutic effects of clean linen may well have been a major motivation for the governors of the hospital to provide the incoming patients with underwear. Providing patients with underwear when they were discharged, however, would have been more to do with the social propriety of clean linens. In Ipswich the Tooley Foundation, which operated more as an almshouse and provided long-term care, had an orderly clothing supply system, with regular purchases of cloth to make a stock of hose for both the men and the women, as well as cloth to make up batches of shirts and smocks. One entry in 1577, for example, shows that the Foundation bought fifty-two and a quarter ells (a measure of forty-five inches) of canvas at eleven pence per ell to make up nineteen smocks, four shirts and three pairs of sheets, and paid five shillings and eight pence for someone to do the sewing. It also had regular laundry expenses, which indicates that these stocks of shirts and smocks were sufficient to allow changes for the inmates. A canvas shirt may not have been the softest and most comfortable of garments, but it could still have provided a basic, socially accepted level of healthy cleanliness.

The picture that we can put together is one in which linen underwear was an essential part of cleanliness and respectability, but was not always achievable. All clothing was expensive, and while shirts and hose were generally cheaper than doublets and gowns, they still represented a significant investment. As we saw from the Tooley Foundation accounts, towards the end of the sixteenth century a basic canvas shirt suitable for a poor person cost around two shillings new (based upon two ells of canvas at eleven pence an ell, plus sewing costs). A second-hand shirt with plenty of wear still left in it could be valued at one shilling and six pence, while an old worn-out shirt fit for turning into dishcloths could be worth only two pence. Meanwhile, bread – the cheapest of all food – cost a penny a loaf, and just six pence a day was considered to be a working man's wage. It took considerable time, therefore, to save up two shillings from the family budget to buy a new shirt. While it was usable as a garment the price remained relatively high, and there was no shortage of potential customers for decent second-hand shirts and smocks. The difficulties that a labourer faced in clothing his family are clear when you look at the economics of everyday life. Imagine a family of five. The father, working six days a week, brings in three shillings; the wife manages to make another shilling from spinning; and the oldest child, at around eleven years of age, brings in another shilling – a total family weekly budget of sixty pence. Five people eating bread and water alone would cost thirty-five pence if they had not grown their own grain. If they replaced the water with small beer and perhaps had one hot meal of pottage a day, there would be precious little left even for rent. Basic clothing could be a luxury that required additional resources – the produce of a little plot of land, perhaps.

So even if you do have the requisite clothing, does this system actually work? Did people in the Tudor era stink to high heaven? Were they endangering their health as they tried paradoxically to preserve it from evil miasmas or foul air?

I have twice followed the regime. The first time was for a period of just over three months, while living in modern society. No one noticed! It helps, of course, if you wear natural-fibre clothes over the top of your linen underwear. I used a fine linen smock, over which I could wear a modern skirt and top without looking odd, and I wore a pair of fine linen hose beneath a nice thick pair of woollen opaque tights (these, of course, did contain a little elastane). I changed the smock and hose daily and rubbed myself down with a linen cloth in the evening before bed, and I took neither shower nor bath for the entire period. I remained remarkably smell-free – even my feet. My skin also stayed in good condition – better than usual, in fact. This, then, was the level of hygiene that a wealthy person could achieve if they wished: one that could pass unnoticed in modern society. While we know that some people did follow the full regime outlined above, we have no way of knowing how many. Several advice books that include some form of early-morning hygiene regime don't mention the rubbing cloth at all, stopping short after telling young men to wash their hands and face and comb their hair.

I have also followed the regime in a more Tudor context while filming a TV series, during which I wore all the correct period layers and head coverings. I was working on a farm, so this entailed a much heavier coarse linen smock, woollen hose and far fewer changes of underwear. Although I was working mostly outdoors, often engaged in heavy labour and also lurking around an open fire, I found that just changing my linen smock once a week proved acceptable both to me and to my colleagues – including those behind the camera, who had more conventional modern sensibilities. The woollen hose I changed just three times over the six months; the linen parts of the head-dress I changed weekly along with the smock. There was a slight smell, but it was mostly masked by the much stronger smell of woodsmoke. Once again my skin remained in good condition. This, of course, was much more representative of the majority of the population's experience in Tudor times, in the frequency of changes, the lifestyle and the types of material that the underwear was made from.

A friend and colleague has also tried it the other way around, washing his body but not the underwear. The difference between the two was stark and revealing. He continued with a full modern hygiene routine, showering at least once a day and using a range of modern products, but wore the same linen shirt (and outer clothes) for several months without washing them at all. The smell was overpowering, impossible to ignore. He looked filthy too.

Many modern writers have presumed that without hot soapy water being regularly applied to bodies, Tudor England must have been a place inhabited by people who smelt like the long-term homeless. Much play has been made about the difference between beautiful clothes on the surface and an imagined filth and stench on the inside. I would refute that reading of the situation. The sixteenth-century belief in the cleansing power of linen turns out in practice to have some truth to it. The laundry makes a vast difference. The smell of the past undoubtedly was not the same as the smell of the present, but we need to be aware that cleanliness and being neat and sweet-smelling were important issues for Tudor people. Charitable institutions were eager to ensure that their inmates conformed to the social norm, and masters wanted their servants to be so attired. There must of course have been the occasional 'stinking beast' among those having a particularly hard time, but it appears to be the absence of laundry, rather than the absence of washing the body in water, that has the biggest impact upon personal hygiene.

However, there were some who washed their bodies in water in Tudor England, and even some who bathed. The public baths south of the river Thames in London were open for business until 1546, while those in the city of Chester had been running until 1542. At around the same time, John Leland, who wrote a traveller's guide to England, described three of the ancient Roman baths in the town of Bath as being in daily use when he visited: the warm-water Cross Bath, used by people with disfigurements and skin diseases; the Hot Bath, which along with the Cross Bath was close to the hospital and patronized by humble people; and the large King's Bath in the centre of town, with an arcade of thirty-two niches where men and women could stand privately and which the gentry favoured. Such public baths served many functions: some people used them for their perceived health benefits, such as softening overtight sinews; many appreciated them as social spaces where you could meet, lounge around, perhaps take a glass of wine; some sought them out as gateways to brothels; and others went in order to wash themselves. It was the public nature of the baths, with many people coming together in hot steamy atmospheres with their pores exposed and opened, that made them seem like places rife with infection both moral and physical. Their link with the sex trade at a time when syphilis, almost unknown before 1490, was rampaging through the country made them doubly dubious places. As urban phenomena frequented primarily by young wealthy

men, they had never been part of the daily routine of the majority of people.

For men and boys (modesty prevented women and girls from
following suit) there was also the option of bathing naked in
rivers, streams, ponds and other outdoor bodies of water. Swim-
ming is often recorded as an activity for pleasure and exercise,
but it could also be for cleanliness. The intentions of two such
men, John Strete and John Jerret, were made clear at the coroner's inquest after they had lost their lives one August afternoon
in 1592 in a pond in Mountfield, Sussex, where they were said to
be washing naked. Both men were ordinary labourers who
strayed in too deep and were unable to swim. They are by no
means a unique example of men and boys getting into trouble
while bathing in Tudor times: coroners' records across the country are scattered with similar tragedies.

Private baths carried few of the negative health connotations
of the public baths. Henry VIII famously had a brand-new
bathhouse built for him at Hampton Court, along with a steam
bath at Richmond Palace, facilities that his daughter Elizabeth is
recorded as having enjoyed regularly. A slightly less costly
option for those wishing to enjoy a steam bath – as recommended by some physicians, such as William Bullein in his
Government of Health (1558) – was promoted by Sir Hugh Platt in
his magnificently entitled *Delightes for Ladies* (1603). Sir Hugh, a
gentleman with a lively interest in the world about him and in
what later came to be called 'science', also wrote upon subjects
such as distillation, food-preservation techniques and the nature
of salt. To make a steam bath, Sir Hugh explained, you needed a
brass pot with a lid, a lead pipe, some flour, an egg white, a fireplace, a wooden bathing tub 'crossed with hoops according to
the usual manner', a large sheet and plenty of appropriate herbs.
You began by boring many small holes in the bottom of your
tub. Then it was necessary to make a hole in the lid of your pot

big enough to take one end of the lead pipe. The flour and egg white was mixed to a paste and some of it was to be used to seal the pipe into the lid. Now you could set your pot on to the fire, full of water and fresh herbs, put the lid on, with its integral pipe, and use the rest of the egg and flour paste to seal it in place. The free end of the pipe was then fed under the bathing tub so that herb-scented steam could make its way out from the pot, along the pipe, under the tub and up through the many little holes. The hoops were put in place and a sheet draped over to make a tented chamber within. Sir Hugh was concerned that a lady should make sure that the chamber she was using was secured against draughts, which might 'offend you whilest your bodie is made open and porous to the aire', before she began her steam bath.

The herbs were an important part of this bath, for just as evil airs could access the body through open pores, so too could beneficial ones. This could be a form of delivering medication into the system, and transformed bathing from a dangerous activity into a therapeutic one. Such baths seem to have been restricted to members of the gentry and a few aspirational merchants, and were not everyday experiences even within this elite group.

Perfume

It wasn't just through the pores of the skin that fumes, vapours and airs entered the body: breathing the herb-laden air of the steam bath would also have an effect. With every lungful of air passing up the nose, scent entered the body and made its way directly into the brain by means of two small nipple-like organs at the very top of the nostrils – or so the doctors and surgeons of the day believed. In the Elizabethan surgeon John Hall's English translation of the work of Lanfranco of Milan there is a description of how, alongside those scents, 'vital spirits' would be carried to the 'marvelous net' surrounding the brain, bringing the very spark of life that transformed our bodies from lumps of meat into living beings. Modern anatomical studies show that neither of these two physical structures actually exists within human beings. There are no nipples in the nose and no marvellous net encasing the brain. There is a net-like structure around the brains of sheep, however, and with human dissection still being both rare and crude in the sixteenth century (Vesalius' groundbreaking work, first published in the late 1530s, took a long time to be accepted) surgeons had mistakenly assumed that a structure that was familiar from butchery was present in all living creatures. After all, most of our internal organs and structures do closely resemble those of other species. Air quality was therefore of the most intense importance, and smells, be they good or bad, were believed to change us, altering the balances within us and causing either sickness or a host of other effects. The smell of rosemary, for example, was believed to stimulate the function of memory, directly strengthening the brain. Lavender was thought to help to calm and cool an overheated brain. Perfume was important stuff.

In 1485 only a couple of hundred people in the entire nation could afford an essential oil that you might put on your skin. By 1603 there may have been as many as 10,000 people in a position to procure a vial of such an oil, but that still left the other 2 or 3 million without.

Perfume for most people came much more directly, and less intensely, from natural sources: a posy of violets; a small linen bag filled with lavender flowers; the smoke of herbs burnt on the fire; lady's bedstraw in the bed. Sir Thomas More planted a hedge of rosemary beneath the window of his study so that its scent would waft up as he worked, stimulating his mind, a practice that he advised other scholars to follow. Rosemary also accompanied the main rituals of life: moments when memory became key. At weddings, someone would walk in front of the bride on the way to the church holding aloft a branch of rosemary, gilded if the family could afford to do so, so that she might remember her marriage vows. Rosemary was also prominent at funerals, to help people remember the dead, a dried sprig being carried sometimes long afterwards as a token. Christenings, too, called for rosemary, so that all present might recall the promises they had made on the child's behalf. Within the home, bedrooms were often redolent with lavender, as its calming nature was believed to help induce sleep – as it is today. It was tucked among the straw of the bolster in poorer homes, and hung in bunches on bedsteads in those of the better-off. Those who had stores of bedlinen popped sweet bags of lavender in the chests with them so that sheets and pillowcases would become impregnated with the smell over time. Natural insecticides such as tansy, rue and wormwood were strewn on floors and mingled with bed straws, giving a sharp smell to many domestic interiors. These scents were believed to be both stimulative and purgative, driving out sloth and idleness along with the unwanted pests.

Rooms that had become nasty for one reason or another, perhaps a room where someone had lain sick, for example, could be purified and purged by fumigation. It could be a simple matter of setting fire to large green bunches of rosemary and marjoram and wafting them around the room so that the smoke they generated touched all parts of the space, or a pot of burning charcoal could be placed in a room and handfuls of sweet herbs thrown on at intervals to drive out bad and polluted airs and fill the space with wholesome scented smoke. When the Lord Keeper visited Ipswich in 1568, the town laid on a banquet (not a feast with meat and veg: the word 'banquet' in the Tudor period meant sweets, cakes, cheese, nuts and fruit with a glass or two of wine). They were obviously concerned that everything should be perfect, buying in large quantities of the best wines and sweetmeats and two pence worth of perfume. Robert Dudley, the Master of the Queen's Horse, and the queen's favourite, spent £1 7s 9d in 1558 upon herbs to strew in his chamber. A mixture of tansy and daisy roots was mentioned on one occasion, obviously an attempt to repel insects; roses and flowers are mentioned on another, when he was more interested in creating a sweet smell. Lavender would have made people drowsy; the preferred herb for daytime clothing was marjoram, a scent that was considered to be especially 'sweet' and capable of inducing a 'merry' state of mind. Roses, too, are often called upon for clothing for much the same reasons. For those who could afford a little help from the apothecary, these sweet bags could be made to hold their scent much longer if dried powdered orris root was mingled in among the crushed dried leaves and petals of the scented herbs.

It wasn't all herbs, though. For everyone, high or low, the most distinctive and well-known deliberately created smell of the early Tudor years was the incense used in church. Its cost restricted its use in the majority of rural parishes to twice-yearly experiences around the feasts of Easter and Christmas, but incense burning could accompany the funerals of wealthy parishioners, or saints' days when supported by the financial contributions of a religious guild. As incense was made primarily from frankincense and imported from the Near East, its exotic origins and its links with the biblical stories, as well as its costliness, combined to keep this smell strongly associated with sanctity, with sacred rather than domestic spaces. To breathe in the fumes of incense was to turn your mind to spiritual matters not only by association, but also by the physical action of the smell upon the brain. It was special, separate from the ordinary airs and smells of daily life, an aid to prayer and meditation.

However, as everything has its time and place, the smell of incense belonged in the main to the beginning of the era and faded away over the sixteenth century. The very physicality of such a spiritual experience was both important to many people and a source of worry to the reforming spirit that was sweeping across Europe. The smell of incense could bring you closer to God, could help to waft your prayers up to heaven (the traditional interpretation), or it could be a sensual distraction from more intellectually focused prayer (in the mind of someone like Erasmus or Luther).

The essential oils that offered a more concentrated nasal experience to the super-rich in 1485 were generally imported from Spain and Portugal ready-made, but the early years of the sixteenth century saw the knowledge of the art of distillation spread out among apothecaries and the educated elite. As home-grown production increased, the price dropped. The production of distilled 'waters' was, and is, much easier than that of oils. The same quantity of raw ingredients will produce around fifty times as much of herb, flower or spice waters as it will essential oils. Naturally, therefore, the waters were a fraction of the price and both produced and sold much more widely. John Cumberland, for example, who had a shop in Ipswich in 1590, had a total stock of essential oils valued at five shillings, whereas his waters were valued at £1 6s. There are no quantities given for the oils, but he had four and a half gallons of distilled rose water. These waters could be used in food – particularly the case for rose water – but also as medicines, as scented hand and face washes, or sprinkled upon linen collars, ruffs and handkerchiefs, where they would be close to noses. Producing the waters required investment in a little equipment, but only basic skills.

Stills were made of pewter, lead, copper, glass and pottery, the pottery ones being the cheapest. They were roughly conical in shape. Those made of metal or glass usually had a small bent pipe at the top that carried the cooling steam down to the receiving vessel; those made of pottery had a glazed interior, an unglazed exterior, a small rim around the inside of the base to collect the condensed steam, and a spout from this rim to carry the liquid to the collecting jar.

The process began by infusing the herbs in water. Since rose scents were by far the most popular sort, let us begin with them. They are also the scents that I have most experience of making, although rosemary, lavender and thyme scents are also fairly straightforward to make. Any scented rose will do, but the best are damask roses; newly arrived in England in the 1520s, they have the strongest smell of all. The petals are best gathered in the early morning with the dew still upon them, for this is when they exude the most scent. The petals are spread out on a sheet to dry a little and then the white nib at the base of each petal where it joins the rest of the flower must be pinched out. The petals are packed into a glass jar, water is added, the top sealed and the jar put out in the sun. The next day a second batch of petals is gathered and prepared, packed into a clean jar and the water from the previous batch is strained and poured over them. This jar is sealed and put out in the sun. This process is repeated three or four times. The infused liquid is then put into a bowl over a steady gentle fire and the still, or alembic, is put over the top. The essential rose oils evaporate at a lower temperature than water, so if you are skilful enough to control the heat precisely, the condensed liquid will be pure rose oil. If, however, your control is a little lacking, both water and oil will drip into the receiving vessel and you will have produced rose water. A rag wrapped around either the pipe of your metal or glass alembic or around the top of the pottery version can be regularly doused in cold water to help the evaporated oils and steam to condense. Absolutely pure oil on the first run through the still is exceptionally difficult without modern thermometers; however, simple separation can improve a batch that has gone reasonably well. Pour your rose-oil mixture into a tall, thin glass vessel and allow it to stand. The oil will float to the top and can be very carefully poured off into another small bottle. All of the above techniques are described in manuals aimed at apothecaries, learned men and gentlewomen alike.

Rose oil was used as a body perfume, particularly at the court of Henry VIII. As the symbol of the Tudor royal dynasty was a white and red rose combined, rose perfume was especially apt. Huge quantities were purchased by the king and members of the royal household both for personal use and for splashing around on festive occasions. As well as being a deeply patriotic aroma, rose oil on the skin could also be used as an aphrodisiac. Roses were considered to have a warming, strengthening nature, able to quicken the blood, and their sweet smell was believed to induce a merry frame of mind. While a splash of rose water on a ruff was pleasing, the intensity of the oil upon the skin was arousing. Perfume bottles – or casting bottles – exquisitely made, using the most expensive materials, and filled with oil of roses, made perfect aristocratic love gifts.

By the end of Elizabeth I's reign, complex blends of many ingredients, generally including musk, civet and ambergris, had begun to compete with rose oil as the perfume of the court and high society. As imported ingredients they had held their high price and thus their exclusivity, while the scent of roses was becoming more available to an increasing segment of the population. One of Sir Hugh Platt's recipes for a casting bottle, for example, called for oil of spikenard (a herb), oil of thyme, oil of lemons, oil of cloves and a grain of civet to be worked together in a silver spoon with some rose water. If at the end of the procedure you didn't think that there was enough civet smell in the mixture, you could double the number of grains.

Casting bottles holding liquid perfumes were far less

common than pomanders, however, which generally contained a solid perfumed mixture. A pomander could be a very humble item, just one step up from a lavender bag. Herbs and spices were worked into either a ball of wax or a lump of resin; naturally the herbs and wax, being home-grown, were much cheaper than the imported spices and resin. If you had access to essential oils, they could also be added. The resultant mixture was generally put into a perforated wooden or metal box that could be suspended from a cord and worn. At least one of the men who served aboard Henry VIII's flagship took his to sea with him; it was found within the wreck of the ship up on the main deck, attached by a plaited silk cord to his scabbard. A woman would wear it on a long cord suspended from her girdle. This allowed the pomander to be knocked and moved against her skirt with each step, effectively swinging it like an incense censor in church, wafting the scent into a cloud around her body, where it could act as a barrier to incoming evil miasmas. Without a skirt, such an arrangement would have tangled up one's legs, however, so men wore their pomander much higher. The cord allowed both sexes to bring the pomander up to their faces when confronted by a particularly invasive odour.

Teeth

Sweet-smelling breath was a highly prized attribute, which encouraged an active oral hygiene regime. Remaining food particles, general poor health and 'worms' in the gums (associated with decay) were all seen as causes of stinking breath. Rinsing the mouth out first thing in the morning with clean water was as important as washing your hands and face. After eating, it was polite to use a toothpick to remove any fragments of food, although almost every guide to polite manners deplored using your knife or fingers to do the same. Robert Dudley evidently used disposable toothpicks: they were a regular bulk purchase made by the groom of his chamber, setting him back a full ten shillings in 1558.

A range of powders for cleaning the teeth often combined breath sweetening with tooth whitening. Soot was particularly good at both, and clean soot from a wax candle was best. It could be collected by holding the candle flame against a clean polished surface, such as a mirror, pane of glass or glazed earthenware pot. Rubbed directly on to the teeth and gums with a finger or a small cloth, it acted as a soft abrasive and a deodorizer. It is the Tudor method that I personally prefer, having tried all of them. It removes plaque without damaging either teeth or gums. Chalk and salt were both useful for general abrasive cleaning of the teeth, and both had a small deodorizing effect, although not as good as soot.

John Partridge, who wrote on several subjects but especially upon bleaching, cleaning and dyeing, thought that the ashes from burnt rosemary wood were the most effective. He suggested gathering them up into a little piece of linen and tying it up into a small pouch which could be rubbed all around the mouth, combining the abrasion of the cloth with the cleaning power of the ashes. Such ashes would have been quite alkaline, just like the main cleaning chemicals of other aspects of domestic life, which means that you must rinse very thoroughly after use or the alkali will make your gums sore.

The more elaborate tooth powders found in recipe books used by Elizabethan gentlewomen frequently had a perfuming purpose rather than simply removing smell. Cloves predominate, perhaps in part because they can also ease pain. They also have a powerful smell, which advertised to everyone that you had used something to clean your teeth, much as the strong 'fresh' mint ingredients of modern toothpastes do. Other ingredients included pulverized alabaster to polish, and civet and musk for their smell.

Toothbrushes are not mentioned, but tooth cloths are. Akin to small linen handkerchiefs, they were used to rub around the teeth and tongue before mouth and cloth were rinsed out. Those who were particularly concerned about the appearance of their teeth could visit the barber surgeon, who, among his other roles, offered a tooth-scraping service and tooth bleaching with 'aqua fortis', although as Sir Hugh Plat points out in his *Delightes for Ladies*, overuse could require a person to 'borrow a ranke of teeth to eate'. Aqua fortis was a strong distillation of an alkali or acid – recipes varied. But either would strip a layer of the surface enamel off the teeth, making them appear whiter. It would also attack the gums. A very careful application would be no worse than some modern-day tooth-whitening procedures, but mistakes or repeated use could easily lead to tooth loss. The barber surgeon, whose day-to-day business included tooth pulling as well as hair cutting, shaving, bloodletting and minor surgery, was the obvious professional to turn to for the application of aqua fortis. Barbers needed a steady hand and were accustomed to dealing with frightened patients.

Haircare

In September 1568, Richard Tye's ship the *Grace of God* docked in the port of London. She had sailed across the Channel from Rouen in France; on board was a mixed cargo owned by sixteen different merchants. Canvas and paper made up the bulk of the goods on board, but John Newton had also brought twelve gross of combs (a gross is 144, so this makes 1,728 individual items). He wasn't alone: Humphrey Broune brought in twenty gross of half-penny combs on the same ship, and John Challener had another three gross of boxwood combs among his shipment. Docked close by was the *Mary Ann*, which had landed another twenty-six gross of halfpenny combs only days earlier. In total during the previous twelve months around 90,000 combs were imported into London, around 46,000 of which had been brought in by Richard Pattrick, who obviously dominated the trade. Such vast numbers point to the ordinariness and ubiquity of combs as part of the nation's personal hygiene regime. Regular annual imports on this scale would have been sufficient for every single person to have had two combs in his or her lifetime, even if none was imported through any other port and none was produced within these isles at all.

Many of those brought in by Richard Pattrick and others are specified as 'pennyware' or even 'halfpennyware' combs, and shopkeepers' inventories reveal that there was a plentiful supply at a range of prices, none of which was especially high. Some combs came in their own leather cases, others in small wooden boxes. Combs could be made out of box wood or cow horn, bone or even ivory. Most were two-sided with widely spaced teeth on one side and very fine teeth on the other, capable of removing fleas and lice. When the wreck of the *Mary Rose* – which sank in July 1545 as Henry VIII watched in dismay from the shoreline – was recovered, eighty-two combs were found on board, some inside the sailors' small personal chests, some found with human remains. All but one were made from box wood, and were part of the personal effects of ordinary men going about their daily lives. All the manuals about health or manners agreed that you should comb your hair at least once a day; it was essential first thing in the morning, but advisable to repeat it at intervals during the day.

Many modern writers assert that the people of Tudor Britain were all infested with fleas, head lice and body lice. I am not sure how they can know that. Yes, the combs were designed to act as lice combs; yes, there are images (mostly from later in the Tudor period, as are almost all our images of Tudor daily life) of women checking over the heads of children for evidence of nits and lice; and, yes, there are satirical pieces of writing about dirty, infested people. But does any of this mean that the majority of the population was infested? It does point to there being enough of a problem for people to wish to take precautions, but surely it also highlights the desire to be free of lice and fleas. One does not need to be flea-infested to get a plague-ridden flea bite: a casual encounter with an animal will do that for you. Modern Londoners, it is often said, are never more than eight feet from a rat. We can't, therefore, cite the prevalence of the Black Death as proof of bodies crawling with insect life. Close combing with a fine-toothed comb is a very effective method of removing head lice; a daily comb will prevent any arriving louse from getting a hold and laying its eggs. So perhaps once again we are looking at a personal hygiene regime that works so long as you actually use it.

Some people didn't, or couldn't. Combs might have been both cheap and widely available, but there was always a fringe of people for whom life had become too desperate even for that. Prisoners in gaols are often described as 'lousy', and then there is the unhappy story in 1608 of Mary Duffin in Norwich, whose master, responsible for her physical well-being while she was bound to his service by indenture, kept her 'very unclean and full of lice', according to the mayor's court proceedings. In his *Government of Health*, William Bullein claimed that 'Plaine people in the countrie, as carters, threshers, ditchers, colliers, and plowmen, use seldom times to wash their hands, as appeareth by their filthyness, and verie few times combe their heads, as is seen by floxes, nittes, grease, feathers, straw and suchlike, which hangeth in their haires.' However, Mary Duffin, who was only around twelve years old when she was recorded as being full of lice, was seen as a victim of unfair and unacceptable treatment. The mayor's court freed her from her duties to such a neglectful master and apprenticed her instead to Ann Barber, who, it was hoped, would maintain common decencies. William Bullein's assertion about the common people, incidentally, smacks of snobbery and misunderstanding. Note how he assumes that they have not washed their hands or combed their hair. He hasn't asked them. Anyone whose work involves shifting straw, looking after livestock or transporting coal, as his 'plaine people' did, knows only too well that you can begin the day as clean and well groomed as you like and still be covered in dirt by lunchtime. And when the Londoner Humphrey Richardson was publicly called a 'lousy rogue, nitty britch knave, and scurvy nitty britch knave' in 1598, he was deeply offended. Fleas and lice were certainly a part of life (fleas were discovered within the sediment samples taken from the *Mary Rose*, for example), but Richardson's reaction goes to show that they were also something to be vigorously and enthusiastically combated.

Washing the hair was unusual, but not unheard of – an occasional ablution undertaken in the summer or in well-heated indoor spaces. However, even then the hair was simply rinsed in cold, herb-scented water. Hot water opened pores on the face and scalp, and was therefore to be avoided for the sake of health. Even rinsing the hair in cold water could be dangerous in the Tudor mindset, the chill of the experience upsetting the internal balance and making a person catch cold.

Michel de Nostredame, also known as Nostradamus, worked primarily in France, where he held the position of court physician for some years. In addition to his famous mystical prophecies, in 1552 he published a small book of recipes. These were luxury products for the aristocracy and royalty. Two are for hair and beard dyes, one producing a 'golden' colour and the other dyeing grey hairs black. Both require a person to first wash the hair 'with a good lye, for if it were greasy or dirty it would not take the colour so well'. Using such grease-dissolving liquids upon the hair or body was, however, problematic. They could be very caustic, leaving the hair brittle and the scalp damaged. The soap derived from lye – a strongly alkaline solution – was a little kinder, but still not something that lent itself to frequent use.

3.   Dressing

The sacred Muse that firste made love devine
Hath made him naked and without attyre
But I will cloth him with this penn of myne
That all the world his fashion shall admire
His hatt of hope, his band of beautye fine
His cloake of crafte, his doublet of desire
Greife for a girdell, shall aboute him twyne
His pointes of pride, his Ilet holes of yre . . .

   Sir John Davies, *Gullinge Sonnets* (1584)

Once hands and face were washed, clean linen underwear put on, hair combed and teeth cleaned, it was time to finish dressing.

All his wearing apparel

A man's clothes were a matter of great public importance, a woman's less so. With his clothes a man advertised his place in society, a fact that had serious consequences in Tudor England. Laws restricted a man's rights to wear certain fabrics and colours to those within particular social strata, so thoughtless dressing could land a man in legal trouble. As our period opens, the statute of 1483 was still fresh in the minds of people. It limited the use of 'cloth of gold' and purple silk to members of the royal family, and velvet cloth to those of the status of knight or above.

The servants of small-scale farmers, labourers and their wives could by law spend no more than two shillings per yard upon any cloth for clothing. Even within the law, the cut and style of a man's clothing could indicate either occupation or the membership of a specialist or elite group, something that was fiercely protected. A man's public appearance also denoted his creditworthiness. With no formal banking system and most trading operating upon credit, the well-dressed were more able to acquire goods and services. Those looking for work needed to advertise their skills and experience by appearing in the correct working gear of the relevant trade.

As with shirts, all clothing was fearfully expensive by modern standards. The costs involved in making a garment, particularly in processing the raw materials, were enormous. Take sheep, as the most important example. A Tudor sheep, while not miniature, was considerably smaller than those that graze in modern fields. Pictures of sheep with their shepherds, the bones of butchered animals recovered archaeologically, and the weight of butchers' carcasses recorded in the accounts of the great households all point to smaller animals. Twin lambs were a rarity among Tudor flocks, whereas nowadays it is the singleton lamb that is uncommon and triplets are not unknown. Flocks grazed outdoors upon upland pastures and overwintering arable fields without the supplementary feeding that helps modern sheep to bulk up and fatten. The resultant fleeces were both smaller and lighter. Direct comparisons between fleece weights can be a little misleading since modern fleeces are sheared all in one and the entirety is weighed, while records of Tudor fleeces often include only the best-quality wool from the back and haunches when weighed for sale, but nonetheless a twenty-first-century fleece of twelve pounds in weight is in a different league from a one-and-a-half-pound fleece of the sixteenth century.

At the end of May, when the weather was warming, shepherds drove their flocks down to streams and ponds where they could wash their charges, herding them up on to clean pasture to drip and dry out. Shearing was a massive operation that called on all the local labour. Modern electric clippers permit the professional shearers of Australia and New Zealand to work their way through many hundreds of sheep in a working day; the equally skilled and hard-working men of the sixteenth century, armed with a pair of hand shears, did well to complete thirty. Once shorn, the fleeces had to be sorted, rolled and packed for sale. Cloth production began with the combing or carding of the wool to clean out any grass, twigs and other filth and to untangle any knots or matted locks. This was all done by hand, keeping many women and children busy. Next it was spun on simple drop spindles, or increasingly, as the era progressed, with a spinning wheel, work again carried out mostly by women or children. It took twelve skilled spinsters working at full pelt to supply enough yarn to keep one weaver in business. Few women totally escaped the job of spinning; indeed the work became synonymous with the unmarried woman (hence the change in meaning of the word). Like the baking of bread or the brewing of beer, spinning was a regular female task, whether for yarn used in the home or for the few pennies it earned.

Weaving itself was mostly men's work, requiring the careful warping up of the loom (threading each of the long threads that run the full length of the finished bolt of cloth through the various parts of the loom and carefully winding up the length on to the back beam) before cloth could be woven. Lengths of twenty-two yards were generally worked at a time, although different types of cloth were legally prescribed at slightly differing sizes. This single length or piece could take a man six weeks to produce. Once woven, the majority of cloth needed some form of 'finishing'. Most webs needed washing, and many were fulled (a process akin to felting, where the fibres are encouraged to mesh together) to tighten up the fabric, improving its ability to keep the wind and rain out. Dyers got involved either in dyeing the wool before it was spun, dyeing the yarn or dyeing the piece once woven. The wet webs were stretched out on tenterhooks to dry and regain their legal dimensions. (Non-conforming lengths of cloth could be confiscated, and there was a system of fines to be paid for every small deviation.) Naps were raised by combing over the surface with teasels and the surfaces sheared smooth and flat.

All of these people in their many and varied places of work needed to earn a living from their labour, each adding a little more to the cost of the finished product. It was a complex industry, involving tools and machinery that required significant capital investment and skilled professionals to operate. The fleeces, yarn and cloth itself moved from workshop to workshop, bought and sold many times over.

With cloth being such an expensive commodity, a man needed to be careful how he laid out his hard-earned cash. The few items of clothing that he would be able to afford needed to do multiple jobs. Primarily he needed protection from the cold, the wind and the rain. He needed clothing that would be able to withstand the wear it was going to be subjected to, and that would last until such time that he could afford to replace it. In addition, his clothes needed to be socially acceptable, so that he didn't get into trouble for 'indecency' by being underdressed or become the butt of jokes and ribaldry for his extravagance. They also needed to fulfil his desires to project an image of himself to the world, to look respectable or attractive or like one of the gang. His self-image, social image and bodily comfort were all bound up in a few precious items of clothing.

For many men, the garment to aspire to was a gown. This could be short, around knee-length, or long, around ankle-length. Gowns fell from the shoulders and were generally worn loose as overgarments. There were several styles running simultaneously throughout the period, with a gradual shift over time towards the longer gown and full-length, straighter sleeves. As an unfitted, voluminous piece of clothing, it could be cumbersome to wear whenever physical exertion was called for, and it required a lot of cloth in its making. This was not the day-to-day wear of an agricultural labourer or blacksmith; it was a signifier of those whose daily lives were more sedentary and those with additional resources. Lawyers, clerics, aldermen and academics sported gowns as part of their daily workwear, and most gentlemen had several in their wardrobes. Shorter gown styles that allowed more freedom of movement were considered suitable for younger men; the grave and serious opted for the full-length version. The successful blacksmith or labourer might, with the requisite finances, have a gown for Sunday wear.

Something of the aspirational nature of gowns can perhaps be seen in the records of Philip Henslowe, whose main line of business was the theatre, but who also appears to have run a pawnbroking business as a sideline. Gowns form a significant proportion of the goods being pawned. On 13 May 1594, for example, he 'lent upon a sylke grosgren gowne garded with velluet and lined with saye of mr Burdes for iij li xs [£3 10s]' and two days later 'lent upon a manes gowne un lined of brode cloth blacke for xiijs [13s]'. They were high-value items that were easy to sell on, and were the sort of garment that a person could manage without when push came to shove. The first of these two gowns, made out of a heavyweight silk fabric with velvet strips sewn on around the hem, up the front and around the collar, and lined with a good-quality lightweight wool, was a luxury item even for a successful merchant and its pawn value reflects this. The second gown, while much simpler and cheaper, was still a substantial item for a successful craftsman, being made of broad-cloth, one of the highest-value woollen cloths available.

When men came to write their wills, the gown was frequently the only item of clothing that they specifically bequeathed. A gown, after all, was likely to fit pretty much anyone and with so much cloth involved it could always be cut up and used for something else. It could also be the item of clothing in which a man had the most emotional investment, representing his position and success in the world. This was particularly true of those ordinary craftsmen who had risen to positions of urban power: aldermen and mayors. Gowns formed the official uniform of such men, in specified colours, cloths and trimmings, and they were encouraged to wear them on all official business and even when generally out and about. In Exeter the mayor wore a gown and cloak of scarlet cloth ('scarlet' can denote a high-quality woollen cloth, the colour scarlet, or indeed both, since the majority of scarlet cloths were in fact dyed scarlet). The stewards, one step below, had violet gowns and the aldermen had murrey-coloured gowns. The brightest shades were the most expensive to produce, so a very clear visual representation of the municipal power structure was on display here. In some towns the requirement to wear mayoral gowns extended beyond the mayor himself to his wife. In 1580 Winchester issued a ruling that all mayors forthwith were to buy their wives scarlet gowns, and scarlet gowns are seen on some mayoral wives in portraits and within the wills and inventories of others in several towns and cities. Our culture is a little wary of such sartorial display. We value a form of casual negligence of dress, especially in men, so it can be hard sometimes to see how men of the Tudor era enjoyed and sought out formal clothing as genuinely respected badges of success, to be worn with pride.

While a simple form of gown was achievable by a significant section of the population, making them fairly common if not ubiquitous garments, the details of fabric, linings, cut and trimmings gave gowns an almost infinite number of social gradations. A frieze gown was a very lowly thing when compared to one of broadcloth, and a broadcloth gown was negligible against that of damask. Richard Brett, for example, worked as one of the bailiffs in the borough of Maldon, Essex, a position of some local authority. His wool gown was lined with 'budge', one of the cheapest furs and one permitted by the clothing, or sumptuary, laws for men of non-gentry status. Richard was well off and had three separate houses and parcels of land to leave in his will. He could have afforded a more elaborate and flashy gown had he chosen to do so, but instead opted for sober and restrained respectability. Stephen Caterall was a curate in the parish of Layer de la Haye in Essex. His two gowns are both described as 'long' in his will of 1567, a style synonymous with the clergy.

Beneath the gown, men wore doublets and hose. At the very start of Henry VII's reign these still gave men a slim appearance, closely following the contours of the body. Doublets were generally functional garments that gave a layer of warmth to the upper body and held up the hose. They were not major items of display at this point in history, and were generally covered up in formal situations such as going to church, market or any other public outing. If a man did not have a gown to go over his doublet, he would wear a coat over the top. His doublet was only on display when working hard.

The hose that accompanied these early doublets were full length from waist to toe. All around the top, at the waistline, was a row of paired holes that allowed the hose to be tied to the doublet as tightly or loosely as you required. There is something of an art to 'trussing'. A lovely neat look where the two garments join perfectly all round is fine as long as you don't intend ever to move; too loose and you will be embarrassingly exposed.

Those whose work involved a lot of digging or bending double often left the ties (or points) completely undone at the back while tightening the front points to their maximum. Of course, when you stand up the back sags down in a traditional 'builder's bum' fashion. Bruegel the Elder's paintings of the Flemish peasantry are particularly good at highlighting this phenomenon, although shirt tails lend some modesty. A little looseness at the front helped to prevent any pull when walking or running. It was therefore the fastening at the sides that most men relied upon for supporting the hose, and these were often tied a fraction higher and tighter than the others. You can see such careful adjustments among all those aristocratic young men in the painted illuminations of fifteenth-century manuscripts. I have watched a lot of modern men dressed in reconstructions of full-leg hose struggle to achieve the right balance. It is interesting to note that once they have found the perfect pointing strategy, they almost all leave the two garments fixed permanently together, stepping in and out of the complete suit, rather like a cat suit.

A fully footed pair of hose put more pressure on the knees than a pair of trousers might do. Trousers are free to ride up and down at the ankle as people sit and kneel, but when the leg and foot are in one piece this ease has to come from somewhere else. Fitted hose were therefore often a bit baggy at the knee, where the cloth stretched to accommodate movement. A young man wishing to look his best could well achieve a more flattering look, showing off his calf muscles, if he tied a garter just below the knee, confining the bagginess to the knee area and holding the hose smooth, slim and snug against his lower leg. At the front a small piece of cloth tied across the front opening, fulfilling the functions of the modern zip fly. This was the codpiece, for most men a modest simple covering and at this date rarely padded or otherwise exaggerated. Hose wore out much more quickly than doublets, coats and gowns as they bore the brunt of movement stresses. Wearing replicas, it becomes clear that there are two main areas that suffer: the feet, and the holes for points around the waist. Repairs to both are fairly cheap and simple to do, requiring small oddments of cloth. It seems likely, therefore, that a large proportion of hose as actually worn had replacement feet sections, or were worn footless. In the Kloster Museum in Württemberg, Germany, there is a pair of sturdy, natural-coloured linen hose made somewhere between 1495 and 1529 that are footless, showing signs of having once been footed and heavily worn.

Most of the coloured images we have for men of Henry VII's reign are those found in illustrated manuscripts. Gorgeous, jewel-like creations, they suggest a world inhabited by colourfully dressed young men in tight-fitting hose, the origin of the 'men in tights' idea of male fashion. These were always idealized images, however, often intended to portray holy perfection and harmony, the men's physical beauty a signifier of inward purity and godliness. The colours may also be symbolic, with green hose indicating youthful vigour, for example, and red denoting passion. Other illustrators consciously tried to portray the livery colours and heraldry of particular royal and aristocratic houses. Some of the depicted styles were pure fantasy, bearing little relation to actual garments but rather sartorial indicators of the exotic, foreign, historical and mythical.

The written record tells a different story. An analysis of wills from the first half of the sixteenth century shows only a smattering of bright colours in the hose that were bequeathed. This selection of wills is heavily dominated by the more wealthy members of society and has an urban rather than rural bias, yet by far the most common colour of hose mentioned is black, with white the second most popular. The few bright colours are mostly to be found in the wills of the aristocracy. Of course, not everyone mentioned their hose at all and those that did generally made no mention of the colour (only 44 out of 247 in an analysis by Maria Hayward). Maybe the rest of the hose were undyed – a range of creams, beiges, greys and browns, perhaps, reflecting the colours of different breeds of sheep and the natural colour of linen. Fabric could also alter the picture. In 1520, when the Lestrange family provided hose for their kitchen boy, they bought a yard of 'blanket cloth'. In 1558 Robert Dudley provided 'russet' cloth for his kitchen boys. Both types of cloth are cheap, fairly sturdy, a bit hairy, and loosely woven so they have an element of stretch; with the best will in the world they are too bulky to make up into smooth, sleek, elegant hose.

Portraits of Henry VIII standing full square, feet apart, and staring straight at us, show where doublet, hose, coat and gown had gone by the mid sixteenth century. The sheer quantity of cloth used to make that super-wide pleated gown was beyond most men's means, but letting your more modest gown hang wide open to reveal the layers beneath was easy to copy. Doublets and hose, as a result, attracted more attention right across the social strata. The law, too, was focusing more closely upon the details of male dress. Henry VII had been largely content to simply reiterate the sumptuary laws of his predecessor; his son was much more concerned with fine-tuning and updating the regulations. Within a year of ascending the throne, he passed the first of four Acts of Apparel. It was most detailed in dealing with those at the top of society, those directly around the king himself, but its rules would have an impact on almost every man. The vast majority who worked the land – shepherds, labourers and small-scale farmers (husbandmen) – were banned from wearing imported cloth of any type, and were even restricted to the cheaper types of natively produced wools. They could wear broadcloths, for example, only if they cost less than two shillings a yard, and hose had to be made of cloth costing less than ten pence a yard.

The clothing regulations addressed a number of issues that bothered successive Tudor governments. The balance of payments was obviously one of these worries. By restricting imported cloth to a small minority of the population, it was hoped to prevent large amounts of money from flowing out of the country. The encouragement of home-produced textiles was also intended to stimulate manufacture, providing or sustaining a market particularly for the cheaper sorts of cloth that were not in much demand abroad. This was seen very much as a duty of job protection or creation among those in authority. As well as worries about national cash flow, there were also powerful concerns about individual indebtedness. The luxury imported cloths were seen as deeply desirable, tempting citizens into unnecessary financial danger. In their preambles the sumptuary laws sought to put a brake on the self-destructive desires of people to indulge themselves in textile luxury. But perhaps more important than these concerns was, in the words of the Act of 1533, the 'subvercion of good and politike ordre in knowelege and distinccion of people according to their estates, pre emynences dignities and degrees'. Fashions and monarchs might change, but this remained a central worry.

There is no doubt that for many people these regulations posed little problem since they could barely afford the cheapest of cloth anyway, but what did you do if you were left a good broadcloth gown in someone's will? It could also be that the second-hand clothes available locally, originally owned by more prosperous people, were made of something a little better, though well worn. Imported wools from Ireland were very cheap, well within the reach of the working majority, and yet it was technically illegal for working men to wear them.

The price restrictions also had a bearing on colour. The bright reds, the solid blacks, the deeper blues and verdant greens were all costly colours to produce, pushing fairly humble types of cloth up in price over the legal boundaries. Undyed remained the cheapest option. Paler blues derived from woad, and the more muted orangey-pink reds dyed with madder, along with mustard-yellows from weld, were the colours to be found in the mid-price range.

Cheaper cloths were generally less 'finished' and made from the hairier sorts of fleece, so the law enforced a certain look upon the rural working man. There were also some very practical reasons for the working man to stick to the legal fabrics. Frieze is a bulky cloth with a raised hairy nap on one side, made of coarse wool spun and woven fairly loosely. It is warm, trapping lots of air between its fibres, and good at shedding water, especially if the nap is lying vertically downwards. The coarse, cheap fleeces that are used to make it have a high proportion of 'kemp' fibres, which are the longer, thicker, stiffer hairs that allow sheep to keep dry in the rain, channelling rain away; the under-hairs of the sheep are shorter, softer, more crimped and better at holding in body heat. A frieze coat therefore looked a little shaggy, and as it didn't take dye very well (the kemp doesn't absorb it as well as the under-hairs) it was generally left in a natural grey or brown colour. It made excellent coats. Russet cloth could be dyed more successfully: it was a bit softer than the frieze and had more 'drape', but was less water-resistant. Russet therefore tended to be used more for doublets and hose and less often for gowns and coats. Canvas lent itself to doublets where wear was more important than warmth. Those whose work involved lots of hauling on ropes, for example, could benefit from a canvas doublet. Canvas was rarely dyed. It began life a beigy-grey colour and was slowly bleached over time in the sun and rain to a creamy white. Frieze, canvas and russet dominated the wardrobes of this the largest section of the population.

Sailors really stood out from their shaggy-coated landlubber brethren. Not for them the frieze coat and russet hose. Not just in materials but also in the cut of their garments sailors were easily spotted in any crowd. The 'sea gown' that appears in the inventories of those who title themselves mariners was cut more like a knee-length smock. Images of sailors engaging with indigenous people in John White's watercolours made on his various trips to the New World show stiff, full, long-sleeved garments, rather smock-like, covering everything underneath. They either buttoned up the front or were just slipped on over the head. A tightly woven canvas offered a degree of wind- and waterproofing over the top of the men's other clothes. The Museum of London has a garment that may well be one of these sea-going gowns, made of linen that has been tarred. Working linseed oil into canvas is another waterproofing method open to men facing everything the weather could throw at them. Leather clothing was also popular among the seafaring fraternity – generally sleeveless jackets known as jerkins, but you also come across leather doublets and very occasionally leather hose. Martin Frobisher, the famous captain who led the search for the North-West Passage to Asia, was painted in a very upmarket version of leather jerkin and breeches in 1577, deliberately choosing to highlight and commemorate his sailing experiences.

The law, however, did not remain static. By 1533, when the fourth of Henry VIII's sumptuary laws was passed, the rules became much more detailed, changing along with economic and social realities. The cloth for a common man's hose could now cost up to two shillings per yard, and canvas or fustian could be worn even if they were imported. This was just as well, as prices had been rising and a huge amount of linen cloth was entering the country. It was probably simply an acknowledgement that change had happened and that the law was dragging on behind. But it did add a new layer of legal complexity by splitting the common man into two groups, with only the husbandman being permitted the two-shilling cloth; his servants and apprentices were restricted to sixteen pence per yard.

The new rules also gave a nod to a new fashion, that of splitting the hose into two garments at thigh level. The lower part of the leg remained visually much the same in garments that could be called stockings, hose or nether hose. Garments for the upper part, variously named hose, upperstocks or trunk hose, were more substantial. With the split above the knee there was less need for stretchy fabric: the two garments could overlap, allowing movement. Upperstocks could therefore be made of a wider variety of fabrics, and could also be more heavily tailored or decorated. My favourite pair of upperstocks is the yellow knitted silk pair that were worn by the elector Augustus of Saxony between 1552 and 1555. For me they embody the quirkiness of fashion with the exquisite skill of craftspeople. The leather foundation is shaped down to the lower thigh just as the older, full-length design was, providing a familiar and comfortable fit and a strong stable base for the delicate top fabrics. The knitting is very fine and must have taken weeks of solid work. Mimicking a design of applied braids, it has openings, or slashes, where a sheer yellow silk lining can be pulled through in eye-catching puffs. At the front is a full-blown explicit codpiece. According to wardrobe accounts the elector had several pairs like this, and so did Henry VIII.

Large graphic codpieces were a little less socially acceptable at humbler levels of society; they were associated with power and lordship, with masculine assertiveness. Soldiers, perhaps unsurprisingly, were another group for whom the codpiece could be prominent, bravado and display being seen as linked to aggression and courage. The young swashbuckler about town, dressed in gaudy colours, his sword audibly swashing against the buckler (a small hand shield) suspended from his belt, could sport the

most outrageous of codpieces with impunity. Images of craftsmen and those working on the land are noticeably lacking in
prominent codpieces, but some humbler men, at least, sported
smaller woven twill versions as three were found in the ground
at Worship Street in London among other cloth fragments.

Edward VI took clothing so seriously that he drafted the
1552 bill for restraint of apparel personally. Elizabeth I issued a
series of proclamations throughout her reign, tracking the
changes in fashion, the imports available and the continued
worries about social mixing. The sumptuary Act of 1562, four
years after Elizabeth took the throne, saw the first concerns
about the 'monstrous and outrageous greatness' of men's hose.
The new double ruffs were also singled out as outrageous, and
particularly unsuitable for anyone outside the court. What was
comely fashion for a lord was ridiculous on a carpenter. The
phrase 'aping your betters' was one that took visual form in an
engraving of 1570 that has apes, dressed in middle-class clothing, laundering and setting ruffs. By counterfeiting that which
they were not, the non-gentry were themselves degraded as well
as cheapening that which they were copying.

There was felt to be an inherent natural rightness to the strati-
fication of society and to clothing as an indicator of that layering.
Clothing was supposed to visually place a man within society –
not only to indicate his wealth, but also to indicate the nature of
his position, whether craftsman or professional, master or servant, owner or renter of land, father or son. If you knew who a
person was, you would know how to interact with him, how
much respect you should show, whether you should bow or doff
your cap. Should you enter into business relationships with him,
ask for his help or employ him? In a society where most men
were armed in some way and where social respect was taken
very seriously indeed, mistakes of behaviour could quickly esca-
late into violence. Court records are brimming with cases of

brawling and stabbings over issues of respect and honour. Take the coroner's records for just two months in 1596, in the rural county of Sussex. On 13 April, Geoffrey King killed Thomas Horne, beating him over the head with a staff. Robert Hall used a horsewhip on the 26th of the same month to beat Henry Smythe to death. On 9 May, John Almon clubbed to death a man who would not let him pass in the street. On the same day Richard Norrys was stabbed in the face by Richard Rumnye, and on the 31st William Furner murdered Richard Kymber by stabbing him in the stomach.

Until 1574 all of the legal clothing restrictions applied only to men. It was, after all, the social position of men that affected public life most strongly. It was men who might own land, possess the freedom of the city, sit on juries, lead the community in the Church, fight for their country, attend university, and men, ideally, who were to be head of the household. Since each of these functions served the good ordering of society, it was believed that they needed to be acknowledged in a manner that was apparent to all. Clothes formed a perfect universal vehicle for expression of these ideas, even the humble cap, as in this late Elizabethan ballad:

> The Monmouth cap, the sailor's thrum,
> And that wherein the tradesman come,
> The physic, law and cap divine,
> The same that crowns the muses nine,
> The cap that fools do countenance,
> The goodly cap of maintenance,
> And any cap, whate're it bee,
> Is still the sign of some degree.

By your cap alone a person could tell if you were a doctor, lawyer or countryman, a fool (with bells on), a sailor in a shaggy thrum cap, a churchman, or if you followed a trade.

Most caps were knitted in the round upon four needles, then fulled and felted to make them almost completely waterproof. Indeed, in 1577 it became law for all men and boys over the age of five and below the rank of gentleman (with the exception of gentlemen's servants) to wear on Sundays 'one cap of wool knit, thicked and dressed, in England'. The law did not, however, specify colour or shape. We are extremely lucky in that several dozen of these caps have survived the vagaries of time when almost no other working men's garments have. The majority are round, flat and with one or sometimes two brims all round. They are also generally associated with an urban context – the Thames foreshore mud being a particularly successful preservative medium for this type of garment. According to Thomas Dekker's *The Honest Whore* (1604):

> Flat caps as proper are to city gowns,
> As to armours helmets, or to kings their crowns.

Portraits, woodcuts and other images bear this out: respectable begowned merchants, aldermen, guild officials and mayors all wear such caps, almost always in expensive black. The surviving caps, however, were originally in a variety of colours – reds and blues as well as black – indicating that some were more likely to have been the caps of ordinary craftsmen and tradesmen.

Those wishing to indicate a professional status, rather than just a mercantile or trade identity, frequently combined a flat knitted cap with a black coif. In the personal chest of the barber surgeon aboard the *Mary Rose* was found just such a coif in black velvet, cut from a single piece and seamed together with ten darts, each covered with a length of braid. Several of his professional colleagues are seen wearing just such a cap in the 1540 painting of Henry VIII and the Guild of Barber Surgeons by Holbein the Younger. Soldiers, meanwhile, favoured 'Monmouth caps'. These were also knitted and fulled, but in shape resembled a simple 'beanie' or bobble hat without the bobble. The thrum caps of sailors were also knitted, but with a shaggy covering of loose threads that were particularly good at keeping the water out. Out in the countryside, small, round, brimmed felt hats graced the heads of ploughmen.

But what if a man, be he sailor or farmer, flouted the law? What if he bought, having had a successful year and wishing to strut his stuff, a silk hatband, for example, or a pair of black kersey hose? Well, in truth he was very unlikely to be prosecuted. A few people were: Richard Bett, for example, a tailor from Essex, was convicted in 1565 for the size of his hose; and in the same year Richard Walweyn, who worked as a servant in London, was arrested for wearing 'a very monstrous and outraygeous great payre of hose', a charge that closely followed the wording of the 1562 proclamation. But, even at the time, people were aware that policing the sumptuary laws was almost impossible. To begin with many people were exempt: not just women, but churchmen, those in service to the crown, servants of rich men, those who held office within a town government structure, graduates, ambassadors and – while working – actors and musicians. It was therefore a little tricky to know whether someone was breaking the law with that pair of black kersey hose or whether they were a member of an exempt group. Social pressure about what was 'fitting' kept most people on the straight and narrow, but there were always those who were willing to push at the boundaries of fashion and personal display, and a few who were happy to manipulate social understandings of clothes to fool, cheat and defraud others.

Clothes were the stock-in-trade of con artists. In a society where the vast majority of people displayed their status and wealth sartorially, a suit of clothes was taken at face value. Enter an inn wearing a good black gown, and the proprietor was only too happy to show you into the private parlour and fetch out all the best table linen and pewter dishes. Send him to fetch a jug of wine and sugar, and you could pack it all into a bag and climb out of the window. In 1552 a book entitled *A Manifest Detection of the Most Vyle and Detestable Use of Diceplay* was published anonymously, purportedly as a warning to young men about the dishonesty and tricks of London's criminal fraternity. Written in a decidedly tabloid style, it caught the public imagination and spawned a number of similar works. Though a pinch of salt is probably required when reading these accounts of confidence tricks, loaded dice and card sharps, the nuts and bolts of the business ring true. The sting begins with catching the attention of the intended victim with clothing. 'Haply as I roamed me in the church of Paul's . . . there walked up and down by me in the body of the church a gentleman, fair dressed in silk, gold and jewels, with three or four servants in gay liveries all broidered with sundry colours, attending upon him.' The victim was impressed and flattered by the attention of such a personage. Where he might have been wary of talking to a commonly dressed stranger, he implicitly trusted one 'fair dressed in silk' and was soon accompanying him to a tavern where they began to play dice for high stakes. He was fleeced, of course.

St Paul's Cathedral in London was reputed to be the regular haunt of well-dressed thieves whose business relied upon recognizing and intercepting unsuspecting countrymen, distracting them with gentlemanly friendship and either picking their pockets or leading them into rigged gambling sessions or dubious places where they could be more systematically robbed. According to the slang of the day, playing a confidence trick in this way was known as cony-catching, a cony being a young rabbit or a gullible fool. In his *Notable Discovery of Cozenage* (1592), Robert Greene writes: 'The cony-catchers, apparelled like honest civil gentlemen or good fellows . . . they see a plain country fellow, well and cleanly apparelled, either in a coat of homespun russet or frieze, as the time requires, and a side-pouch at his side – "There is a cony," saith one.'

Most of these deception crimes used clothing of a social status higher than the wearer should have been attired in, but clothing could also mislead when a person dressed down. Thomas Harman, a magistrate in Kent, wrote about just such a case in his *Caveat for Common Cursitors* (1565–6): Nicholas Jennings was famously prosecuted for wearing rags to beg in when in fact he was in possession of a black frieze coat, a new pair of white hose, a fine felt hat and a shirt of Flanders linen, all of which was valued at sixteen shillings. By day he wandered the streets of London naked from the waist up, apart from a sleeveless, ragged leather jerkin, his legs clothed in a series of dirty rags tied in place and a bloodstained coif upon his head. He carried a battered old felt hat in his hand as a begging bowl, and he claimed to be a sufferer of the falling sickness, or what we would call epilepsy. The use of clothing to extract false alms provoked both outrage and notoriety. He was put in the pillory, where he had to stand alternately in his rags and in his good suit. A picture was put up at the house of correction 'for a monument', and the anonymous *Groundeworke of Conny-Catching* (1592) further published his shame, including a woodcut showing him in both outfits calling him a monstrous dissembler.

The business of clothes

Off-the-peg clothing was a scarce commodity in Tudor England. Hats, stockings and gloves could be purchased as finished new items, but almost all other clothes were made to the customer's specification. For the more prosperous, shopping for a new doublet began with a trip to buy cloth and trimmings. Tailors rarely carried much in the way of a stock of cloth, restricting themselves in the main to the sorts of fabrics that were used for interlinings. With a budget in mind, a man visited the mercer's shop, or went to market to look over the colours, qualities and prices available. The range was rarely large. Few mercers could afford to carry large stocks of cloth; they tended to play safe, stocking a few popular neutral shades in the cheaper fabrics with perhaps a couple of small pieces of flashy silk to enliven the display. The larger the town, of course, the more choice there was: larger pools of potential customers allowed for faster turnovers and a wider range of personal tastes. But even mercers in the biggest of towns and cities outside London had trouble getting hold of the full range of fabrics. London was dominant in the cloth trade, pulling in fabric from all over the Continent as well as the home-produced wares.

Buying cloth for clothes does require a little technical knowledge: some weights and weaves make up better than others; some are suitable for coats, some for hose. Sticking to the tried and tested was one way of ensuring that you didn't waste your money; other people took someone with them to help make the choice. With your precious cloth in hand, you then visited the tailor and discussed the style and finish you wanted. Measurements were taken with a long strip of parchment – not a tape measure with the units of measurement written on it, but a plain strip that the tailor made a series of notches or marks upon. This was your personal measure, the measure of a man. The tailor's next job, and one of the most important, was to work out how to lay out the pattern of the garments upon the length of cloth as economically as he could. People, understandably, were very stingy with the amount of cloth they bought, and any excess was by tradition the tailor's perk, his to keep and sell on if he could. Even the tiniest shreds of cut-off material – 'cabbage' or 'garbage' as it was called – had a value as patching or stuffing, or even as rag for paper.

The very first surviving tailors' patterns are not patterns as such but laying-out plans to show how to get each style of garment out of different widths and lengths of cloth; they have nothing to do with fit. There is a black silk suit in the reserve collection of the Victoria and Albert Museum that reflects something of this relationship between the tailor and his customer. Tucked away in a drawer at Blythe House, it is deteriorating fast: the black dye has broken the fibres over the intervening 400 years, and fine black dust lifts and floats away at every tiny shake or movement. Too fragile to go on display, there is sadly no conservation method currently known that can stop the decay. I have had the great privilege of studying it closely, trying to unpick the story of its construction before it is gone for good.

The owner of this suit, in the early seventeenth century, chose a black silk fabric for the body of his doublet, with some fearfully expensive cloth of black silk interwoven with real silver thread for the sleeves, black velvet for the breeches and a sky-blue silk for the lining. The style was conventionally up-to-date, with a heavily stiffened straight front, high collar, skirts at the waist and a tabbed wing at the shoulder. A little more unusually it also has hanging sleeves in addition to the main sleeves, to show off that black cloth of silver, perhaps. They had no practical function but were simply formed from extra cloth that hung down from the back of the shoulder. The whole suit is covered in black silk 'guards'. These guards, rather like elaborate constructed braids, were almost certainly made separately, not by the tailor but by a professional embroiderer, and bought in on a roll. They are not woven braids but assembled pieces: a strip of canvas was cut and a strip of black satin laid on top, possibly glued in place, and turned around under the raw edges of the canvas, then a series of black silk cords were stitched on to the surface, forming a running repeating pattern. Over the top of these cords a black silk thread was embroidered with satin stitch and French knots to create a repeating vine motif. Black upon black, this is all about textures, about how the light catches on different silk surfaces. Rich and gorgeous and yet restrained at the same time.

It is clear, looking at the surviving fragments, that the tailor knew his business, had access to the best materials and was experienced in creating such high-fashion garments. It is also clear that he was open to saving a few pennies here and there, had a team of workers and was under extreme time pressure. The first stage of the work was done very carefully and frugally. The black silk for the doublet was cut to have two joins right down the front, which could be carefully hidden by the guards later, allowing the tailor to squeeze more out of the cloth, and the final layout of the guards was planned to the sixteenth of an inch. There can't have been much of the black velvet for the breeches as they have a number of irregular piecings fitted together out of small offcuts. Then it seems the work was divided between several people, each working on a separate component, something that can be guessed at from the details of the different stitching styles. One person worked on the collar, assembling two layers of cardboard, two layers of canvas sewn together in a curve, then adding the black silk and a cream silk lining. The tabs, the skirts, the sleeves, the lacing band and belly piece all began life as separate pieces, interlined and stiffened with a variety of materials, from bundles of bents (reeds) for rigidity in the belly piece to at least six different grades of linen canvas. The workmanship is good but not overly fussy; there is not an unnecessary stitch anywhere. If the stitch was to be invisible in the final garment, there was no attempt at making it neat. Knots and stray ends of thread abound, hidden within.

When it came to putting all the pieces together, huge stitches in a thick strong thread did the trick. The bought-in guards were then laid over the top and invisibly stitched down. Perhaps our tailor had a lot of orders on his books, or maybe it was our customer who was in a hurry. This is the most speedily constructed high-class suit I have seen. Corners were definitely cut. Only the skill and experience of the tailor, who knew exactly where and what he could skimp on, saved it from being a bit of a bodge job. Oh, and someone sewed three pins into the waistband of the breeches by accident – they're still there.

But our tale does not end with the customer taking away his rush job. He was soon back: the breeches were not right. He might not have noticed the pins, but he had certainly decided that the length was wrong. Five inches had to be added to the bottom of each leg. There was none of the original black velvet left, so this alteration was patched together out of fragments left over from another job. Nor did the tailor have very much of that roll of black guarding left. Luckily he had some bits very like it, with a slightly different pattern – well, another three different patterns in fact, but since they were all black on black and roughly the same width this wouldn't be too noticeable. His careful arrangement of the guards also had to be compromised: they had all met perfectly edge to edge at the bottom, but to carry on the line he now had to pleat them in a bit at the new lower hem. Had he got the measurements wrong? It is an unlikely place to make a measuring mistake, and there were no alterations elsewhere, so perhaps this is the call of fashion. I like to imagine our customer, having procured the suit in a hurry, perhaps on an infrequent visit to court, had worn it once or twice and gone back to the country. When next he visited he thought, 'Oh, that's all right, I still have that new black suit – that will do.' But to his annoyance he soon realized that the fashion had moved on over the last couple of months and above-the-knee breeches were just not the thing any more. A quick trip back to the tailor's was required: 'No, just alter them with what you've got, I haven't got time to mess about.'

But what if you could not run to tailor-made clothing? What did everyone else do? Underwear could be made up at home. Shirts were simple shapes, just a series of rectangles that were easy to plan and cut out, and the sewing skills needed to turn them into a garment were part of the general education of women – and many men. Outer clothes, however, were much more of a risk. When one had spent vast sums on the cloth, a mistake in cutting could be disastrous, and outer clothes were generally much more complicated shapes to produce. Many very humble and cash-strapped people therefore did take their cloth to a tailor. The making-up costs were a fraction of the cloth costs. The alternative to a tailor for most people was not home production but second-hand clothing. The market for pre-worn clothes was huge, and at all levels of society. There was no shame at all in wearing clothes originally tailored for someone else; even the aristocracy did it. Clothes were inherited, given as gifts, pawned, bought and sold, and were often part of someone's wages. A doublet originally produced as Sunday best for a country gentleman, with all its interlinings, stiffenings, braids and buttons, could pass at his death to his brother or nephew, who had it altered to fit. As it became a bit worn, the buttons and braids could be stripped off for reuse and the doublet handed on to a servant. With new but basic buttons it may have been worn for a while, or sold on to the petty chapman who called at the door. Weeks later, it could have been on the back of a husbandman, having been given a good clean by his wife. As it grew more worn, patches and darns would have accumulated, until one day it would have been considered too tatty and was probably passed on again, this time, maybe, to one of the labourers who worked seasonally upon the farm. By this time it could have been ten years out of fashion and very heavily stained, but because it was a good, well-made garment in the first place it would still have provided warmth and protection, even a touch of faded style.

The second-hand clothing market in London was centred around Long Lane in Houndsditch. Clothes of almost any quality could be bought here, from the sumptuous gowns of peers of the realm to the oldest ragged frieze coat of an apprentice. These clothes could be cleaned, patched, repaired and altered to fit, and buttons and trimmings could be added and alterations done to turn them into more fashionable or practical garments. A merchant's old gown made Sunday best for a craftsman, and a source of heavily worn and patched workman's clothes meant that there was something within the reach of all but the very poorest to buy.

About a quarter of Tudor wills make some mention of clothes to be passed on to family members, servants and friends. People generally left their nearest and dearest their best items, but even those clothes described as 'old' or even 'worst' are individually bequeathed by some. In Essex in 1576, Thomas Peyre, for example, left his best coat to John Benton, a relative even though the surname is different. He also left a blue livery coat and one pair of his 'best hosen' to Henry Norton. Thomas Bocher got his best frieze coat, while two other men got an old coat each and John Hubbarde was left an old pair of hose. Two years earlier, Robert Gainsford divided up his stock of hose among his servants: Nathaniel Eliot had a russet pair, as did William Felsted; John Gilbet got the best white pair, while John Nice got the 'worst russet' pair. But even a worst russet pair of hose was worth having. Not everyone who was left clothing in someone's will actually wore it themselves; indeed, when, as occasionally happened, men left their clothes to women, or vice versa, it is clear that they intended them to be reworked into something else or sold on. In a world without banks, a pair of hose could sit easily enough in a chest until a person converted them into cash either by sale or pawn.

Those with good clothes could raise serious money: in the late 1590s the Elizabethan theatre manager Philip Henslowe lent Mr Crowch £3 10s against the security of his wife's gown, and a similar sum to Mr Burdes against a silk grosgrain gown guarded with velvet and lined in yellow say (say is a woollen fabric, often used for bed curtains). This amount of money was eighteen months' wages for a maidservant in London at that time, but only represented about two-thirds of the resale value of the garments. Even that second-hand pair of worst russet hose could be expected to bring in around four shillings, and who in modern life would turn their noses up at a bequest that equalled two weeks' wages?

A woman dresses

Start with a smock made of linen cloth, sewn at home from rectangles and two triangular gores at the sides, giving a fullness at the hips and hem, a hem that sits at mid-calf length. This is a woman's underwear, the layer that can be laundered easily, and the layer that touches her skin. There are no knickers, at least not for Englishwomen. Some foreign (especially Italian) women wore under-drawers similar to those worn by men. But even on the Continent they may have been associated with the dress of courtesans, where an additional man-like layer offered titillation and an aura of transgression. The ban that St Paul placed upon cross-dressing within the Bible, calling it an 'abomination', may have played its part here.

A smock, then, provided modesty, hygiene and comfort. When you first stepped out of bed, this is what you slipped into. Now, linen is a very cool fibre even on a warm day, and first thing on a frosty February morning it's a shock to the system. In aristocratic or royal households, servants warmed it in front of the fire before handing it to their mistresses, but for the vast majority of people that morning nip was best avoided by pulling it into bed with you for a bit to warm up. Hose came next. While men's hose were on display as outer garments, women's hose were largely hidden from view; they were shorter too, more like socks than stockings, most ending at the knee. There were linen-cloth hose, woollen-cloth hose, and increasingly there were knitted hose of wool for most and silk for the super-rich. Linen-cloth hose survive a lot of laundering and could be worn on their own or under another pair for comfort and cleanliness. Woollen hose, whether cloth or knitted, require surprisingly little laundry. Pure wool copes very well with the sweat and bacteria of feet. If you are accustomed to modern socks with a percentage of man-made fibres, and modern shoes with synthetic soles, foot odour and fungal infections are probably a part of life. Pure wool socks and leather shoes provide a much healthier environment where both smell and athlete's foot find it much harder to get a toe hold. Both materials allow the sweat to evaporate quickly, both are resistant to the bacteria that produce the pong, and wool in particular is resistant to the fungi that like to colonize human skin.

After hands and face, feet were the most likely part of the body to be regularly washed in water. When in 1575 Dorothy Clevely, a London wife of dubious morals, told her maid Judith to wash her feet and put out a clean smock as she might have to share a bed with some gentlewoman who would be 'loath to lie with her if her feet were foul and her smock not clean', she was expressing common sensibilities. Feet needed a little more attention than arms and legs as they quickly picked up the dirt of the street, and should be clean before you put your hose on. Woollen hose were also washable, if not as robust as linen; nonetheless, for these small items a periodic rinsing out was a simple matter. Cloth hose didn't have the stretch of knitted; they could be crudely shaped affairs that bagged at the ankle – after all, they were not on display all that much – or they could be carefully fitted to every contour, which was much more attractive but harder to get on or off. Woollen hose, whether cloth or knitted, will soon felt beneath your foot as the heat, the wet and the constant pounding bond the fibres together. My daughter, wishing to avoid the work of darning her woollen stockings, simply slips a bit of carded wool now and again into her shoes and waits for them to felt themselves on. It's highly effective, but don't wait until there are holes before you do this: add the wool when the fabric begins to look a bit thin and there is still something for the new wool to bind to.

They all need holding up by a garter tied below the knee. A good garter has a bit of stretch in it, is fairly broad and is either buckled or tied without a knot as such. A selvedge strip of loosely woven woollen cloth works well, as does a woollen inkle braid; knitted garters, like the surviving mid-sixteenth-century one on display in the Museum of London, knitted appropriately in garter stitch, are very good. Buckled garters are still worn to this day by members of the Order of the Garter, and a lot of small buckles turn up in archaeological digs and in the mud along the Thames. Many of these may have been garter buckles. To tie your garters with the method that I have found most comfortable, begin by folding one end of your garter over to form a three-inch loop, lay that loop vertically against the outside of your leg, loop up, ends down. Now take the long end and wrap it twice around the leg, taking care that the wrap crosses the loop, trapping it in place. Now tuck the long end over and down under the resultant binding. This should stay snugly in place without any hard lumpy knot to dig in, and still incorporate a little play for when you move.

This, then, provided the full washable covering of the body; smock and hose together represented a barrier between the skin and the outer world of dirt and disease. They also protected your valuable outerwear from the sweat and grease of your body. An intimate, personal and protective layer, a second skin and a very conservative layer, remaining almost unchanged throughout the whole Tudor period. Yes, sleeve shapes went in and out of fashion, embroidery styles changed, different forms of lace were employed and necklines moved around a bit, but essentially the body layer remained inviolate, its practical role holding firm.

In 1485, when our period begins, the smock was covered by a kirtle, a full-length dress that was sleeved and laced together. This was a sturdy piece of clothing, following the shape of the upper torso and flaring out from the waist. In an ideal world you had a gown to go over the top. This could be of a similar shape and material to the kirtle. The point was to have two layers – for warmth, of course, but also for show. As the outermost garment and therefore the most prominent, gowns were generally of a slightly better cloth than kirtles. But more important than showing off your gown cloth was showing off that you had a gown at all, that there was a kirtle layer beneath. Gowns therefore had lower collars or shorter sleeves, which showed off the other garment. A medium-quality kirtle-and-gown combination displayed more gravitas than a good kirtle alone. Gowns were generally worn at formal occasions, such as going to church (very chilly places, with lots of standing still), receiving guests and trips to market. Naturally, in the cold of winter you just piled everything on regardless.

Putting your kirtle on in the morning was a matter of wriggle and shake. It is often opined that only those with maids to help them dress had back-lacing kirtles. Yet there are images of working women whose lacings are definitely not at the front. A kirtle could be side-laced, but there is nothing to stop a woman from getting into and out of a back-lacing kirtle by herself. The trick is a good long lace and a spiral lacing technique. The few clothing fragments and even rarer complete surviving female garments that have come down to us show many tightly packed lacing holes. This gives a smooth, supportive fastening to a kirtle. Widely spaced eyelets lead to large puckers, which are not only unsightly but uncomfortable. It is also worth looking at the alignment of those eyelets. They are not parallel across the opening, but staggered; they are not designed to be laced across like shoes, but in one long continuous spiral. Tie one end of the lace to the bottom of the run of holes and lace up from there with the one free end. Now, if your lace is long enough, you can loop it very loosely, leaving a gap of four or five inches open down the length of the back. This turns the garment into a largish tube that is loose enough to be pulled on over the head in one go. Once you are in and everything has been smoothed into place, grab the unsecured end of the lace and haul away. Spiral lacing will tighten from this one end. Getting out again is a matter of another wriggle to loosen the lacing; you may have to reach round to the back of your waist to give it a hand. Once slackened off, cross your arms, lift up the back of the kirtle over your head and pull it off, like skinning a rabbit.

A kirtle is a good working garment, generally warm enough on its own when you are engaged in something physical; it is close fitting enough for nothing to flap around and get in the way. Made of good, strong, hard-wearing wools, it shields you from the heat and sparks of the fire, the splinters and thorns of fences and hedges, the irritants of plant saps, the burn of the sun, and the friction of tools, ploughs and carts. With the sleeves rolled up and an apron tied over it, you can cook and wash up, milk the cows and do the laundry. Out in the mud, or working in the stream, the skirts can be 'kirtled' up, out of the way.

Just as important was your head gear. Young girls could show their hair; it was a symbol of maidenly innocence, and as such a young woman's hair was combed out and worn loose upon her wedding day. Elizabeth I tellingly chose to be crowned 'in her hair', invoking the marriage ceremony and making a declaration of faith that all her subjects would have understood. In day-to-day practice, however, most girls and young women were almost as covered as married women.

First the hair had to be controlled. There were no hairpins in the modern sense; the work was done instead by laces or tapes. There were two main methods: the bound ponytail and the plait, both of which could be a single one or in pairs. Hints of both methods can sometimes be glimpsed in the shape of the final headdresses and in images of young girls and even saints.

Let's begin with the single form. If we are willing to move across Europe and slip a little later in date, one surviving example of the single bound ponytail method was found upon the head of a young woman who died in 1617 in the Czech Republic, when her tomb was opened in 2003. A little ghoulish though it is, this is a fantastic survival. Her blonde hair has been combed out and a sausage of cotton padding laid down the length of the hair. A long ribbon has then been tied to create a ponytail, with the padding caught up in place. The two ends of the ribbon were evenly wound down and around, crossing each other to the end of the hair and padding. The resultant thick, long, bound braid of hair was taken up and coiled upon the top of her head and a cap put on top. It gives a luxurious appearance. A woman's hair was private, her crowning glory. Introducing the padding gave an illusion of enormous sensual volume, provocatively hinted at under her headdress. Of course, the binding works just as well if you stick with your own, less impressive hair. A single bound braid can be secured in place with a long pin – like a hatpin. A pair used at an angle to each other is even more secure, and it is noticeable that many wealthy women at the end of the fifteenth and early sixteenth century include two silver pins in the gifts they bequeath. Two well-polished slivers of bone or wood will do the same job. The bound braids are much less slippery and much more manageable than simply twisting your hair up into a bun, which is just as well without lots of modern bent wire pins.

The plaiting method was easier to do by yourself. Plait the hair as normal, but as you begin lay a hair lace in with one of the bundles of hair so that it is plaited in. Use the lace to tie off the end of the plait, coil and pin as before.

The double bound or plaited method simply involves making two bunches of hair and binding or plaiting as before, but this time leaving a long free end of lace on each one. The two braids of hair can be crossed at the back of the neck, brought up over the head, crossing them again on the top, then taken back down and round before you tie the ends of the lace together; the laces can continue even when the length of hair runs out. You do not have a bun or coil to draw attention to your possession of concealed sexy hair, but it is very much more secure, a more practical method of hair control for those who are likely to be physically active.

With the hair in place, a cap or band can be tied or pinned around the head to act as an anchor point for the veil. At its simplest, a strip of hemmed linen two inches wide can be wrapped around the head horizontally and pinned to itself. It needs to be a snug fit and cover the hairline above the forehead. A simple piece of linen or woollen cloth draped over the head and pinned to this band to keep it in place provided all the headdress most women needed. A little fashion could be had by how you pinned the head rail or veil. In 1485 many women still pulled it smooth and round over the brow, but within a handful of years a pointed gable look was sweeping the countryside. This was an element of very cheap fashion. Store your veil overnight, folded in half under a weight of some kind to create a prominent fold crease that ran front to back on the top of the head, move two pins slightly, and, hey presto, the latest look. Not quite the full English gable hood worn at court, but definitely reminiscent of it.

By the 1580s whole new garments had emerged, gowns were undergoing a retreat and headdresses looked very different. The clothes of the court are familiar to us all, Elizabeth in her great white ruffs, long, slim, pointed body, and wide skirts supported by farthingales (hooped or padded undergarments). This iconic style was reliant on a number of sartorial innovations. New garments were accompanied by new materials and new techniques. The small linen ruffles around shirt collars could only swell into true ruffs when there was starch to stiffen them, a technique that arrived from the Low Countries in 1564, according to Philip Stubbes's *The Anatomie of Abuses* (1583). Whalebone joined glue-stiffened canvas and bundles of reeds as a method of supporting and stiffening fabric, allowing sleeves and farthingales to assume not just larger shapes but more complex ones. Meanwhile, bobbin lace arrived from the Continent, supposedly with Catherine of Aragon's retinue, to add another decorative technique to the English repertoire, and knitting moved from being a foreign oddity to a major domestic industry.

Ruffs instantly call the whole period to mind, yet they are primarily the signature garment of the Elizabethan period. So how many people actually wore them? What emerges from images and documents is near universal ruffage among the aristocracy and senior gentry from around 1564, when the technique for starching became established in this country. When Elizabeth, Countess of Worcester, died in 1565, for example, she left some clothes to her daughter and a tranche to her niece, the as-yet-unmarried Ann Browne, including 'all my linen clothes, smocks, partlets, ruffs and sleeves'. Ruffs, or 'bands' as they are often called, are rarely mentioned among the general population till late in the century, and then mostly among up-and-coming urbanites, men like the ironmonger Edward Hadley who lived and worked in Banbury and had two ruff bands to his name along with some silver buttons and a small stock of books. Out in the countryside ruff-wearing seems to have stopped at gentle-man level. It was, however, London that was ruff city. In 1569 a maidservant discharged from St Bartholomew's Hospital was given back her clothing, which included 'three pair of ruffs'. The royal court generated a lot of work for laundresses and maidser-vants, cleaning, starching and setting the ruffs of the aristocracy as they circulated between court and their country estates. Gen-tlemen up on business created more demand, and so did the resident population of professionals, the doctors and lawyers. Mayors, aldermen and wealthy merchants all found ruffs to be the acceptable face of fashion, setting off their sober black gowns beautifully and marking them out as wealthier citizens.

Ruffs may have been signifiers of status, but they were not intrinsically all that expensive. Half a yard of fine linen was enough to make one, a quarter of the amount needed to produce a shirt. It was a fairly simple matter, therefore, for a woman whose work had taught her the skills of sewing and starching to make one – or three – for herself. Professionally the tailor Edmund Peckover was charging three shillings and eight pence for 'stitching of a ruff' for Nathaniel Bacon's family. As the brother of Sir Nicholas Bacon, Queen Elizabeth's Lord Keeper, Nathaniel would have been purchasing the very best and most complicated of ruffs, so this represents the top-end costs of the garment. Something within the reach of a determined young person about town, then, and certainly a very affordable element of high fashion when set against the £2 2s 4d that Nathaniel paid Edmund for a simple, workaday fustian doublet. The impresario Philip Henslowe and Edward Alleyn, one of the most famous actors of the Elizabethan era, both had a hand in the ruff business. They put up the money for a 'howse to macke starche in', while their partners in this enterprise, John Ockley and Nycolas Dame, were to supply the various vats and equipment. The theatre would itself have been a major customer for starched ruffs, necessary for the costumes of all wealthy and important characters onstage, but Henslowe and Alleyn clearly expected there to be plenty of other business for this new venture as they were to take three-quarters of the profit in lieu of rent for the starch house.

Over the years I have made somewhere in the region of forty to fifty ruffs, starching and setting them in many different patterns and several different colours. I have made huge cartwheel ruffs, tiny wrist ruffs, layered ruffs, soft loose ruffs and perky pink ruffs. They give, I think, a flavour of the complexity of Elizabethan clothing and the levels of labour and skill involved. They all begin with a long strip of linen, cut not down the length of the cloth but across, so that the weft thread runs along the length. The stronger warp threads can now all radiate out from the neck. You need to join several pieces to obtain the long strip that you require. The most basic ruff in relatively chunky cloth needs a yard and a half, while fine ruffs can contain up to twelve yards of cloth, and later in the seventeenth century the most elaborate of Dutch examples used nearly twenty yards. Once you have joined the pieces together into one long strip, all of this fabric will have to be pleated into a neck-sized band. The strip is first given a minuscule hem along one edge (those on surviving ruffs are one-sixteenth of an inch, or one millimetre, wide) and then three rows of parallel running stitches are worked along the unhemmed edge. These must match up exactly, just like the cords on curtain ruffle tape, but unlike chunky curtains the stitches that make up your running stitch must be no more than a quarter of an inch long.

When you pull these three threads the strip concertinas up into tiny pleats. It is best to spend a little time at this stage combing the ruff into place with your fingers, encouraging the densely pleated fabric to lie neatly and untwisted. Now the neckband can be sewn on. This is a simple doubled-over straight strip of linen long enough to go around the neck. The band is folded over the raw edge, so that the rows of running stitch are tucked inside. Each of the tiny pleats is sewn to the neckband on both sides of the band, one stitch for each and every pleat. This is fiddly work but must be done evenly so that the neckband doesn't twist and pucker. Further stitches can be worked along the neckband over the top of all the ruffled edges within to help hold everything firmly in place. A little neatening at the two ends, and eyelet holes, ties or a hook and eye added as fastenings, and the ruff is complete. But while that is the end of the sewing, the ruff is not yet ready to wear. There is starch to be made and poking-sticks to heat.

Any starch-bearing plant could be used; grains were easiest, but several different roots were also employed (not potatoes, though: the common potato only arrived in Britain at the very end of the century and was too much of an expensive exotic for starch production). If you look at the wonderful engraving of the apes setting ruffs that I mentioned before, you may see, on the right-hand side, some of these roots lying on a counter beneath a line of drying ruffs. I have managed a successful set with parsnips, sweet cicely and bluebell bulbs. The plants must first be cleaned and boiled for several hours to release the starch, then the softer part of the pulp is forced through a sieve, leaving any fibrous material behind. The best starch is then reboiled, and forced through a finer sieve. The resultant jelly-like substance can be used directly or spread out in thin sheets to dry. Dry starch can be pounded back into a fine powder and stored. A little boiling water will ready your starch for use.

At this stage you must choose the colour of your starch. Natural white was the most common, but there are references to yellow, pink and blue starch being used too. The resultant starched ruffs acquired only the palest of shades from the coloured starch, and the effect can sometimes be missed on a dirty or over-restored painting. Nonetheless, coloured ruffs are visible among the images we have of Tudor people. Pale pink (a colour associated with male youth in the Tudor era) ruffs appear on a picture of an unknown boy holding a book and flowers, painted in 1576. His doublet is also pink, slashed through to show a red lining. A 1578 portrait of Ulbe van Aylva, a Calvinist Dutchman from Friesland, by an anonymous German painter, shows him wearing a deep-brown doublet and Venetian hose, with a set of matching pink starched wrist and neck ruffs. Yellow starch was especially fashionable in the first few years of the seventeenth century, but fell rapidly from favour following a political scandal involving Anne Turner, who along with the Earl and Countess of Somerset was convicted of murdering Sir Thomas Overbury. Anne was hanged in 1615, her penchant for yellow ruffs receiving much attention in the popular ballads and broadsides that reported the affair. Blue, meanwhile, fell from favour when it began to be associated with prostitutes, whose vast ruffs, according to Robert Greene, were 'gloried richly with blue starch'. Elizabeth I went as far as ordering the Lord Mayor of London to inform Londoners that 'her Majesty's pleasure is that no blue starch shall be used or worn by any of her Majesty's subjects'. Fashion in coloured ruffs was especially easy to follow, however, since the colour was not in the garment itself, but in the starch, which could be washed out. The same ruff band could be pink one day and white the next.

The shaping is also dependent upon the starching. You can form your sets around your finger, a narrow stick, or a wide one, which can be circular or flat like a ruler. The clean ruff is first dipped into the starch, ideally so that the band part remains clean and free of the substance, which is stiff and uncomfortable, while the frill part is entirely saturated. Then it needs to be worked and massaged between the fingers to evenly distribute the starch and remove any excess. Skimp on this stage and you will end up with a streaky look and unsightly lumps, with some areas stiff and other places limp. As the starch begins to dry it is necessary to rework the ruff in your fingers a number of times to prevent the linen from sticking together and to stretch out any creases. Once dry, a glossy finish can be achieved by polishing the linen with a glass smoothing stone. This is an exceptionally lengthy process, taking three or four hours to work your way down the length of the gathered strip. It's fiddly, too, trying to get into the heart of the pleats, but the effect is much more impressive than the unpolished ruff.

At last you are ready to heat your poking-sticks and begin forming the final shape. The early poking-sticks were made from polished wood, and you used them by pulling the linen tightly and sharply around them to force a shape. But the wooden sticks were quickly replaced with metal ones that could be heated like irons on the fire. It helps to dampen the ruff very slightly before using hot poking-sticks – a moment or two in the steam above a boiling kettle is perfect. Fingers are still key, though: each poke of the stick needs the linen to be wound tightly against it and held for a few seconds under pressure. More than one size and shape of stick can be used in a single starching. Where the ruff has a strong pattern upon it, from lace embroidery to cutwork, certain elements of a repeating design can be highlighted by the way you set the ruff. One day, perhaps, a large square motif might be brought uppermost with a wide stick while the bottom curve of the set is worked with a smaller stick, so that on the upper surface just that one motif is showcased. On another day the set is so arranged that a smaller circular motif is prominent on the upper surface, or with careful variations the two motifs can alternate. With the starching complete the ruff can be kept in shape by catching together the sets where they touch each other. Tiny little blobs of beeswax were sometimes employed for this purpose. Small fragments were rolled in the fingers to round them and warm them, then popped between the linen and firmly pinched to glue the cloth in place; equally important, they would simply wash out when the ruff was laundered, allowing access for the new starch and set. More common, perhaps, were pins to do this job, particularly upon the large wide sets that were popular in Elizabethan England (the Dutch liked smaller, tighter shapes). A pin inserted radially from the outside towards the centre not only held the sets in place but provided a little more stability. With a pin at every place where the looped linen kissed another, a light metal framework surrounded the wearer.

It's a huge amount of work to prepare a ruff for wear. The elaborate sets with polished linen can take an entire day, and even a simple, unpolished, small version requires a couple of hours. Luckily they last quite well. Unless you are caught in torrential rain, a well-starched ruff will stand for several weeks of wear. The real limiting factor is how dirty the neckband becomes.

Wearing a ruff requires a little care. Those at the neck can restrict your ability to turn the head, a fact that can add a certain elegance to movement, requiring a turn of the whole torso. Indeed, posh Elizabethan clothes for both men and women also inhibit twist at the waist, so the turn must be from the feet. It enforces a mannered, considered style of behaviour which was much admired, an indicator of civility, breeding and sophistication. Eating is more problematic. Not that it gets in the way as such, more that the merest speck of fallen food shows dreadfully. Crumbs on the ruff are not a good look, stains even worse.

The ruff wearer therefore needs to be exquisitely careful to follow Tudor dining etiquette to the letter, lifting only small, manageable morsels without haste. Wrist ruffs are much more difficult to wear than neck ruffs. Arms cannot be rested on tables without crushing the ruffs, nor laid in the lap or allowed to hang close by the sides. It is very tiring supporting your forearms away from the body all day. Gentlemen had the easier option of the hand resting on the hip and sword, which gives some relief. This was an essentially masculine pose, however, quite unsuitable for women, which is perhaps why you see more and larger wrist ruffs on men than on women.

Pins and points, buttons and laces

One of the ways that Tudor people coped with the scarcity of clothing in their chests and wardrobes was to have many small separate elements that could be assembled into a full outfit in different combinations. A woman might own gowns, coats, cloaks, frocks, kirtles, petticoats, pairs of bodies, stomachers, foreparts, sleeves, partlets, kerchers, cross cloths, coifs, hoods, rails, veils, supportasses, rebatoes, aprons, smocks, stockings, garters, girdles, billiments and upper billiments, waistcoats, mufflers, crepins, safeguards, farthingales, cassocks, forehead cloths and bongraces, though few owned all of them.

Naturally a modest wardrobe of two gowns and three kirtles allowed for a number of combinations, but if a woman also owned a pair or two of separate sleeves that could be laced in place on to more than one of her kirtles, a much greater variety of outfits could be achieved at a reduced cost. A forepart was another way of sprucing up a tired clothing selection. This was just a triangle of cloth that could be tied or pinned at the waist, reaching down to the hemline beneath the open front of the gown, giving the impression that a whole different kirtle lurked below the outer layer. Queen Elizabeth had many such garments to ring the changes, often with matching sets of sleeves and foreparts, while a second pair of sleeves could enliven the wardrobe of a maidservant. Stomachers could fulfil similar functions. These were even smaller triangular pieces that were pinned across the front of the body from neckline to waist, again beneath the front opening of the gown. If a woman changed shape, a regular occurrence with multiple pregnancies, the stomacher covered a bigger or smaller gap while also giving a bit of visual variety. Headdresses could be particularly varied and were again assembled from a number of smaller, simpler parts. A straight fillet band or a triangular forehead cloth controlled the hairline while a coif or cap could be used to contain the rest of the hair. Kerchers (a square or triangle of linen), rails (more of a mystery, but probably a different-shaped piece of linen) and veils could be pinned on top in several different styles, or you could choose to wear a hood over the cap. A crepin (a pleated or embroidered silk band) might cover the juncture between headdress and hair; a hood could additionally have a bongrace (a long, thin, bag-like structure hanging at the back) to tip up over the top or to the side of the head. Billiments were strips of decoration that could be pinned on to the hood, often luxury jewelled items. Although billiments and crepins were expensive, the plain linen kerchers, rails, veils, cross cloths, coifs and caps were much more affordable, sufficiently so for very ordinary women to have a selection thereof that could be worn in a variety of ways to please themselves.

Once the attire was chosen, then the elements had to be fastened together. For women this largely meant pins, for which a woman needed pin money. In the 1580s they could be purchased for as little as two pence per thousand for small fine ones, with thicker and longer dress pins fetching anything from six pence per thousand to three shillings per thousand. As well as being manufactured here, they were imported through the port of Antwerp into London in vast quantities. On board the *Benjamin of Lee* when she docked in May 1567, for example, were '374 dozen thousand' pins (about 4.5 million), and this was not in the least unusual. At the very least a woman needed a few pins to secure the various parts of her headdress. Neckwear also required pinning in place, even if it were a simple kercher worn over the shoulders. Indeed, an alternative name for the cloth worn about the neck and shoulders was a 'pinner'. Those who had pretensions to more elaborate neckwear needed a lot more pins. Even the most basic ruff calls for around fifty to hold the sets, and the garment itself was often pinned in place to prevent it rotating in wear. The turn-back collars of gowns could need pinning in place, and some gowns with no other form of front fastening were pinned down the front to the underlying kirtle. A practical pair of linen oversleeves worn to protect kirtle and gown sleeves, like aprons for the arms, could also be secured with a pin. At the end of the sixteenth century when wheel farthingales were high fashion, the skirt was tucked up in place, forming a ruff-like ridge where it turned through a right angle from the horizontal to the vertical. These tucks all had to be individually pinned in place daily, and those who had stomachers and foreparts to their name used pins to fasten them against the plainer fabrics beneath. A labourer's wife might be wearing four or five pins, a lady at court could be wearing a thousand at any one time, and with the best will in the world some got lost, regularly. Mudlarks sifting through the silts along the river Thames find vast numbers of Tudor pins, long and short, fat and thin.

Laces were also a feminine fastening. Hair was controlled with hair laces, kirtles were closed with long laces, and corsets were laced up too. These laces were not twisted cords, but woven braids that are very much stronger and hard-wearing (necessary when a lace is repeatedly passing through eyelets). Flat woven inkle braids worked well for garters and hair laces, but where eyelets were involved round braids, generally produced by a technique known as finger-loop braiding, were preferable. Silk was what everyone wanted: it was pretty and shiny and very strong and smooth running. Because such laces were small and long-lasting, they were affordable as little personal touches of luxury quite far down the social scale. They formed an important part of the stock-in-trade of petty chapmen who traded at markets, fairs and door to door. In his small shop in the quiet market town of Winslow in Buckinghamshire, William Davis had nine ounces of silk lace at sixteen pence the ounce in 1588, as well as thirteen yards of another quality and four odd ends. They made excellent courting gifts, too.

Points were a more masculine fastener. Short strips of leather, cloth or braid, they had metal aiglets, or points, riveted on both ends. Like a short shoelace, these were used to lace male garments together, slipping through eyelet holes. They were most importantly used to hold hose to doublet but could also be employed to close doublet fronts and, in the early years of the Tudor period, to lace sleeves in. These were fiddly pieces of metalwork to manufacture, but were produced in vast numbers at knock-down rates. Thin sheet metal was cut to shape, two holes punched into it, and the sheet was rolled up to form the point, either as a cylinder or a cone. The metal aiglet was slipped over the end of the braid (and it was usually braid, due to its superior wear quality) and a piece of wire was forced in through one of the holes, through the braid and out the other hole. The section of wire was trimmed off and a sharp tap with a hammer flattened the ends, creating a tiny rivet. Where pins were sold by the thousand, finished points were sold in dozens. In 1588 William Davis had 3,000 pins and fourteen dozen points in stock in his Winslow shop. Four years earlier, in the much larger town of

Ipswich, John Seely carried a stock of 1,500 pins and twelve dozen points. These were common, everyday items, and essential ones.

Buttons were again very masculine. They were also an item of display: gold, silver and even diamond-encrusted buttons litter the inventories of the aristocracy, who tried to cram as many as possible on to the front of their doublets. The front of the black silk suit that was such a rush job at the tailor's had forty-one buttonholes with evidence of a further four button loops on the heavily stiffened collar. Each sleeve was fastened down the forearm to the wrist with a further seven buttons. The buttons themselves, sadly, have gone, perhaps stripped ready for reuse on another garment, too valuable to waste. They were set so close together on this doublet that they would have been touching each other, something that would have made it difficult to do the garment up but would have looked wonderful.

The masculine nature of buttons becomes evident when you encounter the abundant complaints in the second half of the sixteenth century about women dressing like men. The 'problem' is discussed in righteously shocked tones of voice. Claims are even made that it could be hard to tell the two sexes apart. What they in fact meant was basically buttons and hats. Women accused of dressing like men were still in skirts, as contemporary woodcuts that accompany some of these rants make clear, but their bodices, done up with buttons, mimic the male doublet, and a felt hat rather than a hood or veil was surely a mannish garment.

4. Breakfast

'And then to breakfast, with
What appetite you have'

William Shakespeare, *Henry VIII*, III, ii (*c.*1613)

Should you have breakfast? It was a point of some discussion. Sir Thomas Elyot, in his *Castel of Helth*, finally concluded: 'I thynke breakfastes necessary in this realme.' He was refuting more ancient advice that claimed healthy adult men should wait until dinner. Small children, pregnant women, breastfeeding mothers and the sick had been granted the indulgence of breakfast in medieval advice, but it is clear from the household accounts and rules of aristocratic regimes that breakfast was not part of the usual routine for their menfolk. Mind you, many of these households had dinner at ten o' clock in the morning, so waiting for this meal was not too problematic for the healthy. By the 1530s, when Sir Thomas Elyot was writing, dinner was slipping to a later time, midday being the more fashionable hour. Sir Thomas's argument was more climate-based. The old abstention till dinner had been advice written by and for those living much further south, around the Mediterranean. The cold and damp of the English climate, he argued, required a different regime: a person needed the fuel.

Andrewe Boorde, an ex-monk, traveller and physician writing some twenty years later, was more concerned with what you ate at breakfast. Bacon and fried eggs, such as labouring men ate, was not good for a gentleman, in his opinion. No, a gentleman should have his eggs poached. It is our earliest record of the full English breakfast, and already it is being marked out as unhealthy and associated with workmen. How many working men could actually afford bacon and eggs for breakfast, though, is another matter.

The majority of the population had to put in an hour or so's work before breakfast. John Fitzherbert, in his *Boke of Husbandry*, tells wives that before they make breakfast for the family they should sweep the house, tidy the 'dishboard' — a sideboard or dresser where the dishes were kept — and set all things in the house in order, then milk the cows and strain the milk, feed the calves and dress the children. Their menfolk, meanwhile, were out feeding livestock, mucking out horses and oxen and sorting out harnesses. As people rose at 4 a.m. in the summer months, breakfast in the countryside had to wait until around 6 a.m. It was a family meal, and included any live-in servants. Since it was made a little later in the day, it was possible for a hot dish to be prepared alongside the bread and ale, something quick to make and sustaining. Fried bacon and eggs, or kippers, or porridge, would have been very welcome when they were available. Pancakes are mentioned in later texts about rural life, and a variety of pancake and fritter recipes turn up in Tudor books of cookery, my favourite being slices of apple dipped in an ale, flour and egg batter, then fried in butter.

The same hours held for tradesmen and labourers in town. The first legislation upon working hours came in an Act of 1495, which in its preamble complained that some workers came late and sat too long at their breakfasts when they did get there. The new law stipulated 5 a.m. as the beginning of the working day, and in the winter they were to be at their work 'at the springing of the day'. James Pilkington, Bishop of Durham in the first half of Elizabeth's reign, complained that 'The labouring man will take his rest long in the morning; a good piece of the day is spent afore he come to his work; then must he have his breakfast, though he have not earned it, at his accustomed hour, or else there is grudging and murmering.' Six o'clock then seems to have been the general breakfasting hour, even among those who liked a lie-in, and it was a meal taken as a break within the working day, not before the work began. As a meal taken away from home among workmates, the tradesman's breakfast may well have been simple bread and ale brought from home, but those working in town had the option of popping over to a pie shop or hot meat seller for something more substantial.

With people dressed, washed, combed and fed, the day could now begin in earnest. For the younger members of society, a busy round of work and education was bundled together.

5. Education

... what a worthy worke it is to bring up Children vertuously
in good learning, and what singular fruit it bringeth to all
kind of people, to all estates and degrees ...

William Kempe, *The Education of Children* (1588)

For all our assumptions about the complexity of modern life, there was nothing simple about that which was lived half a millennium ago. High or low, boys or girls, there was a great deal that all children needed to know. Most toddlers had to get to grips with the habits and care of poultry and dodge the vats of boiling water moving on and off the fire. Almost as soon as they could speak they needed to learn a series of prayers by rote, and nursery rhymes and the rudiments of garden and farming lore quickly followed. By four or five years of age many children were minding younger siblings, weeding alongside their mothers, feeding pigs and chickens and fetching water.

Social etiquette

The young had a host of social rules to learn and behaviours to acquire, with lessons interspersed throughout the day – codes and conduct that were marked out according to their gender and social status from the very first moments of life. How they walked, ate and spoke needed to fit the ideology of the day, with boys encouraged to be bold and outgoing in all their actions – 'signifying the courage and strength that ought to be in a man', as Sir Thomas Elyot put it – while girls were guided towards more physical control and quietness, the 'pleasant sobernesse that should be in a woman'. Those whose parents held social pretensions were tutored to avoid 'boorish' habits, from squinting to nose picking. Some rules of polite behaviour were dressed up as health issues (exhortations to avoid sullen faces, for example, which would produce sullen, dull minds), some were common across all classes (talking with your mouth full), while others, such as resting your forearm, not your elbow, upon the table, were synonymous with the boundary between the simple countryman and the prosperous elite.

The simple business of walking, standing or sitting could communicate social position, and all required different postures according to gender and age. A way of standing that was admired in an adult man as redolent of strength and virility could be wholly inappropriate for a young boy, and there were other pitfalls too. Standing with the arms crossed, for example, was considered foolish by the Humanist Erasmus, and it is noticeable that it is exactly this posture that the king's fool Will Somers adopts in a miniature featuring him alongside Henry VIII. The king's own famous stance – looking straight ahead, legs apart, with his weight evenly balanced between them, toes pointing forwards and a little out, and hips pushed forward of the shoulders – was one that few dared emulate completely. This stance was generally associated with young adult men with martial aspirations, and was thought to be insolent and faintly ridiculous in a young boy. When Henry's son Edward was portrayed in the pose, to echo his father and assert his authority as his rightful heir, it is very slightly softened by an oblique angle to take some of the edge off the incongruous sight of a boy in a man's stance. Standing with your hands behind your back was a position associated with the merchant classes, a habit that is mocked in literature and drama, part of the visual comedy associated with playing sententious old men of middle-class origins. Stooping was linked both with the aged and with labourers.

Learning to walk came with similar subtleties. Just as today, where a person's nationality can be guessed at by their gait, there were numerous modes of perambulation. Ploughmen were described as having a 'plodding' gait, slow and deliberate. Their working lives were walking lives, back and forth across the fields, covering twenty miles or so within a few small acres as they guided each furrow in turn across the earth, their feet gathering clumps of the freshly turned soil as they went. No wonder, then, that they developed a style of walking that was deliberate and a little flat-footed, and not so surprising either that young boys should learn that gait from copying their fathers and the other men of the village. In arable-dominated communities the ploughman's plod was the walk of men. Townsmen often laughed at the countryman's gait; it was instantly recognizable on the city streets among the much quicker-footed locals. Young gentlemen swaggered with a certain style, and the older apprentices copied them more or less successfully, thrusting their hips forward and encouraging purses, daggers – or, if they had them, swords and bucklers – to swing about and make a clattering noise. You could hear a 'swashbuckler' from some distance as he made his way down the street, eager for everyone to notice him. Some of the clergy, as Erasmus pointed out, adopted as part of their occupational identity a halting gait that was thought to denote intense internal musings, a habit (or affectation, according to your viewpoint) that was still being satirized by Jane Austen at the start of the nineteenth century. Back in the countryside the ploughman's walk was contrasted with that of the shepherds of the upland areas, who were renowned for their light and springy step, striding out across the hills.

Most children learnt to stand, sit and walk by watching those around them, emulating those they admired, and corrected by laughter and ridicule if they transgressed, but a few received more formal instruction in the arts of movement from parents, schoolmasters and dancing masters, ensuring that they learnt the very latest styles in posture. Late-fifteenth-century fashionable posture as displayed during the first few years of Henry VII's court favoured an emphasis upon long, sinuous lines. The upper body, from the bottom of the ribcage to the shoulders, was inclined backwards and young people were encouraged to extend one leg a little in front when standing to give a long, smooth flow of line from toe to forehead. The chin was to be gently tucked in a fraction, stretching out the back of the neck, a particularly elegant look for women with large headdresses. Naturally, if you overdo these adjustments you look ridiculous and awkward. The trick was to hold everything in proportion to hint at the posture, and to maintain it smoothly in movement. This is not easy to pull off and requires regular practice from early childhood, the difficulty and training providing the whole point of the exercise. Perfect posture was achievable by those bred to it, and almost impossible for a newly wealthy merchant to acquire later in life.

Within Henry VIII's court, fashions changed quickly and posture was as much part of that as clothes. The elegant Italian method of sitting with one's legs crossed at the ankle fell into disfavour; when seated it was now considered to be most pleasing when both feet were fully flat upon the floor. Mid-sixteenth-century fashion called for full-square postures, the emphasis for men firmly shifting to movement that spoke of solidity, stability and martial prowess. The fashionable walk now led from the hips rather than the bottom of the ribcage, and when standing those in the know preferred to be depicted square on, with the feet slightly apart, in a toned-down version of the king's stance. The fashionable male walk maintained a small distance between the legs with the weight well back and the buttocks tight, body shapes that work well with the more elaborate upperstocks and trunk hose of the period, giving room to the codpiece and holding the shoulders open and broad. The extreme masculinity of this style of movement made it wholly inappropriate for fashionable women to adopt it. Instead the feminine walk was more focused upon the movement of the skirt. If the main thrust of the walk comes from the hip, rather than the thigh, a bell-like resonance to the gait can be produced. Waist seams on the gowns and kirtles of fashionable dress (rather than the all-in-one flowing lines of the previous century) drew further attention to this more up-to-date method of locomotion. Feet and legs were kept demurely together, especially when seated with hands in the lap.

After Henry VIII's death in 1547, aggressively masculine postures fell from favour and fashionable men turned increasingly to the diagonal. When Philip II of Spain married Queen Mary seven years later, ambassadors' letters record a brief upsurge in Spanish manners at court; a greater rigidity of torso and well-turned-out feet is evident in the few images of Philip himself that have come down to us. All across Europe, new Renaissance ideas about beauty were making themselves felt, ideas that drew upon classical statuary as an exemplar for the human body. By 1589 the French dancing master Jehan Tabourot (who wrote under the pseudonym Thoinot Arbeau) was telling his students that the most attractive stance was one in which one foot rested at an oblique angle to the other, 'because we observe in ancient medals and statues that figures resting upon one foot are more artistic and pleasing'. Women, however, were to stand with their feet together and their toes turned out (a balletic first position). As these opinions spread, more and more children were schooled to stand in what is called fourth position in ballet, their weight upon one turned-out foot with the other leg resting casually upon the ground in front with the toe also turned out. A slight bend in the resting leg added elegance and helped the supporting hip to swing outwards. Poise and sophistication were further enhanced if the torso was allowed to twist naturally to the diagonal rather than held rigidly frontal. It is a stance that speaks of casual cultured ease and seems to naturally draw the hand to the supporting hip, where a gentleman's sword hilt hung.

In the early seventeenth century the manner of walking that was recommended to complement this stance is described by another French dancing master, François de Lauze, as proceeding in a straight line 'without bending the knee, the toes well outwards, in a manner that the movements, free from all timidity, proceed from the hip'. This is the walk used on stage by modern classical ballet dancers, and just like all the earlier fashionable court walks requires a great deal of practice to pull off in a seemingly effortless way.

Portraiture of Elizabethan gentlemen shows that they also took careful note of how they sat as well as stood and walked. Fabritio Caroso, an Italian dancing master writing in 1600, advised resting your left arm along the arm of the chair and placing the right so that the 'right hand drops from the wrist', a very familiar pose, or else leaning one elbow on the chair while holding a handkerchief, glove or flower. A gentleman was best served by sitting only halfway back upon the chair so that the feet rested comfortably upon the floor almost together, not crossed or spread.

If all children needed to learn to walk in one style or another, they also needed to learn the gestures of respect. Basic attempts at bowing and curtseying were expected from four- and five-year-olds, with proficient bows and a more nuanced understanding of the degrees of courtesy expected from older children.

Your cap put off,
Salute those you meet;
In giving the way
To such as pass by.

   Francis Seager, *The School of Virtue* (1534)

A simple removal of a cap was sufficient for the very young boy,
and any sort of bodily dip would serve for a very young girl.
They were easy movements to master, and they were courtesies
that were very frequently required. Age carried a great premium
of respect throughout the Tudor years, and young children were
called upon to show deference to almost all adults, even those
who were quite significantly below them in social station. A six-
year-old gentleman's son who failed to doff his cap to a respectable elderly villager and stand politely aside to let him pass might
well find his ear being clipped by his father. The manner of
doffing your cap was obviously very well laid out by Desiderius
Erasmus in his *Civilitie of Childehode* (1532) as it was copied out
almost word for word in several subsequent publications, including Fabritio Caroso's work for adult Italian dance students
more than sixty years later. The hat was to be removed by its
brim with the right hand and lifted from the head rather than
sliding it off and rumpling the hair. This is most successful if
you take it from the back of the head rather than the side or
front. The hat was then to be carried down to the front of the
body, taking care not to display the inside of the hat to anyone.
Showing the hat's inner surface, where there might be a little
grease or dandruff, was most uncouth and discourteous. As a
twenty-first-century person you have probably witnessed the
repeated waving around of hats in this uncouth manner upon
stage and screen, where some modern-day actors have been
sadly bereft of Tudor teaching.

   The well-tutored sixteenth-century boy, meanwhile, now

swapped his hat from his right hand to his left and held it either against his left thigh or against his waist, leaving his right hand free to make a wide, sweeping, open-handed gesture. To bow he brought one foot back behind the other and bent his knees, letting his body incline a very little forward. A fuller, more formal bow meant dropping to one knee, generally with the right knee forward. Towards the end of the sixteenth century the French style of bowing, whereby only one knee was bent, gained in currency. This was a matter of sliding the right foot forward, keeping the weight upon the back foot and bending the back knee while inclining the body forward. Such a bow requires the feet to be well turned out and accords very well with the more diagonal standing postures of the Elizabethan age, whereas the older English-style bow is much more square on and is most stable when the feet point forward. The two most common period terms for bowing are accurate summations of the two different movements: the older style was referred to as 'going upon bended knee', while the later French style was termed 'making a leg', as the straight leg that pointed forward during the bow was its most visual feature.

Girls had a much simpler time of it. Their hats remained firmly welded to their heads and they had only to lower their eyes and bend their knees. A well-tutored girl kept her head perfectly erect while she gazed downward, and her back perfectly straight as she executed a slow, steady *plié*, as you might in ballet, with her hands open and slightly to the side.

The hard part, however, for either sex was not so much perfecting the physical gestures but learning exactly when to use them and to what degree. How deeply should you bow, how long should you remain bowed, and should you replace your hat immediately or hold it in your hand? A flick up of downcast eyes could be flirtatious, or might imply that you were worried or even, if held a millisecond longer, being insubordinate or insulting. Too exaggerated a bow could seem like parody and sarcasm, too fleeting could indicate disrespect and contempt. The inside of a hat could be accidentally revealed or deliberately shown to undermine a gesture that looked respectful from a distance. A bow could be beautifully executed to reveal the depth of elegance and sophistication of the bower, or clumsily muffed in a hurry.

Physical education was not restricted to walking and bowing: children needed to know the 'right way' to carry out numerous daily activities. A constant stream of manners books laid out rules for eating, dressing, talking and playing, covering such basics as spitting, trailing your clothes in the mud, washing your hands before meals, not shouting over other people, taking your turn without pushing, and trying not to fart at table. These were all aimed at young upper-class boys, lads of seven or eight years old who would soon be taking a more prominent role within the public areas of great houses. Take, for example, the instructions on blowing the nose. A handkerchief was obviously the preferred method for those who had one, but, if you did not have one available, good manners could be preserved by using finger and thumb to clean the phlegm away and drop it to the floor, where it must be trodden into the ground with your shoe so as not to leave a mess for others to step in. Wiping your nose on your sleeve was very much frowned upon, and apparently smacked of the behaviour of ploughmen. It's hard to know how far down the social scale such social rules were followed. Did ploughmen all wipe their noses on their sleeves as a matter of course? Or was this a social slur used to chivvy seven-year-old boys into compliance? Certainly handkerchiefs were in short supply among rural workers, but the fingers method is both free and eminently suitable for the outdoors. Many rural children needed to assimilate polite behaviour every bit as well as their richer brethren if they were to find work in other people's households and had any hopes of social advancement.

Life skills

Farming and housework, the most fundamental of skills, were largely learnt directly from other people, from watching and doing. But, as Adam Fox details in his *Oral and Literate Culture in England, 1500–1700*, there was also a source of readily available advice and simple tuition in the form of proverbs, sayings and local lore. Such sayings may sound like platitudes to our untutored ear, but when the yeoman farmer Richard Shane, who lived just south of Leeds, wrote some of them down in his commonplace book around 1600 to 1610, he was recording a form of practical teaching, one relevant not only to the jobs and lives of those who learnt them, but to the particular locality with its specific climate and soils. Many of these sayings laid out an order of work, so that nothing was forgotten and each task was carried out at the optimum moment for that region. Shane noted down a calendar poem, for example, which in one of its verses reminded him, his workforce and neighbours that:

> September is come, and therefore applie,
> In lande that is stronge, to sowe wheat and rie,
> Nowe reape up your barlie, least that it be lost,
> Youre beanes and your peasome, to quite care and coste,
> Remeberinge allwaies, the age of the moon,
> So shall you do nothine, to laite or to soone.

Further south, sayings and lore advocated leaving some of these jobs until October, but in the West Riding of Yorkshire it was best to get all the grains and pulses harvested before September was out. Wheat and rye could be planted out as early as the beginning of September in 'stronge' ground, meaning highly fertile clayish soils, but it was worth waiting until spring if your soil was poor and sandy. The rhyming made it easier to remember and indeed to teach to the young. In addition to learning all twelve verses of this poem, youngsters could be taught valuable lessons from a host of short sayings or couplets. 'A bad ewe may bringe a bad lambe, yet shee spoyles but one; but an ill tuppe is likely to spoyle many' was a saying that pointed out the importance of obtaining a high-quality ram for the flock and encouraged the shepherd to concentrate his resources there even if he had to compromise elsewhere. The couplet 'Whiles the grasse groweth, Ewe dryeth, lambe dyeth' warned against the dangers of moving a ewe and her newly delivered lamb on to pasture high in the hills where the grass had yet to spring forth. The rhymes served as mnemonics of longer discussions and explanations, summaries of the teaching that came from parents and neighbours.

In the dairy, rhymes passed on elements of recipes. The Somerset rhyme 'If you will have good cheese, and have'n old, You must turn'n seven times before it is cold' (If you want good cheese and don't have any ready matured, make sure you turn your new cheeses seven times before winter storage) details the regime for the rich moist cheeses the region was renowned for, for example. One of the early cookery manuscripts is couched entirely in rhyme, delineating the full list of recipes that a professional chef was required to know, rhymes that could allow a lad apprenticed to a cook in an aristocratic household to get a toe on the ladder. This is the recipe for a tansy, an omelette-like dish flavoured particularly with the herb tansy. It was a popular dish, especially at Easter when fresh eggs were first available after Lent. The herb was believed to help clean the blood after the winter diet of dried peas and salt fish.

> Breke egges in bassyn and swing hem some,
> Do powder of peper ther to anone
> Then grynde tansy, the juce outwring

To blynde with yo egges without lessinge
In pan or skelet thou shalt hit frye
In butter wele skymmet wyterly.

The recipe is identical to several other prose versions telling the cook to break open some eggs in a basin and swing them through a cloth to beat them together. Next the cook is required to season them with ground pepper, then to bruise the tansy in a mortar and wring the juice out into the eggs. The resultant mixture is then fried in well-skimmed butter in a pan.

Rhymes such as these helped the illiterate or semi-literate to store knowledge. The most famous of these instructional rhyming texts is Thomas Tusser's *Hundreth Good Pointes of Husbandrie*, a book so popular that after several editions it was expanded into *Five Hundreth Pointes of Good Husbandrie* and continued as a teaching text for rural people well into the eighteenth century. Much of its appeal lay in its suitability for rote learning, and as a familiar document it was easy for the just barely literate to work out and follow if memory failed. It begins with an exhortation for husband and wife to pull together in their endeavours:

A hundreth good pointes of husbandry,
Maintaineth good household, with huswifry.
Housekeeping and husbandry, if it be good:
Must love one another like cousinnes in blood.

Since Tusser's agricultural year begins in September, when the grain harvest is in, the verse then moves on to an instruction to prepare the next season's seed, threshing it from the straw and winnowing it to clean away weed seed and chaff: 'Threashe sede and go fanne, for the plough may not lye.' Rye is to be sown dry and as soon as the husbandman has given his ploughed ridges a thorough harrowing. The winter wheat follows closely behind.

With his rye and wheat planted, he is to look to ditches and land drainage so that winter rain does not wash away his crop and soil: 'The ditches kept skowered, the hedge clad with thorn; doth well to drain water, and saveth the corne.' Hedges need laying so that thick growth will fill any gaps, crows must be scared off the new seedlings, and acorns and other pig fodder must be gathered.

Rote learning unprompted by the written word taught another range of lessons to the young. The tradition of beating the bounds, for example, sought to instil local geography in the next generation. The boys of the parish were walked around the perimeter of the parish with landmarks pointed out along the way. Fields, meadows and woodlands were named, the acreages and associated common rights were often rehearsed, with refreshment stops to help set memories, and in some parishes a few beatings were meted out to further stimulate retention of the lesson. Lists of plants, their cultivation and their uses were taught to girls, along with the basic skills of fire management and spinning. Thomas Tusser himself includes several such horticultural sayings. In November, for example, he tells wives to sow garden beans, but not until the feast of St Edmund has passed (on the 20th) and at the waning of the moon: 'Set gardeine beanes, after saint Edmonde the King; the moon in the wane, thereon hangeth a thinge.'

All in all there was a good deal for the young to learn by rote, both temporal and spiritual, and a variety of different people to learn it from. Before the Reformation, the Church required a child to be able to recite the Lord's Prayer, the Ave Maria and the Creed in Latin as a bare minimum, teaching that was supposed to be carried out by the parish priest. Protestantism replaced this with the recitation of the catechism, an even longer piece to be learnt by rote.

Reading and writing

Reading was not a universally taught skill, although it was becoming a more common one as the era progressed, and one that remained much more widespread than the skill of writing. In the modern world the two skills are taught simultaneously and form the fundamental core of what we think of when we see the word 'education'. Neither of these things was true of Tudor Britain. Education referred mostly to spiritual teaching in the Tudor mind and need have nothing to do with literary skills, while reading and writing were two separate activities taught at separate times, often by separate people. For those lucky enough to get any teaching at all, reading came first, and for many people that was also where book learning stopped. It did not even need to be a lesson particularly well learned to be useful. Those who could read a familiar text at even the most halting level were in a position to use the written word as an aide-memoire in personal devotions. This was a valuable spiritual skill, one valued both before and after the Reformation. Very few lessons indeed are needed for a person to begin to follow the words of something as short and well known as the Lord's Prayer, even if it is in the Latin that was heard and learnt by rote pre-Reformation. Moving on to a small repertoire of four or five short prayers was well within the literary reach of many whom we in our schooling-rich world would now discount as functionally illiterate. Nor do these people turn up in the written record to be counted as literate. Unable to write, they cannot leave us traces of their reading, a frustrating problem for a historian.

People learnt to read by first recognizing and naming letter shapes. These could be printed on a piece of paper and stuck on to a wooden board with a sheet of protective, transparent horn over the top, or simply scratched into the dirt. The alphabet was chanted and individual letters were pointed to. Printed sheets often arranged the alphabet into a cross shape to help children memorize them by reference to their position on the page. When people talked about learning to read, they often referred to learning the 'criss cross' (a common shorthand for Christ's cross), referring to this layout, or to 'conning their horn book', meaning learning from one of these horn-covered printed texts.

When that lesson was learnt, the vowels were picked out and combinations of vowels and consonants were taught, for example *ab, ad, af, ag, ba, da, fa, ga* and so forth. Each one was sounded out and learnt independently before the groups were assembled into words. The Lord's Prayer usually formed the first actual words that people attempted to read, familiarity helping children across the great intellectual divide between symbol and sound. For the bright and the motivated, this could be enough to open the doors to a much fuller and deeper exploration of the written word, allowing a few to teach themselves the finer points and go on to become confident consumers of literature. Others remained within a half-literate world, able to sound out printed texts, to work their way through popular ballad sheets or the Ten Commandments written up on the church wall, but all at sea with a handwritten letter or a longer, more complicated religious tract.

The basic reading lessons could be taught at home by mothers, fathers and older brothers, or picked up from fellow servants and neighbours. The clergy were encouraged to teach basic reading skills to their young parishioners alongside the rote-learnt prayers and catechism, and there was a patchwork of small, informal and often temporary schools in place across the country offering the same simple lessons. It was very hit-and-miss whether any young person had access to reading lessons or not. The very poorest were, of course, less likely to be able to spare their children from productive labour for long, so theirs were the slimmest of chances, but even for this group there was the occasional stroke of literacy luck. In the 1597 census of the poor in the town of Ipswich, for example, the nine-year-old daughter of Robert Michaelwoode is mentioned. He was bedridden and his wife spun shoe thread to bring in a few pence. The parish was supporting them to the tune of an additional ten pence a week. This, then, was a poor family, and their daughter was surely the last person you might expect to receive any formal education, yet it was recorded that 'she goeth to school'. Three boys among the list of the poor were also recorded as attending school, and three other girls were recorded as attending a knitting school. It is possible, of course, that young Miss Michaelwoode was at the knitting school; we have no way of knowing if a little reading was taught alongside the knitting, although that was common in later petty schools that taught craft skills.

The end of Elizabeth's reign seems to show a surge in the provision of schooling, with several English counties recording that one in four of their villages had a resident schoolmaster. The county of Essex, for example, had schools in 258 out of its 398 parishes at different times within the Elizabethan period. In 1593, for example, the villagers of Willingham in Cambridgeshire set up a school of their own by public subscription. There had been a schoolmaster operating in the village for the previous thirteen years and it is clear that the idea of schooling was a popular one among the locals. One hundred and two people donated between them £102 7s 8d. This was a sizeable proportion of the entire population of the village, and the sums were substantial. Three-quarters of those who subscribed did not sign the relevant documents but made their mark. This, then, was a community deeply committed to the education of its children, one that perhaps hoped that the next generation would be more learned than themselves. Moreover, the enthusiasm for literacy was not confined to the gentry and yeoman families at the top of the local social tree, but extended down to men like Henry Bedall, who contributed ten shillings and two pence, despite only holding three and a half acres of land, or the entirely land-less cottager William Ridley, who somehow managed to give eight shillings. A school nearby offered opportunities for those willing to pay for lessons, but of course that didn't mean that all the local children attended it.

Only when children had mastered the skill of reading was the skill of writing taught. Those whose labour was in demand out in the fields or within the home could be quickly called back from book learning and would never get the chance to master writing. Writing also called for more resources than tuition in reading. The first steps in letter formation could be made in sand or upon a slate, but soon paper, ink and pens became necessary and this further reduced the numbers of the poorest sectors of the community remaining in schooling.

John de Beauchesne, a Huguenot Protestant refugee from France, was the first to publish a book teaching the skill of writing in the English language, in 1570. Interestingly, he chose to couch the main body of the text in verse, indicating that once again this was a text designed to be memorized:

> Keepe even your letters at foote, and at heade;
> Wyth distance a lyke between letter and letter;
> One out of others shows much the better.
> Scholer to learne it may do you pleasure,
> To rule hym two lynes just of a measure;
> Those two lynes between to write verie juste,
> Not above or belowe that he must . . .

Rote learning remained at the heart of teaching.

Neither pens nor ink came ready-made from the shop but had to be produced by the writer him- or herself. Making the tools of the trade therefore formed part of the lessons that a child had to learn and became part of the morning routine of both school-children and secretaries. Cheap ink could be made from the ash of woollen cloth mixed with vinegar, but it didn't run well on to the page and quickly faded. A simple ink could be made from gum arabic and soot, the same ingredients as black watercolour paint, but this had a tendency to block up the pen and was of course soluble. For an indelible ink that ran smoothly as you wrote, a more complex mixture was required. This consisted of oak galls, copperas (copper sulphate), wine and gum arabic. The galls came from the structures that gall wasps make on oak trees; these structures contain high concentrations of tannin, which reacts with the copperas. The galls had to be crushed and soaked in the wine before the copperas was added, then stirred and strained. The resultant ink was then thickened with gum arabic. Two ounces of gum arabic was sufficient for five ounces of pow-dered galls and three ounces of copperas. If the resultant ink was too thick, it could be watered down, ideally with wine or vin-egar, but many schoolboys obviously resorted to their own urine for this purpose as several teaching texts make a point of telling them not to.

Pens were generally made from goose quills. Other feathers could be pressed into service – both swan and raven quills are mentioned at various times – and pens could also be fashioned from fine dry reeds. A small number of metal dip pens have sur-vived, made of brass and even silver. Goose quills, however, predominated: they are cheap and easy to make and have a longer working life than reed pens. Wing feathers make the best pens. Some people claim that you need a right wing for a right-handed person and a left wing for a left-handed person, but in truth it makes very little difference. Most of the fluffy feather is cut off, leaving only the spine of the quill. This gives a better balance to the pen, making it easier to use. The quill has to be cleaned and any membranes or fluff removed. The point is then shaped with a penknife.

According to the teacher Peter Bales, who was writing in 1590, 'Sheffield is best' when it comes to penknives. Knives and steel were already seen as the town's speciality and as products of the highest quality. It needs to be a particularly sharp knife if it is to give a good clean cut without cracking the quill. The quill is held in the left hand between the third and fourth finger with the feathery end pointing away from you. The tip of the quill is laid upon the pad of the thumb and held firmly in place by the forefinger. A scooping cut is made towards your chest, taking away just under half the width of the quill. Then a second smaller cut is made at the top of the first one of about the same diameter as the quill itself. This gives a stepped shape. The tip can then be squared off and a slit made vertically from the nib up. This takes practice. As each of us writes with a slightly different angle and pressure, a marginally different cut works best for each of us. Using someone else's pen was never very successful. Pen making was a personal matter and a very frequent task, as the writing tips of quills wore down very quickly. It could be necessary to recut your quill several times as you wrote a single document.

The letters of the alphabet that you wrote were mostly recognizable to a twenty-first-century eye – a letter *t* looked much the same, for example – but some were radically different. A letter that was written as a twenty-first-century lower case *r* was in fact the letter *c*. The letter *s* had three different forms, depending on where it appeared within a word, with one shape used exclusively at the end of words, another as an initial letter, and a third that could be used either at the start or in the main body of the word, but not as a final letter. This form of handwriting was known as secretary hand. A new fashionable style of handwriting that developed in Italy, known as italic, was beginning to make an appearance among the super-rich with pretensions to Renaissance culture, but the vast majority of Tudor writings were in secretary hand and it was this style that most people learnt. In time the italic would take over, and it is this style of letter shapes that we use today, but such changes lay in the future.

It has been estimated, based upon people's ability to sign legal documents as opposed to simply making their mark, that in 1500 around 5 per cent of men and just 1 per cent of women could write; by the beginning of Elizabeth's reign in 1558 those figures had risen to 20 per cent of men and 5 per cent of women. Further rises pushed the figures towards 25 per cent of men and 10 per cent of women by the end of the sixteenth century. Londoners seem to have been especially well schooled, and tradesmen had a higher likelihood of possessing writing skills than those working on the land.

But if those are the numbers of people who could write, it still leaves us completely in the dark over the question of how many people could read. Presumably those who could write could also read, but there was almost certainly a body of people who could read but not write. Those who were keen to promote Bible reading for religious purposes had far less reason to promote the teaching of writing, and patchy and short periods of tuition favoured the skill of reading without ever necessarily touching upon penwork. There was certainly an ever-increasing amount of cheap material to be read. Before the Reformation in the 1530s, somewhere in the region of 57,000 Latin primer books had been printed, priced at levels that allowed merchants, gentlemen and many yeoman farmers to own one. This middle-income group also bought a wide range of books on more secular subjects. By 1500, fifty-four different book titles had been printed in England, and by 1557 there were over 5,000, covering an ever wider range of subjects. In 1520 John Dorne, a bookseller based in the presumably highly literate town of Oxford, was able to sell 1,850 texts in less than a year, including works by Erasmus, copies of the adventurous tales of Bevis of Hampton and Guy of Warwick, and 170 ballads at only a half-penny each. A couple of generations later, in 1585, Roger Ward of Shrewsbury had 546 different titles in stock, including sixty-nine items priced at a penny each. If the rise in the number of books priced to be within middle-class reach is impressive, the explosion of very cheap single printed sheets of ballads and broadsides is even more striking. Somewhere in the region of 3 to 4 million of these texts were produced in the second half of the sixteenth century, at a time when the population hovered at around 3 million people. As the puritanical preacher Nicholas Bownde moaned in 1595, these examples of cheap print were to be found not just in the homes of the wealthy and middling sorts, 'but also in the shops of artificers, and cottages of poor husbandmen'. He was worried that such unschooled people would be unduly influenced by the printed word.

Apprenticeship

Apprenticeship, perhaps even more than schooling, was restricted to a section of the younger population. The training had to be paid for, generally with a large lump sum up front, which unsur-prisingly excluded children from poorer backgrounds. Fathers of apprentices are usually described in the documents as mostly established craftsmen themselves, or from the more prosperous members of the rural community – yeoman farmers and some husbandmen. Labourers could rarely advance a son into a trade. Girls were highly unlikely to be afforded such opportunities, although there were a few female apprentices, particularly in the early part of our period – girls such as Elizabeth Jaye, the daughter of a Bristol merchant, who was taken on by Elizabeth and John Collys to be trained as a shepster, or seamstress. She was to serve nine years, beginning in 1533. More commonly, girls were apprenticed 'in the arte of hus wifship', as the Bristol apprenticeship enrolment papers term it, a trade hard to differentiate from that of a domestic servant.

The size of the fee for an apprenticeship varied from trade to trade, with the more lucrative areas of business commanding the larger sums. Becoming a goldsmith, for example, required an initial outlay very much greater than that needed to become a tailor. Successful craftsmen with thriving businesses and wealthy clientele could charge more for their training than the struggling small-scale operation. The length of the agreed term could also affect the cost, with longer apprenticeships being cheaper as the master would be able to benefit from a longer period of well-trained unpaid labour.

There were, in fact, two fairly distinct groups of youngsters who were taken on as apprentices. One was generally male, in his mid to late teens, more likely to have been urban born and from a reasonably prosperous background. His family could afford the fee, could hope to give him some capital to set up business at the end of the training period, and had the right sort of connections to find a suitable master. The other was much younger and more vulnerable. He or she was often orphaned, between seven and twelve years of age, and put out as an apprentice by the parish as a way of providing care, supervision and employment. William Maxwell was just such a child, apprenticed in 1584 to a joiner in York, a man by the name of Peter Currer, 'with him to dwell as apprentice from this day for and during twelve years . . . in respect that the said apprentice is the child of a poor decayed citizen', as his apprenticeship record states. Almost all the girls apprenticed to housewifery seem to have fallen into this category. In many ways it could be seen as an early form of fostering. The child's experience, however, was entirely dependent upon the goodwill and character of the master and mistress. There was room not only for love, kindness and a new start in life, but also for abuse, neglect and exploitation.

As the Tudor age began, apprenticeships were becoming more formalized with an increasing number of craftsmen banding together within guilds, each with its own structure and rules governing the length of apprenticeships, the number of youngsters who could be taken on, their ages and the nature of the contract between them and their new masters. A seven-year term had become widely accepted, the guilds in Grimsby insisting on this in 1498, those of Chester in 1557 and York in 1530. The year 1573 saw a new law passed, the Statute of Artificers, which laid down the seven-year term as a national minimum, leaving guilds free to demand longer terms if they chose. Several did. The carpenters of York moved to eight years and the goldsmiths of London demanded ten years. William Maxwell's twelve-year apprenticeship was not a guild regulation but rather a reflection of the fact that he was younger than most. By the time he was released from the contract he would have been the same age as the other young men coming to the end of their term, in their early twenties, and would have already contributed to the profits of the business as a productive, fully trained worker for several years. The local government who paid for his apprenticeship was able to negotiate a cheaper deal because of this period of productive unpaid work, and he received a home until he was fully adult. Francis Long in Bristol was bound for eleven years to his master, Randolph Saunders, in 1533. Randolph was a point maker producing the short ties with metal ends that held male clothing together. This was not a trade that involved any great technical complexity and Francis's father was also a point maker so the boy probably already had a fairly good working knowledge of the basics. What are we to make, then, of such a contract? The lad was not an orphan, but perhaps there were other family difficulties that necessitated paying a colleague to take the boy on.

More common was the apprenticeship of Richard Edmont ap Owen from Bridgend in South Wales, whose father was a prosperous farmer. In 1532 Richard was sent to Bristol bound to Robert Salbryge for eight years to learn the trade of the tucker, a finisher of woollen cloth. This was skilled work that required years of practice to perfect, good connections with fellow tradespeople and capital investment. As an incentive to complete the full training, and perhaps to give him a start in setting up home, at the end of Richard's apprenticeship Robert Salbryge was contracted to provide him with a coverlet, a pair of sheets and a pair of blankets to the value of thirteen shillings and four pence, as well as pay the fee for Richard to become a full guild member and freeman of the city. Paying the fees for membership and freedom was a fairly standard element of contracts, and a substantial number also mention some form of material goods. Most frequently it is a selection of tools of the relevant trade, but bedding and clothes also appear now and again.

Masters were typically supposed to supply all of an apprentice's food, lodgings and clothing, alongside training in the craft, moral guidance and discipline. The lads lived within their master's home and were completely subject to his authority. Working hours were officially laid down in the Statute of Artificers as dawn to dusk in the winter months when days were shorter, with an hour-long dinner break at midday and three other half-hour breaks – one in the morning for breakfast, one mid afternoon, and one early evening for 'bever', short for beverage, sometimes known as 'drinking time'. They should be thought of, perhaps, as the original British tea breaks. From mid March to mid September, when daylight hours were longer, work was supposed to stop by 8 p.m. at the latest, representing

SIR HENRY UNTON (detail)
Unknown artist *c*.1596
The Elizabethan soldier and diplomat Sir Henry
Unton's final hours were spent in the very finest of
beds: a four-poster with red – possibly velvet – curtains
and roof, several deep mattresses, bolsters and pillows
encased in fine white linen, blankets and a matching
red coverlet.

Dow Bucers bones and Daulius Dhagius bones were put into two new coffins and so bound to a stake.

On afore
Onafore

Hold up your torches for dropping.

Salue festa dies

THE BURNING OF THE REMAINS OF
MARTIN BUCER AND PAUL FAGIUS

John Foxe, 1583

Religion was utterly central to people's lives and their understanding of the world. Vehement and often violent disagreements over doctrine spilled into many lives. Torture, executions and book burnings took place in a large number of towns, with especial regularity in Oxford, Cambridge and London.

Een burghers wijf   Een burghers rijck wijf   Een ionghe dochter   Een boerinne. zoo dieme gaen.

FOUR WIVES

Lucas de Heere, *c.*1574

Each with her kirtle (carefully revealed) and gown, these four women indicate the level of individuality that could be achieved by choosing and arranging small and inexpensive items of headwear and neckwear. Note, too, how the kirtle of the woman on the left has separate sleeves in a different fabric.

ALLEGORY OF PRESUMPTUOUSNESS
Hieronymus Nützel, c.1590

One of the central concerns of the sumptuary laws was that people would be tempted to dress in a socially inappropriate fashion, wearing the clothes of their 'betters'. One ruff in this image is even adorning a pile of turds, highlighting the base nature of some unworthy wearers. The devil in the foreground is tending a fire in which poking-sticks to set ruffs are heating, recalling the hot pincers and tortures of Hell that await the social climbers.

ALICE BARNHAM AND HER TWO SONS,
MARTIN AND STEVEN
Unknown artist (English School), 1557
In prosperous homes the first lessons in reading and
writing in the English language were the mother's
responsibility, before male tutors took over with
instruction in Latin when boys were a little older. An
educated mother was a boon in an ambitious household.

SIR CHRISTOPHER HATTON
William Segar, c.1581

An image of a Tudor mind. This is one side of a double-sided panel painted by
William Segar or his workshop. But the highly individual content and layout are
clearly dictated by the sitter. In addition to telling us his lineage (via the heraldry),
Sir Christopher Hatton wants us to know something about his personality and
fortunes (the astrology), his interest in alchemy (the blocks of colour), and that
he is a self-fashioned man (the artist) and learned (the philosopher).

SIR HENRY UNTON (detail)

Unknown artist, *c*.1596

The table is set, the cup board laid out, the yeoman of the ewery, the yeoman usher and waiters stand ready, the gentlemen wear their napkins over their left shoulders and the ladies drape theirs across their laps. Dinner is served.

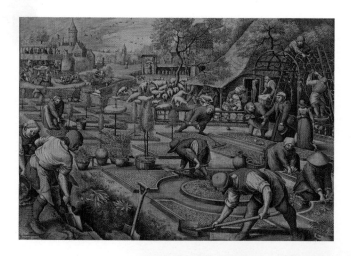

SPRING
Pieter van der Heyden, 1570

(*top*) These scenes of a Low Countries spring contain a wonderful image of shearing time. Notice how everyone pitches in, and how the sheep are small enough to be sheared upon the lap. As for the gardening, men lay out the Renaissance design but planting is women's work.

SUMMER
Pieter van der Heyden, 1570

(*bottom*) As men work their way across the fields, reaping, women and children follow behind, binding and stacking the sheaves. The chap taking a break has undone all of his 'points' save for those holding up his codpiece.

an average of a roughly thirteen-hour day. How close actual hours were to this is hard to say. The work itself also varied. A fifteen- or sixteen-year-old lad at the beginning of his term was useful as a general hefter of water and carrier of firewood, but not much use in the finer points of the trade. Many men record this sort of work as having formed their earliest experiences of apprenticeship. Some investment in training him in a basic repetitive element of the work could be lucrative for a master if he then kept the lad focused on that work rather than expanding his knowledge to the whole of the business. When relationships broke down and attempts were made to nullify the contracts, such dead-end work was often cited as a cause of dissatisfaction.

A smattering of indentures record a master's obligation to provide training in reading and writing in addition to craft skills. In 1548 in Bristol the tailor William Danncer, for example, was required to keep his new apprentice Robert Williams in school for a year. Likewise in that same year Hugh ap Powell insisted that his son Yeven was to have a year in school as part of his apprenticeship to a tanner. Other fathers didn't specify lengths of time but simply requested that their sons stay 'until he can write, and read, and caste accompt'. Occasionally the obligation fell on a mixture of friends and family. When Thomas Roberts of Penzance in Cornwall was apprenticed to Thomas Meredith, a tailor of Bristol, in 1547 the indenture specified: 'the said Thomas Meredith to kepe hym to scole and David Dens his father in lawe to paye for his scole'.

One of the many advantages of the apprenticeship system that people at the time commented on was the propensity for teenagers to behave better for other people than they did for their parents, and the willingness of non-parental authority figures to exert firm discipline. Youngsters put out to a master were not only learning valuable commercial skills that they could not have picked up at home, but also receiving moral and social guidance. This element of the institution is highlighted by the requirement for masters to be married. Each and every indenture carries the name of the master's wife, for her care and authority within the home was of great importance to the lad and to his parents. Husband and wife were both bound by the contract; indeed, if the husband died it was possible for the apprenticeship to continue under the authority of the widow alone.

Naturally, things could go wrong. The discipline element could become a real bone of contention. In 1563 Henry Machyn, a London merchant, recorded in his diary one incident that had a very public outcome. A man called Penred took a leather belt with a metal buckle and beat his young apprentice so severely that he took the skin off the boy's back. What Machyn saw was the aftermath when the authorities stepped in. The master was put in the pillory in Cheapside and whipped till the blood ran down his back. The Lord Mayor of London stood the boy next to him, bare backed, so that all the passers-by could see just what the man had done to the boy. Beating a lad was a fairly normal response to bad behaviour, but there were socially accepted limits, limits that Penred had overstepped in the brutality of his 'discipline'.

Insufficient food and clothing were another common complaint levelled against masters, while masters in their turn moaned about insubordination, idleness, immoral behaviour, fraud and theft. Living and working cheek by jowl could raise tempers and heighten a clash of personalities between even the most honestly intentioned apprentice and his master. Where the evidence survives it becomes clear that two-thirds of apprenticeships failed and were terminated before a lad could reach the end of his indentures and become a freeman of the city, able to join the guild as a full independent member. William Porkar from Horfield must have tried the patience of both masters and parents, for between 1549 and 1552 there are five separate sets of indentures for him within the record books of Bristol, each recording a fresh attempt with a new master.

Thomas and Dorothy Rancock were obviously having trouble finding the right lad around 1550. They were innkeepers, again in Bristol, but the nature of the apprenticeship that they were offering was an unusual one. The first lad they tried, William Drowry, was taken on in March 1548. He had come all the way from York and was the son of a labourer, both of which circumstances were a little out of the ordinary. The explanation, however, appears in the list of goods he was to have at the end of the apprenticeship. Where many spoke of tools, this indenture specifies 'a viol, a lowd shawm and a still shawm' (shawms are mouth-blown reed instruments, like an oboe; the 'still shawm' may indeed have made a sound quite similar to an oboe, but the 'lowd shawm' would have been much harsher and capable of being heard outdoors over a noisy crowd). This, then, despite Thomas and Dorothy being described as innkeepers, was an apprenticeship to a musician, and young William had probably made his way down from York in the company of other players or musicians. The willingness of Thomas and Dorothy to take on a stranger of low birth suggests that he already had some skills and aptitude. But the seven-year term was not completed, for in March 1550 they tried again, this time with John, the son of John Rome, a prosperous man from Draycot in Wiltshire. John junior may have been a bit younger than William, as this time the term is for ten years. At completion he is offered a viol, both shawms and a rebec (a small string instrument often used by dancing masters). This was an even shorter-lived apprenticeship, however, for in October of the same year Thomas and Dorothy are trying again with a third candidate, William Welles from Thornbury in Gloucestershire, the son of a shoemaker.

Either William Welles finally proved to have what it took or they gave up, for no further indentures were signed.

For all the problems with apprenticeships, some work was done, some lessons learnt and potentially troublesome teenagers and young adults were both cared for and kept under someone's watchful eye.

Servants

Those youngsters whose parents could not afford an apprenticeship for them often spent their teenage years as live-in servants in someone else's household. It is estimated that at some points in the sixteenth century 70 per cent of young people were in service. The same basic mix of practical and moral care from masters, and work and obedience from the young, was expected, but this time no fee was paid to the master; instead a small wage was paid to the servant, reflecting the different balance between tuition and productive labour. Service constituted a legal contract, just as an apprenticeship was, but while apprenticeships could last seven years or more, service was an annual contract. Naturally, with board and lodgings provided, the wages were small. Children in their first post, usually around fourteen years old, received next to nothing; youngsters in their early twenties were much more useful about the place and therefore could command higher wages, but still only a quarter of what a master craftsman might earn. The work could encompass almost anything. The servant of a miner might well spend most of his working hours moving coal underground, that of a carpenter might spend their time sweeping up wood shavings or hauling timber. Most youngsters worked upon the land simply because that is how most masters made their living. Girls were more likely to be involved in work about the house alongside the mistress, and boys were more likely to be out helping the man of the house, but the division was by no means complete. Lads were required to sweep floors and carry water, and young women helped out in the fields.

Unlike the nineteenth century, the Tudor experience of service had less to do with social class and more to do with age. It was an element of the usual life cycle, part of growing up. In *The Ties That Bound*, Barbara Hanawalt's analysis of the patterns of fatal accidents recorded in coroners' records shows how the work done by young people changed as they grew older. Lads of fourteen were still falling out of trees and drowning while fetching water, indicating that boys will be boys whatever the century and that their work lives were centred around fairly simple fetching and carrying roles. Young men in their early twenties had accidents related to working with horses and cart gear, a much more adult pattern. After five or more years working alongside older men, they had learnt a useful range of skills and were physically big and strong enough to carry out the main ploughing, harrowing and harvesting tasks on the land. Young women's roles were less reliant on physical strength, but still needed stamina and skill. As horse and sheep care dominated the work routines of male servants, so cows, pigs and poultry formed an important element of the work of female servants. The fields absorbed young male labour, and the yard and garden took that of the girls.

At the big events of the year, such as shearing time and the several grain and fodder harvests, everyone – young, old, male and female – turned out together. The different groups all had separate roles within the main endeavour in order to reflect traditional ideas of propriety, strength and skills. Adult men mowed the hay, girls and women tossed and tedded it so that it could dry, boys led the horses with the carts to collect it, and men and boys together raised the hayricks. But as real life is never neat and tidy, there were of course times when people had to do whatever was needed, regardless of sex or age. Cows, after all, still have to be milked when all the women of the household are otherwise engaged in the business of childbirth, and ploughs pulled when the man of the house is sick.

Nor were the masters and mistresses so very different from their servants in terms of social class; many had, in their youth, been servants themselves. Even small-scale husbandman farmers took on teenagers from other families to help with the daily agricultural workload. There wasn't much physical separation of the living quarters either: servants, masters, mistresses and their children all lived and worked together. Tiny two-room cottages could house an adult master and mistress and their three young children, along with a teenage boy or girl at the start of their servanting careers, the servants and children sharing beds as well as room space. In time the children of the household could well move on to become servants in some other household in search of skills or just a change of scene. The children of a more prosperous yeoman farmer were less likely to become servants, but if they did it was in wealthier households in which a larger range of more specialized tasks was carried out. A prosperous household of a yeoman farmer who managed much larger acreages naturally needed more labour and was more likely to have some commercial specialism, whether that was dairying, the raising of beef cattle or breeding of horses. The work and life within these establishments was therefore more seg-regated. If there were more people, there were also likely to be more rooms and beds split among them, and servants had the opportunity to concentrate upon certain tasks rather than act as general dogsbodies. An ambitious youngster could exploit these differences to climb the servant social ladder, moving perhaps from being an under-dairymaid in a large establishment to the chief maid in a smaller one, before taking on a lead role in a major household.

Some masters and mistresses were better at keeping their servants than others. There are incidents of long, loyal service and lifelong connections, but on average servants stayed two years in each post before moving on. A new post gave opportunities to negotiate a higher wage, to take on a more adult role, to learn a different set of skills and of course to get away from people you could no longer bear to live alongside. The personal relationships within service suffered similar strains as those within apprenticeships, and the opportunities for abuse were there too. The altercation between Marion Graye and Joan Jurden that happened in the kitchen of Joan's house at Iden in Sussex in 1565 was perhaps typical in its beginnings, an outburst of bad temper between mistress and maid. According to the coroner's records, Marion was washing up, scrubbing out the wooden casks and dishes. It was eight o'clock in the morning and breakfast was over. Joan had been out in the garden, cutting some herbs for the pot, when she came into the kitchen to demand angrily who had trampled on the peas. Marion answered 'peevishly, obstinately and haughtily' and told her mistress to go away. Joan hit her with the back of her hand. Marion turned on her and pushed her back to the doorway, where they both fell. Joan still had a knife in her hand from cutting the herbs, and as they fell the knife was driven into Marion's side. She died a few hours later. Many masters and mistresses would have felt that Joan was quite justified in clipping Marion around the ear for her cheek, and would have been indignant that she had retaliated. Respect and deference towards your elders and your social superiors was a bulwark of Tudor life. Obedience to authority was held to be a religious duty, a natural state of being and a necessary ingredient for peace and prosperity. This message was drummed into young people by parents, the clergy, teachers, the government, guilds and masters and mistresses alike. But as cases like that of Marion and Joan show, one of the reasons why the lesson was repeated so long and so loud was the messy reality of daily life.

Certain skills commanded higher wages for both sexes. Ploughing always topped the list for men, while for women it was dairy work, and an ambitious youngster needed to find good masters and mistresses as early in their servanting career as possible if they were to maximize their earnings in the run-up to marriage. In a perfect world a young person in their mid twenties had accumulated not only a pot of savings but also the full range of skills necessary to begin married life as the head of their own household. Average ages at first marriage were twenty-four for women and twenty-six for men, and it was only when the wedding ceremony was complete and the new household established that full Tudor adulthood began.

6. Dinner

. . . but in delycyous metes, drynkes, and spyces, there is at
this day foure tyme so moche spent as was . . .

John Fitzherbert, *The Boke of Husbandry* (1533)

This was the main meal of the day, but eaten rather early by
modern standards. The more conservative great aristocratic
households still dined at ten o'clock in the morning, although
eleven was the more fashionable hour. Having slept in Tudor
beds and risen at dawn to a round of mucking out livestock,
fetching firewood and hauling water, I can attest that the human
body is ready for something substantial by then. As the largest
meal, the one most likely to be hot and the one with the most
potential for variety, dinner had a central importance in everyone's lives.

It had a symbolic importance too, surrounded by echoes of
the central religious ceremonies of the Christian faith. In
wealthier homes a table was set up at one end of the hall upon a
raised dais, covered in a white cloth and laid with salt, bread and
wine. The great households punctuated the simple business of
laying the table with bows and gestures of respect. An order of
laying the table was strictly observed, carried out by a team
of people who all assumed their best clothing for the task and
donned long serving towels over one shoulder or the other, or
around the neck, or napkins over their arms, as badges of rank
and function.

In Viscount Anthony Montague's house at Cowdray Park in

Sussex the ceremony of dinner was overseen by the gentleman usher, who at ten o'clock in the morning, 'ytt being coverynge tyme', rounded up his own deputy, the yeoman usher, the yeoman of the ewery, the gentlemen waiters, the carver and the sewer. The yeoman of the ewery (hand-washing and household linen department) laid out the ewery board with tablecloths, napkins, washing bowls, towels and jugs of washing water. He then accompanied the yeoman usher to the table, who bowed, kissed his own hand and touched it to the place on the table where the yeoman of the ewery was to place the folded tablecloth. He laid the cloth and the two men unfolded it using rods, then bowed and retreated. They then laid out the salt, napkins and plates or trenchers with similar ceremony. The yeoman usher then stood in the great hall and called out in a loud voice so that the whole household could hear, 'Gentlemen and yeomen, wait upon the sewer, for my lord!' When the staff had gathered, washed their hands and donned their livery coats and serving towels, a second shout went out 'for my lord', which alerted the cooks to the imminence of service. The gentleman usher, the sewer and the carver then entered the dining chamber in formation, and when in the middle of the (empty) room they all three bowed in unison before proceeding to the table, where all three bowed again. The carver then made his way to the carving table, and the sewer to the dresser where food would arrive from the kitchen in due course. The yeoman of the cellar then took up his position at the drinks table, otherwise known as the cup board or cupboard. At this point, and not before, the lord and his family came into the room and took their seats. The yeoman of the ewery brought bowls, jugs and towels for them to wash their hands (with more bowing), and the food began to arrive from the kitchen and was placed on the dresser, each dish covered with a second upturned plate. Under the direction of the gentleman usher, the gentlemen waiters, with appropriate bowing, uncovered the dishes and laid them upon the table, removing some to the carver's table for him to prepare and return in due course, ready to eat.

In all it required six named officers and a team of waiters simply to prepare the hall and lay the table, and from the ten o'clock start it was an hour before anyone began to eat. The ritual continued throughout the meal and extended to clearing the table, with no reduction in complexity or expressions of reverence. And this was just the ordinary daily ritual: it became much more elaborate if there were guests, when even more staff and much more bowing were involved.

Lower down the scale, gentlemen, merchants and yeoman farmers dispensed with the vast staff numbers and most of the bowing, but liked to ape a little of the ceremony where they could, setting up separate carving tables and cup boards in their own halls or dining parlours. Noon was the more common time for dinner outside the great aristocratic houses, and the meal was generally expected to take an hour. Even in the humblest home, where people had to take their meals where they could, without perhaps even a table to eat off, the breaking and sharing of bread had some wider symbolic significance and could be reminiscent of a simple church service, a connection that was further emphasized by the saying of grace.

> Let us eate in the name of the lorde and satysfye our body temporally with such meates as he hath sente.
>
> And let us desire hym likewise to satysfye our soule with the gift of goode lyvyng that we may be ever as ready to all good works as we be nowe to our meate.

This grace, 'to be sayd before meate', was one recommended for use in 1546. Henry VIII was still on the throne when the grace was published, and although the break with Rome was well established and English had become the sanctioned language of religion this is still a very traditional grace with its emphasis upon good works.

The grace recommended by Theodore Beza, a committed leading Calvinist, in 1603, at the end of Elizabeth's reign, expresses the same two sentiments, thanking God for the food and asking for His help in prompting us to seek the spiritual life:

> Everlasting God and Father we beseech thee to extend thy bless-
> ing upon us thy poore Children & servants, and upon the foode
> which it pleaseth thee, of thy goodness to give us for sustenance
> of our life, that we may use the same soberly and with thanks
> giving, as thou hast commanded. But above all things give us
> grace to desire and especially to seeke the spiritual bread of thy
> word, wherewith our soules may be fed eternally in the name &
> the glory of the Father, Sonne and Holy ghost, one and true
> God who liveth and reigneth world without end. Amen.

Bread

'Give us this day our daily bread' was a plea of the most literal kind for people of the Tudor age. Bread was the staple foodstuff. It is easy for us now to underestimate the centrality of bread within people's lives. Imagine for a moment every meal that you have eaten this week. It probably contains a number of bready elements, toast and sandwiches being the most common. But now remember every meal that consisted of pasta or rice and mentally replace that carbohydrate with a couple of slices of bread. Now do the same for every potato in every form, from mashed and boiled to chips and crisps. The imaginary pile of bread is mounting up. Your next task is to think how many of the remaining non-bread parts of your diet this week could actually be grown in Tudor England – so that's a yes to turnips and peas, and a no to bananas and sweetcorn. Which of these remaining things are in season right now? Wherever there is a gap, fill it with bread. You are beginning to get a feel for how much bread people ate.

Bread for breakfast, bread for dinner and bread for supper, day in and day out. Although it was often eaten with other foods, for the poorest it was bread alone.

But what sort of bread? Well, here there was a lot of variety. There was bread made of pure wheat flour, barley flour or rye flour, there was bread made of a mixture of wheat and barley, of rye and barley, of rye, barley and oats, of wheat and rye, and of oats and rye. In hard times or for the very poor there was bread made of barley and pea flour, or even of ground acorns. Some bread was made with sifted white flour, some was wholemeal, and cheaper loaves often contained the bran sifted out from the whitest flour in addition to the wholemeal. There was bread raised with brewer's yeast and bread raised with sourdough and a range of entirely unleavened flatbreads. The bread you ate varied according to the local grain, growing climate and soil conditions, your wealth and the quality of last year's harvest. There was also the matter of your personal preference and your social ambitions. And although it could all be said to be organic and locally produced that did not mean that it was all good stuff. Sometimes the flour had spoiled, sometimes it was adulterated, and some loaves were badly baked.

The 'best' sort of bread was 'manchet loaves': pure white wheaten bread raised with fresh brewing yeast. Of all the Tudor styles of bread it is the one closest to that eaten in the modern Western world. But nonetheless it is not the same. Denser, creamier in colour, with a tough, crunchy crust, it is chewier and more filling than that which modern bakers produce. The primary difference arises from the wheat itself. Enormous genetic changes have occurred in varieties of bread wheat over the past 400 years, affecting the look, the yield and the nutritional make-up of the plants. Modern varieties of wheat are knee-high when fully grown, and the uniform grain-bearing stalks are tightly packed together in the field, each ear holding a dense cluster of up to fifty fat grains with plenty of gluten inside to give that soft, light, springy texture to the bread that we have come to expect. A look at the images of harvest time in books of hours or the paintings of artists such as Bruegel the Elder shows us scenes of very different wheat fields. Here the wheat stands more than waist-high and is more widely scattered, holding aloft much lighter, open and varied ears of grain. But we don't have to rely just upon an artist's view of Tudor fields to know what sixteenth-century wheat was like. Deep in the thatch of old houses lie wheat stalks, ears and a few grains of actual Tudor wheat, kept out of the damp of the British climate and away from the predation of hungry animals by the dense bundles of other stalks around them.

In other parts of the world when the thatch of a building, after many years of service, begins to deteriorate people strip it all off and start again. In Britain we just scrape off the worst of the top coat and pile more on top. Many of the ancient thatched roofs here are four feet thick where layer upon layer has built up over the centuries. And at the very bottom lie the original stalks, weeds and grains of the Tudor age. Smoke blackening often provides evidence that this is indeed the original stuff. Before 1500, domestic buildings, with the exception of stone-built castles, had central hearths and no ceilings. The smoke made its own way out, drifting gently up to the rafters and percolating out through gaps in the eaves, open windows and any other cracks and fissures it could find. That bottom layer of thatch was heavy with preservative soot. But during the sixteenth century came the great 'chimneying' of Britain. Home after home was 'improved' by the addition of a smoke hood or full chimney, a second floor was inserted and ceilings put up. No more smoke made its way up to the thatch but was channelled away and out. Find some smoke-blackened thatch hidden above a ceiling in a building where you can date the insertion of that ceiling, and you have proof that that thatch was there before the conversion.

And the wheat in that thatch? It varies enormously. There are short ears and long ones, hairy and smooth ones, red, white and grey ones, some which resemble spelt or emmer or rivet. The only thing they are not is uniform. There is not one variety that could be called Tudor wheat; instead, mixtures vary across the country and from building to building. I have had the privilege of seeing such wheat varieties up close and personal on several occasions, generally in conjunction with lots of field weeds, cobwebs and dust. Gervase Markham, writing in the early seventeenth century, said that one sort of wheat above all others was prized for thatching, a type that he called 'whole straw wheat'. Straw of this type was not hollow but full of pith, and its yield of grain was high, although the flour did not produce the whitest or best bread. You might therefore expect that this wheat would be the dominant stalk among surviving smoke-blackened thatches, but no, all the different types so carefully described in Markham's book of husbandry and in that of John Fitzherbert are there, and still recognizable among the soot: brown pollard wheat, with its large, thick-husked grains, dark in colour and smooth; white pollard wheat, paler, thinner-skinned and smaller; white wheat, bearded and with its grains set four square around the ear; reed wheat, with a broad, flat and very beardy ear; organe wheat, with its red tinge; peake wheat, the reddest of all, with a full beard and a tendency to wrinkle; flaxen wheat, small, pale and delicate; grey-coloured Englysh wheat and the deep-yellow chilter wheat.

Household and manorial accounts, farming advice and

business accounts of the period refer to different types of wheat fetching different prices, being used for different types of bread: grey wheat was often used for second-best bread, known as 'cheat bread', and flaxen wheat for the very best cake, with bakers turning their noses up at brown pollard wheat for its darker coloured flour.

Armed with period descriptions of wheat varieties and examples of surviving thatch, one can now find very similar types among the treasures of Europe's gene banks (much of this detective work has been done by John B. Letts, who now produces what he calls 'Elizabethan Blend Manchet Flour').

It is clear both from the written sources and from the thatch that few fields were ever sown with just one variety of wheat. Seed often came mixed, even when bought at market – Markham warns that if what you are buying 'resemble changeable taffeta' it is likely to be a combination of whole straw wheat, brown pollard, organe and chilter. Most people saved their seed from year to year rather than buying fresh stocks of it, and here the practice seems to have encouraged mixing of seed types, creating a greater biodiversity that offered added security. One type of wheat might flourish in the weather conditions of one year, while another would do well the next year. A mixture ensured some sort of crop whatever the weather. Up and down the country, geography and climate encouraged one mixture or another to thatch people's roofs and provide the bread that they ate beneath them.

But it's not just the wheat that makes Tudor manchet bread so easily recognizable: the yeast, too, is a different beast. Modern yeasts, whether fresh or dried, are grown carefully in controlled circumstances to ensure a predictable, consistent product and contain a particular blend of strains. Tudor yeast was 'do it yourself' yeast. If you lived in a well-appointed farmhouse, you would simply pop into the brewhouse alongside the bakehouse and gather up the frothy yeasts that bubbled to the top of your vat of ale as it brewed, or you would buy a little from the local alehouse. That particular culture would have been saved from the previous batch of ale, and that from the one before. The initial source could have been acquired from a neighbour, or brought upon marriage from a woman's family home or the home of her previous employer. Or if none of these options was possible, you could collect it from the wild yourself. Wild yeasts are present all around us, wherever the air is clean enough. They settle upon the skins of fruits and grains, where if conditions are right they can grow.

Very generally, for brewing purposes there are two main groups of yeast: those that grow on fruit and are suitable for winemaking, and those that grow on grains and are suitable for ale, beer and bread making. To catch your own, simply mix up some flour and water into a warm gloopy mess and stand it outside. In a day or two it will either begin to ferment, meaning that you have indeed caught some yeast, or not, in which case try again. Unsurprisingly, the best results are obtained if your gloop is left near a grain field on a warm day just before harvest. Once you have a fermenting bowl of gloop, skim off the bubbly, yeasty-smelling portion and add it to a fresh bowl of flour and water, cover and keep it somewhere warm for the yeast to grow on. For the best results it is worth growing the yeast on in four or five changes of fresh flour and water for a couple of weeks until the balance between the wild strains has settled down and you are sure that you have a good clean mixture. This yeast can then begin to brew your ale for you. This Tudor system ensured that cultures were highly individual, varying from household to household, and baker to baker. The brewing tubs were also open to the air, and from time to time other wild strains of yeast were able to enter the mix, which allowed cultures and therefore flavours to develop and evolve.

Now that we have established the nature of our raw ingredients, let's turn to the Tudor methods of bread baking, which also contribute to the differences between a Tudor and a modern loaf. The milling of the grain was at this time carried out professionally in watermills and windmills, the grain being ground between two stones. Hand milling at home with a quern stone had long been obsolete by 1500, and indeed legislated against on many manors by landlords who also owned the local mill and wished to maintain their monopoly. There may have been a few obstinate outposts of home milling in far-flung locations, but essentially milling had become a profession and a commercial service.

If you had the luxury of a choice of mill to take your grain to, you looked closely at the type of stone being used to grind the corn. Imported French 'black stones' were recommended as grinding the whitest, finest flour, and the use of millstone grit was widespread, despite the cost of transporting the stone across country; however, all sorts of other local stones were also pressed into service. In general, the harder the stone, the more expensive it was to shape and re-dress when it wore down, but the cleaner the flour it produced. Softer stones wore away quickly, the stone dust mixing with the flour.

It wasn't just farmers who took grain to the miller: many people preferred to buy grain and have it milled than buy ready-ground flour at market. Grain keeps well, each packet of nutrition individually wrapped in its own bran husk container. Once ground, open flour can begin to deteriorate in a matter of weeks. Grain therefore went to the mill in small batches, a few sacks at a time, providing a steady income for the miller and fresh flour for everyone all year round.

John Mayoe was one such professional miller. He was based at Wickham in Oxfordshire, just to the north of the Sor Brook on the Bloxham Road, where he held a long lease on all the mill buildings, a lease that he was able to bequeath to his son. Wickham Mill was water-powered, with two separate mills, and came with a millpond, leats and rights to the local waterways. The fixtures, such as the waterwheel itself and the main mechanism within the mill, belonged to the landlord and were included in the lease, but all the movable 'implements and furniture' were provided by John himself, including the two horses that he stabled there. It was a business that required not just an experienced man to run it, but one with a degree of capital at his command. There was a fair amount of commercial risk involved too, as his need for bridging loans from Sir Richarde Fennys testifies. He ground corn for individuals and for at least one professional baker, Nicholas Berrye, who maintained an account with him.

Men like John were often portrayed in Tudor tales as grubbily well off and quietly unscrupulous. And the practicalities of milling could leave a gap for dishonest dealing. When people handed over their sacks of grain they wanted it all back as flour, but inevitably there would be some losses in the process. The real opportunity for misunderstanding or indeed fraud came if the miller bolted the flour as well as grinding it. Bolting just means sieving, separating out the bran from the flour. The more thoroughly you bolt it, the whiter and finer the flour. By hand it is very slow and laborious work because the cloths that you are sieving through are fine and the mesh gets clogged. Millers could fix up a wooden frame with the cloth stretched tight across it and rig it up so that the moving machinery of the mill knocked against it mechanically, shaking the flour through. At home you can tie one end of a cloth to a hook of some sort, hold the other end in one hand and work a big wooden spoon back and forth over the cloth so that the flour is forced through into the trough waiting below. Your arm aches within minutes (or at least mine does), and it can take an hour to bolt enough flour to make a fine, white, yeast-raised cake. Of course, you don't have to separate the bran from the flour if you don't want to — wholewheat flour makes good wholewheat bread — but white bread and cake need the bran taken out. You can choose to take all the bran out or just some of it; the percentage by weight that you take out is known as the extraction rate. If you gave a miller like John a sack of grain weighing a certain amount, he could return to you a sack of flour weighing just a very little less or, if you asked him to bolt it for you, he could return a sack of flour and a sack of bran to you which together weighed somewhat less than the original sack of grain — and here lay the suspicion. Was the loss just legitimate wastage, or had he kept a little back for himself? Had he in fact kept back some of the good flour and made up the weight with additional bran from another batch?

There is no record of John's honesty ever being called into question. He was certainly living comfortably, but not in any way that would indicate anything but hard work and good business sense. John had married Collett in 1576 and they had two children, John and Frances. They lived, not at the mill itself, but in the nearby town of Banbury, and John commuted to work on a mare that he kept at home, separate from the two horses at the mill. Their home had three rooms upstairs, each with a bed, and three rooms downstairs, with a small stable in the yard at the back. It was well furnished, though not ostentatiously. Collett had a good stock of both bed linens and table linens to launder and pewter to polish, but there were no hangings or silverware, and with two linen spinning wheels being kept in the chamber above the kitchen the chances are that she and her daughter, Frances, had spun much of the thread that had gone into those sheets and tablecloths themselves.

But let's return to the making of the bread itself — in particular the manchet bread that was so highly prized. Manchet loaves were small, generally being about a pound in weight and made of the very finest quality flour, not wheat from the workaday high-yielding fields where brown pollard, organe, whole straw wheat and chilter wheats were all sown together, but from a field of flaxen wheat, milled on hard stones and bolted through fine cloths by a professional miller like John Mayoe. The flour was laid within a wooden trough and a hollow made in the centre. Into the flour went warm liquid barm (the frothy yeast) straight from the brewhouse, three pints to one bushel of flour. A handful of salt was sprinkled in and the mixture was kneaded together with as much water as seemed right – a fairly slack, soft dough in the case of manchets. Now, a bushel of flour is a lot, close to a 25kg sack – this recipe comes from Gervase Markham's *The English Huswife*, written in 1615, the most detailed of the early descriptions of bread making – and kneading a mass of dough that large is no simple matter of hands in a bowl. Markham recommends that you use a 'brake' (for more on which, see below), or, if you don't have one of those, that you wrap the dough in a cloth and put it down on a clean board on the floor, take off your shoes and socks and work it with your feet. I like the feet method best myself, although you do have to work your dough first to the right consistency so that it doesn't stick to the cloth too much, and give your feet a good wash. Feet and legs are so much stronger than arms, but you still have good control over the dough. The 'brake' that he offers as an alternative was a fairly standard piece of kit in a professional bakery. It consisted of a wooden lever attached with a leather hinge at one end to a table. One person held the free end of the lever and worked it up and down with as much force as they could in a chopping motion while another person fed the dough back and forth beneath. As any modern baker will tell you, much of the secret of good bread lies in the kneading. The dough must be worked until it is stretchy and springy. The resultant manchet dough was given an hour to rise before being shaped into smallish, flattish round loaves. These were cut, or scotched, all the way around the 'waist' to help the bread rise, before being popped into the oven.

Manchet bread, however, was luxury bread: much talked about, much desired, but not actually eaten all that often. The kitchen accounts of several great houses show us that even among the super-rich of the day, manchet was for high days and holidays. In 1592 a five-month stretch of daily accounts at Ingatestone Hall in Essex, for example, one of the homes of the Petre family, mentions only 'cheat bread' and 'household bread' in its lists of all the bread baked and eaten, with not a single reference to manchet. At Wollaton Hall in Nottingham, home of the Willoughby family, 10,140 pounds of fine cheat bread was eaten in 1547–8, together with 15,467 pounds of coarser bread, but only around 2,000 pounds of manchet bread.

Cheat bread was also a wheat-only bread, and still regarded as a high-quality product that most of the population could only aspire to. Cheat bread was made of the more common varied wheat grains. That at Ingatestone Hall is described in the accounts as being made from red wheat. The flour could be naturally darker in colour and was often sifted through coarser cloths, allowing some of the bran to be present. Not a whole-wheat flour, then, but not the purest white either. This bread needed different treatment: not fresh brewer's yeast and an hour to rise, but sourdough and cool overnight fermentation. The sourdough was as simple as it sounds: a piece of dough left from the previous batch of bread mixed with a little salt and allowed to sour as the yeasts grew on within it. The lump was crumbled into some warm water before being added to some of the flour, enough to make a batter-like consistency. Covered with a layer of more flour, the batter was left overnight for the yeasts to multiply. In the morning the rest of the flour was stirred in, with maybe a splash or so more water to mix it all up into a stiff, firm dough before kneading, braking or treading. These loaves were twice the size of the manchets and deeply scotched on top rather than around the waist, the different shape advertising the nature of each loaf. They needed a hotter oven too.

But the bread of the people in the south, the east and the Midlands was maslin bread, a mixed-grain loaf, generally containing wheat and rye. The amount of rye versus wheat varied, of course. Rye was always cheaper than wheat and did much better in wet-weather years, growing much better in the uplands and areas of more marginal cultivation. The two grains were often grown together in the same fields. Farmers planted maslin and whatever blend of wheat and rye grew and ripened in time for harvest was the maslin that they and their customers made their bread from. Just as growing a genetically varied wheat crop gave an element of food security, a crop that contained different species insured against larger seasonal fluctuations. Maslin was generally what farmers planted to feed their own families.

Dredge (a mixture of oats and barley grown together in the field) and oats represented the grain and bread of those living in the north and west of the country, where wetter conditions made growing Tudor wheat difficult in any quantity. The different grains needed different cooking methods. While maslin responded well to the same techniques as cheat bread – sourdough, overnight rising and strong kneading – dredge and oats behaved rather differently. The written records of the sixteenth century are predominantly those of south-east England, however, and although there is talk of thin dry oatcakes known as 'clap bread' in Lancashire, of 'grue bread' in Cheshire, and of sourdough-raised oatmeal 'jannocks' and yeast-raised 'dredge bread' in the north generally, we find ourselves with precious little information about the more northerly methodology.

I have been most successful at making both flat unleavened oatcakes and sourdough-raised oat bread when I have begun with porridge-like mixtures of oatmeal soaked overnight in water. For the clap-bread-style thin, unraised oatcake I take a spoonful of the porridge and roll it in dry oatmeal, then begin rolling it out, scattering on more dry oatmeal at intervals if it becomes sticky. I heat a bakestone until it is hot enough to scorch a little dry flour left upon it for a few minutes, then cook the oatcakes upon it on one side only for three or four minutes, and stand them up on end, propped near the fire, to dry out afterwards. I have tried this method both upon an iron 'bakestone' and upon an actual stone heated in the fire. The iron is easier to handle, but I think the stone gave a better flavour. The sourdough 'jannocks' style of bread worked best when I again began with a twelve-hour-old porridge – this time of oatmeal, barley flour and water, then added the sourdough and warm water mix and let it stand another full day in the cool, with a thick layer of dry oatmeal scattered over the top. Then I mixed it up and kneaded it like other bread before baking it on a bakestone, first one side and then the other.

Aside from the oat flatbreads that were baked upon stones, Tudor bread was mostly cooked in ovens. A Tudor oven works much like a storage heater, whereby a mass of stone or brick or dried clay is heated up. Once the mass reaches a certain temperature, it will radiate that heat over an extended period. While a modern storage heater is powered by electricity, ovens were powered by fire, a fire that was built and burnt right at its heart, heating the oven from the inside out. Once the oven reaches the correct temperature, the fire can be removed and the food can be placed on the oven floor, where only moments before the fire had burned. The hot mass of the oven will provide the cooking heat on a gently falling scale as it slowly cools.

Tudor ovens generally sat upon a raised base, bringing the mouth of the oven up to waist height. It was, and is, much easier to work with at this level. At ground level many surviving ovens have an opening that reaches back underneath the floor of the oven. You could be forgiven for imagining that this was where the fire went, but it's not. This is an ash hole, a safe place to push the burning hot embers of the fire as you quickly take them out of the oven. The ovens themselves have a circular base and a domed roof; the only other opening is the oven door. The internal sizes and shapes are critical to the efficient functioning of the oven.

I have had the pleasure – and it really has been a pleasure – to cook in a large number of both real surviving period ovens and historic reconstructions. The reconstructions have been invaluable for highlighting the technical aspects of the originals that might otherwise have gone unnoticed. A reconstruction that goes wrong is as valuable, perhaps more valuable, as a research tool than one that works smoothly. When you first light a fire in the centre of an original oven the flames rise in a column until they are large enough to reach the domed ceiling, where they spread out in all directions. If you keep feeding the fire this will become a continuous sheet of flame playing all over the surface of the dome and curling back down to the floor of the oven. Now the fire reaches its next stage, whereby the exhaust gases are borne by the flames back to the centre of the oven and are reburnt. Very little visible smoke now leaves the oven, with almost all of the energy within the fuel being extracted by the fire. The colours and shapes of the flames begin to change as the temperature rises, from spiky yellow tongues of fire to clearer, bluer flames that move in lazy arabesques. Finally you allow the fire to burn down to a bed of hot coals with small blue flames across the floor of the oven.

A good burn in a three-foot-diameter oven takes around forty-five minutes to an hour. Smaller (eighteen-inch-diameter) domestic clay ovens, known as cloam ovens, found in Devon farmhouses, still need about forty minutes to come up to heat; and very large ovens, such as those used by professional bakers and great households, need about an hour and a half. But in all sizes the same basic rules apply. Use small pieces of fuel: thin twigs that are very dry. They catch more easily and release their energy more quickly, and of course in Tudor times they were much cheaper than timber, which could be used for a thousand things besides fuel. Don't pack the oven and then light it: start with a small fire and feed it. Be careful not to block the flow of oxygen in from the mouth of the oven to the centre point, where the fire itself should be focused. Meanwhile, have the wooden oven door soaking in a bucket of water, so that when you come to seal it in place not only will it not char in the heat, but it will also introduce a little steam into the atmosphere of the closed oven.

There are a number of ways to test the temperature of your oven. Traditionally many Devon ovens incorporated a small 'tell stone' that changed colour as the oven approached bread-baking heat. If you lack the correct geological feature, however, you can throw a small handful of flour at the roof of the oven. If it sparks on contact you have reached the very highest cooking temperature, one that will bake a large coarse loaf, but it will be a bit too hot for a fine white manchet loaf. Personally I use the shape of the heat as an indicator, by which I mean how big and what shape is the area in front of the oven door where the air becomes too hot to hold my hand. The line between fairly warm and 'ouch' is a surprisingly sharp one. In the early stages of the firing the area above the oven door is hot but you still have a cool area at oven floor level, allowing you to manage the fire easily. When it becomes hard to get within six inches of the oven floor you are reaching a good cooking temperature. Each oven is a little different from any other, so it takes a few firings to really pin down the exact shape of the heat of each one, but experience can make one a very accurate judge of temperatures and cooking times for a range of different breads.

Once the correct temperature has been reached, you must quickly rake the fire out of the oven, move the hot ashes away to one side – or into the ash hole beneath the oven – speedily flick a damp mop over the oven floor to clean the worst of the remaining ash out, then slip the bread in, put the door in place and seal around it with a small sausage of flour-and-water paste to keep the heat in. This is all a hurried, urgent business. As soon as the fire is out, the oven is losing heat, so speed is the name of the game. No time to rest, however, once the oven is sealed: you have just forty minutes to prepare the next round of baking. When the first batch of bread emerges from the oven, the temperature will have fallen, but it will by no means be cold. If your first oven-load was large loaves of basic household bread, the reduced heat will now be perfect for pies and pasties, small buns and cakes. An hour later these too will be cooked, and now your oven will have cooled to the ideal heat for setting custards and giving biscuits their second baking. Each firing of the oven can, if you have the ingredients and the organization, cook three oven-loads of food.

If you fancy having a go at building your own oven in the garden, aim to make a flattish dome that internally is no more than two foot tall from floor to ceiling. The cooking happens at floor level, so additional height is simply wasted space and you will waste fuel heating it. Images of medieval village ovens often show an external shape that resembles a cylinder with a hemispherical dome on top. Remember that these are external dimensions, not internal ones. The difference between the two shapes helps to add insulation, particularly at the top, where heat is most prone to escape. The more perfectly rounded the shape, the better the flames will move around inside, and the more evenly the oven will be heated. The easiest way to build such an oven is to construct a stone or brick plinth, then find, or make, a basket of a flattish dome shape. Upturn it upon your plinth and begin building up two-inch layers of clay on top and around it. Work patiently, allowing each layer to dry out before adding the next. Keep going until you have walls of more than six inches thick that seem dry, stable and uncracked. Now light a small fire inside to help dry the oven further and burn out the basket. You are now ready for your first proper firing, so start kneading your bread dough.

Those who lived in well-wooded areas, such as the Wealden area of Sussex, fuelled their ovens with faggots of brushwood. You could make your own if you had trees and hedges on your land, but faggots were also a commercial product, part of the woodland economy. Whenever trees were harvested for timber or coppiced for poles, all the small twiggy bits were bound together into bundles of uniform length and volume. Those offered for sale had to abide by the standards set out in law. This, of course, tended to standardize ovens as well, as people sought a structure that worked easily and efficiently with the commercial product. Those who lived near moorland gathered gorse bushes, old heather and other woody shrubs to fire their ovens with – indeed, many preferred these fuels as the natural resins produced an even hotter, quicker burn. The frugal kept all sorts of woody rubbish to one side as oven fuel; even straw will do the trick if you feed the fire carefully.

But not everyone had an oven. Townspeople in particular had to manage without one. Surviving houses and archaeological evidence show a fairly widespread provision of ovens within the more prosperous farmhouses of yeomen and gentlemen, but very few ovens in ordinary homes or in town houses of almost any social standing. Communal ovens and commercial bakers provided the baking for a large section of the population. The nursery rhyme 'Pat-a-cake, pat-a-cake, baker's man' recalls this history. It calls for the cake to be pricked, poked and marked with *D*, say, something that was necessary in a shared oven in order to distinguish one person's dough from another's. In modern Britain, bakers carry out the whole baking process from making the dough to baking the bread, and many Tudor bakers did the same, but there was also a strong tradition of paying a baker to bake home-made dough, pies and cake (a tradition that still operates in southern Italy, for example). Here, too, marking your bread was an important final touch to the dough.

So what do they all taste like, these different grains, leavens and bakes? In general they are good. The flavours are much stronger than most modern, commercially produced breads, which can be a little disconcerting to those accustomed to bland neutral flavours in their white loaf. Even the lightest, whitest of manchet breads is heavier, nuttier, denser and more filling than most of us are used to, and the commoner maslin and dredge breads are solid indeed by modern standards. They all require plenty of chewing, especially the darker breads. The crusts of the breads are thick and crunchy, sharply different from the softer crumb within, a texture produced primarily by the oven. They also bear the traces of their baking, with specks of ash and charcoal on the base from the oven floor. In grand households the lower crust was often cut off and used in the kitchen or fed to the servants, while the now clean upper crust went to the wealthier and socially elevated members of the household, a practice common enough to have turned the phrase 'upper crust' into a synonym for social superiors. The 'jannocks' are reminiscent of Scottish bannocks, the similarity of the names pointing to a shared origin: quite brown and crispy on the top and bottom, where they touched the bakestone, and softer and fluffier at the sides. Maslin bread would taste fairly familiar to those who eat the artisanal sourdough rye loaves that some of the new breed of master bakers are currently producing, being a mixture of rye and wheat rather than pure rye. It is all hearty stuff, very much a meal in itself, which of course it needed to be in a Tudor world.

Meat, fish and pottage

With bread as the basic element of dinner, what of the other food? While the aristocracy dined upon roasted meats and fish of a bewildering array, for everyone else pottage was the most common dish, and the most varied. The word simply meant a stew cooked in a pot and thickened with a grain or pulse of some sort. As the seasons changed, all manner of fruit, vegetables and herbs made their appearance within the pottage. When the hens were laying and the cows were in milk, eggs, milk, cream and butter would have thickened and enriched the mix, too. The Christian tradition of fasting – abstaining from meat, eggs and dairy products on both a daily and a seasonal basis – meant that fish and shellfish often flavoured pottages on Fridays, Saturdays, Wednesdays, Lent and Advent, and a host of different meats provided further variety on other days. Some recipes were simple and cheap, such as pease pottage, where dried peas were soaked and then simmered in water with a bit of ham or bacon and a handful of mint, while others could be expensive – complex and subtle mixtures of chicken, lemon, wine and eggs, for example, with a pinch of ginger and finely chopped dates and capers. Many of Britain's traditional regional dishes are Tudor pottages, from cullen skink in Scotland to lamb cawl in Wales. Scotch broth, pea and ham soup, cock-a-leekie, kale brose and hodge-podge: the list goes on and on. The basic method was to start with some good stock, add meat if you had any, or fish if it was not a meat-eating day, then the grain or pulses and herbs, and simmer for a good long time, throwing more herbs and vegetables in towards the end of the cooking. It required very little tending or complex preparation, so could be fitted in around other work. It didn't matter too much if the fire died down for a while, so there was no need to be stuck next to the pot watching it. Popping in and out of the kitchen was enough. The same method was effective with any number of ingredients, whatever you had to hand. The end product is both filling and delicious.

Several different handwritten manuscripts of recipes had been circulating in the fifteenth century in numerous copies. The recipe in verse that we looked at earlier was one of them. The first printed cookery book, imaginatively entitled *A Boke of Cokerye* and sadly anonymous, appears around 1500; it probably had a print run of no more than 200 copies. Whether handwritten or printed, in prose or verse, these recipes are clearly intended for use in the grandest of homes by professional cooks. *A Boke of Cokerye*, for example, opens with a recipe for summer pottage. A fillet of pork and a piece of veal are beaten together in a mortar and bound together with egg. The meat is seasoned with ground cloves and pepper, and coloured with saffron. The mixture is shaped into small meatballs, which are dropped into rapidly boiling water. Once cooked through, the meatballs are drained and put to one side and a broth is made. Almonds are blanched, ground and put into a cloth. Hot beef broth is poured through them, and the cloth squeezed to wring out all the almond oils into the broth. Prunes are pitted and roughly chopped along with currants, then added to the broth, which is seasoned with mace and ginger. The broth is brought up to a simmer and the meatballs are dropped in and heated through. A pinch of salt is added at the end of the cooking and the pottage is served. The ingredients for this dish were exorbitantly expensive: all, with the exception of the meat, were imported. The almonds and prunes came from France, the currants from Greece, and the cloves, pepper, saffron, mace and ginger from the Far East — overland, following the Silk Route. I calculate that in 1500 a dish of this pottage sufficient to serve six people would have cost somewhere in the region of two shillings, which at that time was more than a full week's wages for a skilled craftsman.

It was a summer dish because of the two meats used. Both veal and pork were available from late spring to early summer but were harder to obtain the rest of the year. Most of us are at least vaguely aware of the seasonality of fruit and vegetables, but within the Tudor world all foodstuffs had their season. Hens did not lay during the winter (we use artificial light to stimulate them into laying all year round), and cows had a dry period from late September through to the spring, when they were between calves. Supplementary feeding and artificial insemination give us our year-round milk supplies. With almost all calves born in the spring, veal was a very seasonal meat. Pork is best from young pigs, so is once again a meat of late spring, while bacon and ham are usually from more mature animals and were produced later in the year. Mutton is most economically slaughtered just after the annual shearing in June, and geese can be fattened for table when 'green' in early summer when the grass is growing strongly, or 'stubble fed' at Michaelmas when they have grazed on the stubble after harvest. The fish in our oceans follow their own seasonal migration patterns, arriving at our shores on cue at the same times each year. A prosperous farmer, therefore, might well have been eating veal and pork meatballs boiled in a plain broth at the same time as the professional cook was producing this 'summer pottage' for a lord in his castle.

When *A Proper Newe Book of Cookerye* was published in 1545, it was targeting the much larger pool of potential purchasers among the prosperous members of society, rather than the small band of super-rich. The recipes are simpler and cheaper, based upon home-grown ingredients flavoured more with herbs than with spices. And it is here that we begin to see the occasional recipe that could have been produced for dinner in the cottages of labourers. My personal favourite is the one entitled 'To Frye

Beanes'. First soak your beans, then boil them until they are cooked through. Next put a large lump of butter into a frying pan, along with two or three finely chopped onions, add the beans and fry it all together until it begins to brown, then sprinkle on a little salt and serve. Another recipe book adds large handfuls of chopped parsley towards the end of the cooking, which I think is an improvement.

Tudor food is generally very good indeed. It's fresh and seasonal and cooked over wood or peat fires whose smoke is a pleasant flavour addition – unlike coal, which is very nasty. Open-roasted meat is a revelation to those who have only ever had oven-baked beef or lamb. Whenever I have filmed the process, the camera crew have turned into ravenous beasts and devoured the lot in minutes, followed by a sort of dazed guilty silence when they see the scene of destruction and realize that we have not yet actually filmed the next scene in which the meat was supposed to have been eaten. The French call us 'Rosbifs' for a reason.

Open roasting is done in front of the fire, not over it. If the meat is roasted over the fire then fat will drip into it, causing flames to leap up and scorch the outside of the joint. You will soon have a blackened charred rind while the centre remains raw. If a joint is roasted in front of the fire, however, the fat can drip safely into a drip tray, where it can be collected for basting and used in other dishes while the meat cooks much more steadily in the radiant heat. Iron spit dogs supported the spit in place in front of the fire, but the fire itself was contained upon another pair of rather similar pieces of fire furniture known as brand irons. These brand irons held the burning brands.

A good roasting technique that produces meat fit to tempt a film crew begins not only with the fire equipment but also with the fuel. In a perfect world you want to roast over a mixture of three types of wood: beech or ash for your main heat, oak for a long hot heart to your fire, and hazel or birch for a quick boost. You can also introduce other woods simply for their flavour, such as apple. Avoid resinous pines as they are both difficult to work with and don't taste very good, and steer very clear of willow, which has an acrid smoke that taints the meat. The pieces of wood should all be the same size and shape – three feet long and three inches in diameter is what you are aiming for.

To my eternal delight, the wreck of the *Mary Rose*, Henry VIII's flagship, preserved its firewood deep in its hull for the marine archaeologists to find and bring to the surface in the late 1970s. What was found matched almost exactly the wish list of a Tudor cook and the regulations governing the sale of firewood. Over 600 logs were found, comprising a mixture of birch, oak and beech. In this case it is the birch which predominates, probably because that is what works best within an enclosed firebox system, which is what the cook was working with on board: a brick-built structure that supported a huge pot permanently over the fire. The logs had been produced from coppice wood of around fifteen years' growth, which was therefore straight grained and free of branches. The lowermost three-foot section, where the trunk was thickest, had been split lengthways into four; the next two sections, being narrower, were split simply in half, and the top sections were left whole, rendering all the logs roughly three to four inches in diameter. Of all the many wonderful finds aboard the *Mary Rose*, it is this firewood that most excites me. It is a unique find – how else would something so ordinary and fundamentally disposable survive?

A roasting fire is managed a little differently from a boiling fire; indeed, in big establishments the two operations were undertaken separately, which is why you will see in so many ancient buildings two great fireplaces in any kitchen. A boiling fire seeks to establish a series of low mounds of fire beneath each pot, the flames coming together in a column that touches the base of the pot and then fans out around its base. To roast, you begin by lighting a small central pyramid fire to build a hot spot of embers. Next place the two brand irons either side, about two foot six inches apart, and lay some of your thinnest birch or hazel logs across them, next to each other in a rack-like formation. As these begin to catch you can add beech and ash logs and begin to bring them forward to rest against the vertical posts of the brand irons. As your fire builds and spreads sideways, you should aim to create a thin wall of flame. As the brands burn through, kick the unburnt ends inwards, towards the centre; these provide the stock of hot coals beneath the raised brands, keeping everything alight. Once you have established a fire of this shape, it is extremely easy to maintain, dropping on the occasional log and kicking in the loose ends.

Now, ten minutes later, you are ready to put your meat in place. Roasting whole animals is wasteful – a party trick, not an everyday method. Meat will cook best if it is formed into a cylinder with the spit passing through its centre so that there is an even thickness along its length whichever way the spit rotates. If the bone is left in it will change the heat dynamics within the joint, so metal skewers are used to help transfer heat into those areas that are shielded by the bone. The spit dogs are placed slightly in front of and slightly wider than the brand irons, and the spit is laid across. Adjusting the height can affect cooking times, or, of course, with a very big spit dog you could lay several pieces of meat on several spits one above another. The spit needs to turn very slowly, allowing the heat time to do its work. Mechanical devices or small boys can be set to do this, or you can produce equally successful results by making a quarter turn every five minutes. The meat tastes best when it is alternately basted and dredged. The basting liquor can simply be the fat that has dripped from the meat, but you can add flavourings such as honey, wine, herbs and spices to the fat. After each baste, you can also add a dredge. This is a dusting of dry ingredients, with flour, breadcrumbs or oatmeal forming the base, and again flavoured with whichever herbs and spices you please. Alternately basting and dredging builds up the most scrumptious crust, trapping in good smoke flavours as it cooks. It all takes rather more skill than just bunging something in the oven, but boy, does it taste good.

The only problem with Tudor food was getting enough of it. If you were wealthy you could eat very well indeed, but most people were not and frequently had to endure shortages. Even in the great households the best stuff – the roast meat and imported almonds, currants, sugar and spices – was kept for the lord, his immediate family and guests. The kitchen accounts at Ingatestone Hall, for example, talk of cattle being butchered into half a dozen 'roasting pieces' and forty 'boiling pieces', and the volumes of imported ingredients purchased are very much smaller than you might imagine if you simply looked at the recipe books of the era. Late spring was the hardest time for most people. After months living off salted, dried and smoked foods prepared in the autumn, and grain from the harvest, stores were running low across the country and prices at market rose. Despite the green flush of growth, very little was yet ready to eat. Hard decisions often had to be made.

If you had a few animals, did you slaughter them now when they were at their smallest and thinnest, or could you wait till they had grown and fattened? If the harvest last year had been poor, you may have been forced to eat some of your seed corn, so you knew that this year's yields were going to be small too. With the countryside fully settled and all of the natural resources owned by someone, there was very little opportunity to supplement food stocks from the wild. All wild animals and plants belonged in law to the person who owned the land they were on – not the person who rented it, but the freehold owner. This excluded most small-scale and even fairly substantial farmers from the rights to fish from the streams, or take pigeons or even rabbits from their fields. Even hedgerows were owned, with different individuals having the rights to the trimmings, the timber from trees that stood within them and the herbs that grew at their feet. And since those who owned these rights were frequently reliant on these resources themselves, they guarded them fiercely. When the weather turned bad and crops suffered, the whole country looked on with a worried eye. Severe food shortages struck several times during the sixteenth century. The years 1527–9 were particularly bad, as were 1549–51, and almost immediately the harvests were disastrous again in 1554–6 and there was another longer bout of hardship in 1594–7. At such times those who were accustomed to eating wheat bread ate barley, and the humbler people had to move to coarser fare, mixing pea flour and bran and even ground acorns to fill their bellies. Everyone felt it, but the poorest could be in real trouble. The local governments within port towns and cities tried to buy in grain from abroad and offer subsidized bread, the wealthy were urged to open their granaries and sell their stored surpluses, and everyone was instructed from the pulpit to give food to the poor, but still some people starved. Very many more faced severe malnutrition, getting by on one meal a day of bread full of nutritionally poor bran and acorn flour. The bones of several of the crew of the *Mary Rose* show evidence of healed childhood incidents of disease linked with malnutrition: rickets, scurvy and anaemia. Since the ship sank in 1545, these men would have been young children during the bad years of 1527–9. It's likely, therefore, that they were among those who suffered the pangs of hunger. Those pangs have to be severe indeed to leave a trace upon your bones.

7. Men's Work

I have to say of our husbandmen and artificers, that they were never so excellent in their trades as at this present.

William Harrison, *The Description of England* (1587)

Ploughmen

By 1 p.m., when dinner was over, men returned to work. For around 80 per cent of the male population this meant going back out into the fields, and once they were out there the most common work was ploughing. The plough acted as a Tudor symbol for all agricultural work. It was not only one of the most time-consuming jobs on the land, and one of the most physically demanding, but also one of the most important for food production. It was also an exclusively male job, and one for men, not boys. More men spent more time ploughing than any other single activity right across the country, and without their labour everyone would have starved.

When we in the modern Western world think of ploughing, we think of a once-a-year activity taking a couple of weeks' work, prior to planting the seed. Tudor agriculture did not work like that. Ploughing was an activity that served several functions, things that today are achieved in entirely different ways.

First, ploughing provided drainage. Hidden deep underneath a large proportion of modern fields (around a third of those in Britain) lie drainage pipes laid in a network to collect excess water and carry it away into ditches and streams. Without those pipes, the land quickly reverts to a shallow puddle or boggy patch during the winter and wet spells throughout the year. Such waterlogged soil drowns the roots of the crops. If such land is drained it is some of our most fertile soil, but in its wet state crops regularly fail altogether. There were no networks of underground pipes in the sixteenth century; instead the Tudor farmer relied upon the plough to create surface drainage with ridges and furrows. He sculpted the land into long, thin parallel ridges separated by furrows or ditches, which could be joined up according to the lie of the land to drain into the ditches and streams around. 'Waterforow thy ground,' Thomas Tusser writes in his *Hundreth Good Pointes of Husbandrie:*

That rain when it cummeth, may runne away round.
The diches kept skowered, the hedge clad with torne;
Doth well to drain water, and saveth the corne.

To do this a ploughman began at the centre of his ridge and set his mould board to throw the earth to the right. When he reached the end of the row he turned clockwise, set his next furrow as close as possible to the first, and returned, throwing the earth again to the right on top of the earth thrown up before. He continued to work in a long thin spiral out, each time throwing the soil to the centre, gradually moving soil from the sides of the ridge to the middle. If the land was very wet, he might have to go over the same ground several times to create a big enough difference between ridge and furrow to drain the water away.

Wet and heavy soils generally spent the whole of the winter in this configuration. Remnants of this pattern can still be seen up and down the country where old plough land has lain for many years under later pasture, preserving the outlines in grass mounds when modern machinery and methods have flattened out the arable fields. If you spot an area of ancient ridge and furrow, note how closely it is related to the contours of the land, aiming as it does to collect and channel water. In some places you can trace out a ploughman's day, spotting the places where he turned his plough round, and may well have rested to drink from his flask of ale. You will also notice the uniformity of those ridges in both width and length. These reflect the distance that a plough team (whether oxen or horses) could comfortably pull before they needed a quick breather, and the width of ridge that drained effectively. Too wide and the water never made it to the furrows; too narrow and there was little land left to plant. This uniform ridge size had long ago become semi-fixed as a unit of landholding; each could theoretically be rented individually.

In the wettest areas these ridges had to remain high all year round to keep the crop's roots out of the bog, but most land was somewhat drier in the summer and ridges that were too high could suffer from the opposite problem, becoming too dry. For many farmers, therefore, good drainage meant building the ridges up over winter (known as 'ridging up') and then casting them down again before planting to a more even and flatter profile that held moisture in the heat of summer. This casting down was again the job of the plough, setting the mould board to the opposite side of the plough and making furrows a little more widely spaced. John Fitzherbert's advice in his *Boke of Husbandry* was to set the plough three or four feet from the ridge and cast (or plough) down the outer sides of the ridge. He could do this either by having his mould board throw the earth to the left, or by leaving his mould board fixed and working anticlockwise. Then he was to move his plough back to the spot where he began, change the mould board over to the right side (or leave it in place and switch to moving clockwise) and cast the central portion of the ridge up.

In addition to managing the drainage through ploughing, the plough was also the most effective method of weed control. Again, modern agriculture has other methods to call on, mostly chemical in nature, but Tudor agriculture relied upon the physical removal of weeds. Land was ploughed to uproot weeds and to smother them. Weed control was best managed by ploughing deep and wide, 'so that he turne clene & laye it flat that it rere not on the edge, the which shall destroy al the thistles and wedes', as Fitzherbert notes. The depth of the cut was to ensure that weeds were uprooted and not left with a strong tap root in place that could regrow. Thistles are especially pernicious in this manner and a major problem in arable fields, and, as any gardener knows, dandelions positively thrive when you just cut off the tops. The width of the furrow was to prevent the uprooted weeds from re-establishing themselves. If the furrows were narrow and close together the cut section of weed-infested soil would be held up by the surrounding ploughed soil and the weeds would continue to have their leaves in the sunlight and their roots in disturbed soil. A wide furrow ensured that the cut section was thrown on to its side, flat, giving it much less chance to re-root. If the weeds were bad, then a second ploughing in the opposite direction could cut up the soil and weeds further and bury most of the foliage away from the light so that it withered and died. Naturally the sorts of weeds that grew most enthusiastically upon arable fields were those that were best adapted to frequently turned and disturbed soil, plants such as thistles, docks, marigolds, poppies, corncockle, dog fennel and kedsokes (a bit of a mystery which plant this last one is, but the period texts mention it often). Their shed seed lay within the soil, eager to spring up at each ploughing. Getting rid of these weeds required a session or two of ploughing to destroy the parent plants, then a few weeks of quiet for the seeds to resprout, followed by another ploughing session to kill the new seedlings. A diligent farmer, particularly one who was looking for seed corn or premium-priced corn to sell at market, repeated this procedure several times, each time thinning out the weed burden upon the land.

Ploughing also formed part of the fertility regime. Once
again, modern agriculture has a range of alternatives, but the
plough formed the backbone of Tudor endeavours. There were
two main sources of additional fertility available: dung or other
organic matter that could be spread upon the fields, or ploughing up pasture. All sorts of organic matter were employed
whenever they were available, from the dung of livestock to rotten seaweed and silt from rivers. Once spread on the land, it was
then ploughed in to prevent the goodness simply washing away
in the rain. It could be laid directly on to fallow land before the
first ploughing session, or the land could be ploughed both
before and after for a more even distribution. The double-plough
method was considered best by Fitzherbert, as the ploughing in
the single ploughing method had to be deep to break up weeds
and so ran the risk of burying the dung too deep for it to be of
any benefit to the crop. If, however, you spread your dung after
the first deep ploughing, the second ploughing could be much
shallower, a stirring of the soil rather than a turning of the soil.
The usual crop rotations of the era gave every piece of land a
year without a crop, a fallow year, when it was repeatedly
ploughed to destroy weeds; it was on this land that dung was
spread but no crop was planted.

The other main method of improving soil fertility involved
ploughing up pasture, which brought land that had 'rested' back
into use. Atmospheric nitrogen had had time to become fixed in
the soil by various plants within the turf, and grazing animals
had left their manure, so this old pasture was much more fertile
than land that had been regularly cropped. Up and down the
country a cycle was practised of putting exhausted arable land
down to pasture and ploughing up that which had been under
grass for several years. Naturally the process of returning pasture to cropping required repeated sessions with the plough.

All in all, the ploughing season began in early September

with breaking up the stubble on newly harvested fields. The ploughman next moved over to his fallow fields and prepared them to receive the seed for next year's wheat and rye crops, which needed to go into the ground before the end of November. Ridging up to deal with the wet weather of winter came next and kept him busy through the coldest, darkest days. By the feast of Epiphany (6 January) the ploughman needed to begin work on areas which were to lie fallow in the coming year or to receive a crop of oats. Peas and beans were planted in March, so preparing the ground for them was the next job, and the oats went in straight after. March was an extremely busy month as land that had been ridged for winter now had to be cast down ready to receive the barley that was sown in early April. Now, with the pressure easing off a little, he could turn his attention to the fallow lands, beginning the cycle of plough and leave that would kill off the weeds over the summer. Dunging the land was a job for early May, with a really deep ploughing and ridging up in June, just before the weeds had a chance to set seed, although some people preferred to leave this to July. August was often the only ploughing-free month, when farmers and ploughmen, labourers, wives and servants alike turned their attention to bringing in the harvests before September saw the plough back out in the fields once more.

The plough that men used varied from region to region, depending upon a mixture of local tradition and practical necessity. A machine that worked well on the cold, wet clay soils of one area was inefficient upon the light sandy soils of another, and vice versa. At its most basic a plough is simply a spade that is dragged through the ground, breaking it open. A man with a spade can dig a trench one spade wide and one spade deep, turning over the resultant soil very effectively, completing a trench around thirty yards long in a day. Rig that cutting blade up in such a way that a horse or ox can pull it through the earth, and that same thirty-yard trench can be produced in around fifteen minutes. The very first ploughs were simply shaped pieces of wood that could pull a scratch several inches deep through light soils, but by the time Henry VII took the throne in 1485 they had developed into much more sophisticated machines. The first thing to interact with the ground was the coulter – essentially a large and very robust steel knife that cut a slit in the earth as it was pulled forwards. Following directly in its path, with its tip tracing along the slit, came the main ploughshare, a much larger, curved blade that cut under a section of soil and forced it up and out. At the top of the ploughshare was the mould board, which in the fifteenth and sixteenth centuries was generally a wooden board on top of the share that forced the disrupted earth to one side, making it fall over. These three elements formed the main working parts; the rest of the structure held them firmly in place and transferred the force of the pull down into the ground.

Some areas of the country favoured ploughs with wheels, such as Hertfordshire and parts of Kent, where stony ground shook and jolted the plough and would make it dig in and catch without wheels at the front to keep it up and skimming along. Some preferred ploughs without, especially those working uneven ground where wheels wouldn't let the share follow the sharp contours. The plain plough without wheels also turned up wherever money was tight, as it was a much cheaper machine to make. Various wedges and notches allowed a man to alter the depth of the cut, the width of the furrow and the angle at which the earth was thrown off. The distance between the ploughed furrows was a matter of holding the plough in place yourself, a task that resembles trying to guide a supermarket trolley with a wonky wheel. I have not done a lot of ploughing with a Tudor-style plough, but the little bit I have done makes it clear to me why this was work for adult men. You need to use your body weight to hold the bucking, jumping thing true or else your furrows will wander all over the place, missing some patches of ground entirely. It is physical and tiring. The shaking and jolting hurt your arms, shoulders, back, hips and legs. The weather naturally plays a significant part in the experience, not just the cold or the wet on your body, but whether the ground is frozen or soft, sodden, dusty-dry or caked solid. This will affect how much the soil sticks to your feet, and whether every step is a heavy one, how much the plough bucks, how much dust you are breathing in. Every day is different and has its own challenges. As Thomas Tusser writes, 'Good Husbandly ploughmen, deserveth their meate.'

Ploughing was not just a matter of man and machine, there was also the matter of who pulled the plough. Should it be horses or oxen? The sixteenth century saw a gradual move away from oxen and towards horses as landholdings and capital investment gradually increased, but oxen remained important and were much preferred in many areas of the country. Fitzherbert was keen to point out that you could always eat your oxen when they reached the end of their useful working life, but the real question was one of grazing and fodder. Pulling a plough is hard work and burns a lot of calories. To replenish that spent energy, oxen needed long, lush grass when they were not working. Open pasture could not supply this, as other animals – sheep, in particular – nibbled the sward down short. Oxen therefore required a fenced or hedged-off area big enough to supply sufficient good-quality grass. Horses also needed good grazing, but they could be tethered, while the bigger, heavier oxen could not. A horse team could be moved from one little patch to another and tethered, to graze around the edges of the arable land wherever there were wide hedgerows, road verges or areas needed for turning ploughs, such as headlands. Fallow areas that were weedy between ploughings provided another quick free meal. In the winter, things were different. Oxen can digest much coarser fodder than horses and cope with being outdoors in all weathers. They could therefore be left out in the pasture with additional fodder in the form of straw and a little hay. Plough horses were stabled indoors and required more nutritious fodder if they were to maintain their condition and continue to work. Tusser recommended that you used up your rye straw first, then the wheat straw, followed by the straw from the pea crop, keeping your hay till last. Oat and bran mashes helped horses through the coldest and hardest working times of the year, supplementing the dry fodder. Choosing horses or oxen was therefore a matter of weighing up what resources you were able to call upon at different times of the year. There was also the question of local tradition. If one of your beasts was sick, for example, it was much easier to get help from your neighbours if both you and they used the same type of beasts of burden and therefore the same harnesses, yokes and tack.

Caring for your beasts was a vital part of the ploughman's job. They were his first concern, as soon as he was dressed in the morning (around 4.30 a.m. in June and as late as 7 a.m. in December), and his last task of the day was to see them safely settled for the night (from 5 p.m. to 10 p.m., again according to season. The bond could become a very close one, and it needed to be. Man and beasts needed to understand each other perfectly if they were to work well together. The philosophical understanding of the relationship was strongly one of master and inferior: man had been put on this earth by God and given dominion over all creatures. The divine purpose of a horse or ox was to serve mankind. Only man had a soul. If a creature did not obey, therefore, it was a man's right and indeed duty to correct and punish it. This set of ideas could and did lead to forms of cruelty that today make us catch our breath. Capons, for example, had their anuses sewn up while they were alive so that they could not defecate for the last three or four days of their lives, in the belief that it made them put on fat. Bulls sent to slaughter were first goaded and baited in the mistaken belief that their fear and anger tenderized the meat and made it more digestible. Working animals were controlled with the use of whips and goads. Horses were 'broken' into service, and oxen were 'tamed'. But alongside these thoughts also ran a gentler tradition of patience, care and consideration, of allowing animals to get to know their keepers slowly, of singing to them to calm them, of brushing and stroking them and speaking in a gentle tone. Looking after the health of an animal was simple good sense, enabling it to work well. Likewise, good food permitted a beast to work longer and harder. A calm and comfortable animal that trusted the human beings it worked with was much more biddable and reliable than one that flinched with fear.

In his *First Booke of Cattell* (1591), Leonard Mascall's advice on taming oxen to the plough blends authority with care and patience. Begin, he said, with a beast between three and five years of age, old enough to have grown into his strength but young enough to be flexibly minded. First, make him a suitable wooden stall and tie his head so he cannot swing his horns at you. Spend the first two days of such captivity stroking and handling his head and horns as much as possible, letting him see and smell you, talking to him and bringing him all his food and water. Next, yoke the young ox to another ox, taking care that neither beast can touch the other with his horns. Leave them thus for two days, all the while continuing to stroke them whenever possible, approaching always from the head end where they can see you and not kick. Leading the yoked oxen for a walk comes next, and as they become more used to your touch, pick off any ticks, flies or worms and generally try to make the beast more comfortable. Gradually, according to Leonard Mascall, the young ox will become tamer until such time as he can be yoked with an experienced ox and have his first turn pulling the plough, though you must take care that the first work he does is light and easy while he builds up his strength. If you had a particularly stubborn young ox, then it could be yoked between two experienced beasts, who would soon sort it out. Mascall was not in favour of using violence against a beast that refused to work, feeling that there was generally a reason, such as sickness or faintness from hunger, that needed other remedies, but if you really needed to exert your authority then he recommended yoking a stubborn beast between two young untrained oxen, who would pull and push him hither and thither for a day or two until he was only too glad to return to the calmer, steadier regime of work.

It sounds to me like quite sensible practical advice. The oxen that I worked with had had a very easy life for some time, with no work at all and a lot of food. They were quite visibly overweight and out of condition. Being put back to work was not something that the two of them were at all happy about. Wandering about yoked together, they were quite content and biddable, but as soon as you attached a plough and asked for some effort they stood stock-still and refused to budge. Now, if a horse does this you walk up in front of it, hold the bridle in both hands, close to the bit, and lean backwards. The weight of your body pulls the horse forward, and generally once he gets going he will then keep going. This does not work with oxen: they are simply too big and too heavy. Likewise, a smart slap on a horse's flank — you don't have to be mean about it — will often be enough to persuade him to play ball, but oxen barely notice such a thing. Cattle goads, such as whips, can be used gently or cruelly, and it's probable that some horses and oxen experienced their use at both ends of the scale. Being bumped around by enthusiastic youngsters of their own species may well have been a kinder and more persuasive exercise of human authority.

A ploughman probably spent more time with his team than

THE LAST JUDGEMENT

Unknown artist, 1475

Bishops, misers and cheating alewives are all being
herded into Hell in this energetic depiction of the
Last Judgement at St Thomas's church, Salisbury.
Religious art commissioned for sacred spaces formed
a major part of painters' trade right up to the
Reformation. The loss of such work must have
been a financial disaster for the craftsmen.

ELIZABETHAN COAT OF ARMS
Unknown artist, c.1570

This coat of arms at St Catherine's church, Ludham, was painted on canvas to hang over the top of an older, and no longer religiously acceptable, crucifixion scene. Technically this was 'staining', not painting, and is a rare survival of something that was cheap and commonplace – bread-and-butter work for artists.

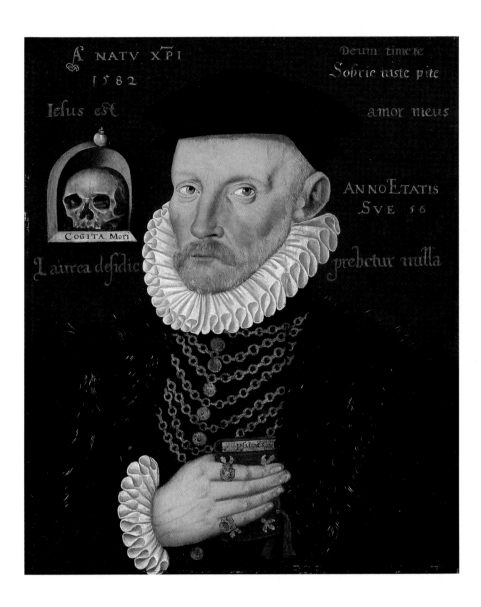

GAWEN GOODMAN

Unknown artist (British School), 1582

Gawen Goodman, a merchant from Ruthin in Wales,
who was looking for more than just his likeness in his
portrait. I love the assertive confidence of Tudor British
art, quite happily employing European techniques but
for its own purposes and in its own style.

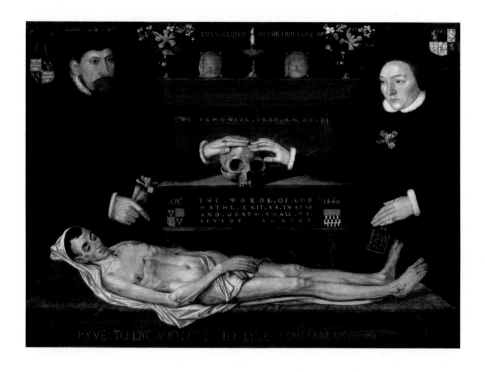

THE JUDDE MEMORIAL
Unknown artist (British School), _c._1560
Typically British, with its flat front-on layout and
emphasis on pattern and meaning, this picture is
crammed with symbolism. In addition to the religious
texts, skull and prominent corpse, there are four
examples of heraldry, two miniature woolsacks,
a lighted candle and two carefully selected flower
arrangements, and both Joan and William have an iris
or fleur-de-lys. Not so much a portrait but a story
of two lives, if you understand the codes.

FOUR GENTLEMEN OF HIGH RANK
PLAYING PRIMERO

Master of the Countess of Warwick (circle of), *c.*1567–9
Gambling was seen as both gentlemanly and highly
masculine in its risk-taking. Note the large numbers
of silver coins on the table, a small fortune. The men are
traditonally identified as (*left to right*) Sir Francis
Walsingham (*c.*1532–90), the statesman and spymaster;
William Cecil, Lord Burghley (1520–98), Queen
Elizabeth's most important adviser, Secretary of State and
Lord High Treasurer; Lord Hunsdon (1526–96), the Lord
Chamberlain; and Sir Walter Raleigh (1552–1618), the
explorer and navigator.

A FETE AT BERMONDSEY (detail)
Joris Hoefnagel, 1570
Dancing was a pleasure sought out especially by the
young of all social classes and both sexes. This may be
the coranto, a tordion or a jig.

A FETE AT BERMONDSEY (detail)
Joris Hoefnagel, 1570
Takeaways or a meal out were a possibility in towns,
where pie shops, hot meat shops and inns set up business.

JOAN ALLEYN
Unknown artist (British School), 1596
Joan was the wife of the actor Edward Alleyn and
the stepdaughter of Philip Henslowe, the businessman
behind the Rose Theatre, a pawnbroker and part
owner of a starch-making house. Her clothes are
very distinctively those of the wife of a London
merchant or professional.

with any other living creature, including his wife. After the basic business of food and water, horses and oxen needed grooming and if they were kept indoors over winter they also needed mucking out. The next job was to yoke the oxen and put the horses in harness. A yoke for oxen was a simple thing to put on, just a wooden frame around the necks to which the plough chains could be attached. Horses needed slightly more complicated gear, made of leather. Each horse had a leather collar, padded to protect the horse's skin. On the outside of the collar sat the hames, two shaped pieces of wood to which the plough could be attached with two chains called treats. Then the belly band and the back band were put in place, so that 'when the horse draws, his collar may not choke him', as Mascall writes, and so that the chains of the plough could be kept up out of his way when he turned. With his gear in place, each beast has to be attached to the plough. Those with the simplest of ploughs working on light soil could manage with a single beast, but most ploughs were pulled by a team of two. Wealthy farmers in heavy clay areas might use much larger teams of up to eight animals for the very heaviest jobs, and the gear to coordinate the movements of such a large team could be complicated. Both gear and animals needed care and attention throughout the day, not only keeping them clean of mud and weeds, which clogged things up, but also untangling ropes, chains and tack, watching out for damage, cuts and broken skin, and managing the rhythm of the work so that the beasts could continue all day. At the end of the day, the gear had to be taken off, cleaned and repaired, and the animals rubbed down, fed and watered.

A farmer wealthy enough to afford a team of eight horses did not always do the actual work himself, and many of those who worked the plough did not own their own plough. Herry Beryes of Clee in South Humberside, for example, was farming on a quietly prosperous scale in August 1557, when he died.

According to his will, he was able to furnish his home adequately, and if he was not exactly rich he was able to have eleven pieces of pewter, which displayed a certain level of prosperity. His real wealth, however, lay in his livestock. He had a pair of draught oxen, who were valued at £4 8s 4d (more than ten times the value of the pewter), together with a wain (cart), wain gear, plough and plough gear, valued at 17s 8d. Herry's oxen ploughed just eight acres for him, with a dairy herd – eighteen milking cows – providing the core of a cheese-making business. He also kept pigs, geese, sheep and horses on the farm. The cash income of the farm came from the livestock sales and the dairy produce, but eight acres of corn allowed Herry to provide both bread for his family throughout the year and fodder for the livestock over the winter months. His oxen and plough gave him a degree of independence and a buffer against market prices.

Nearby, in 1547, Thomas Ramsay had a similar mix of land and livestock but on a smaller scale. His dairy herd was less than half the size of Herry's and he grew two acres of beans, one acre of wheat and one and a half acres of barley. But no plough and no oxen were recorded among his goods at his death that year. He had two horses and other farm equipment, including two harrows, some plough spares – such as a coulter – an old cart and a couple of swathe rakes, but nothing with which to turn the soil. Like many people, Thomas had to borrow or rent a plough and plough team to work his land. The work was almost ubiquitous, but the machines and their power sources were not. The countryside was the scene of complex negotiations, bargains and shared resources. Perhaps Herry lent Thomas his plough and oxen in exchange for borrowing Thomas's harrows, or perhaps Thomas agreed to do some labour upon Herry's land. Or maybe it was a purely financial transaction between both men and their neighbours. However it was managed, men still had to plough their patches of land.

Painters

Tradesmen and craftsmen seem at first glance to have had very different working lives from those on the land, and some of them did. But there was also a significant area of overlap. Between 1560 and 1590 in the county of Essex, eight men described themselves as painters in their wills. Of these, six left bequests of farmland. Being a painter can only have been a part-time occupation for many, something that set them apart from their purely agricultural neighbours, but they would still have had much experience of the plough.

This mixing of craft and farm was a very common one, spreading financial risk for those concerned. In the Ipswich town records there is a clue as to why this was so important. The year 1597 was particularly hard: harvests had been poor for the previous two years and as the summer approached it was clear that, for a third year in a row, grain was going to be in short supply once again. Hunger was stalking the streets, as it had not done for over a generation. Robert Halle was a painter by trade; he had no land and was thus a full-time craftsman. The census of the poor that the town carried out that year included Robert Halle's name and recorded that he was not earning anything at all. In a time of economic hardship few people were willing or able to have their house painted, and work had dried up for Robert. Many of those listed in the census of the poor had developed family strategies for bringing in a little income, with wives and children knitting, spinning or taking in washing. Robert's wife and six children were not bringing in anything, however. The chances are that this poverty was a new thing for the Halle family. They had been comfortably off, a respectable urban family, and may have had servants and apprentices; now, however, there was nothing but a meagre and demeaning eighteen pence per week from the parish and a note in the record that spinning wheels and wool cards ought to be provided for them so that they could begin to support themselves.

Across the other side of the country in Chester, another painter was riding out the economic crisis with more success. Thomas Chaloner was a member of the Company of Painter-Stainers, Glaziers, Embroiderers and Stationers of that city. He, too, was a full-time craftsman, but one whose clientele had more of a buffer against the vagaries of the economy and the weather. He had served his apprenticeship within the guild and in 1584 had been made a free man of the city and a full member of the guild. In his turn he took on the young Randle Holme, second son of a well-to-do blacksmith, as an apprentice. Thomas specialized in heraldic painting, served as an ad hoc deputy to the College of Arms in 1591, and was eventually formally appointed to the role in 1598. Drawing up and accurately painting coats of arms brought him work from all the local gentry, including the Earl of Derby, for whom he is recorded painting an elaborate wooden screen. He and his apprentice had no trouble in supporting a livelihood free from the plough. Their lives were shaped rather by their contacts within the elite of the city and surrounding countryside. Chester was a small- to medium-sized city with a population of around 6,000 people, so maintaining a clientele large and wealthy enough to keep a craftsman in full-time business there required good social skills and networking, along with professional flexibility and a wide repertoire. Thomas and his apprentice were not even the only painters in Chester, the guild recording around six to ten masters of the trade at the time.

The working day of a painter was one that required a great degree of technical know-how and a surprising amount of physical labour. Ready-made paint did not exist as a commercial product. Every painter, whether he was producing heraldic crests on screens and documents, painting portraits or coming up with simple interior design schemes for middle-class homes, had to produce every drop of paint himself. This equates to a lot of grinding, work that generally happened within the 'shop', a word that often means workshop rather than retail outlet. Paint is fundamentally a coloured substance glued on to a surface. Each coloured substance behaves differently, as does each type of glue. Some work best in one combination, and some in others. White chalk, for example, makes a good white paint if it is finely ground and mixed with animal-skin glue to make a distemper paint, but if you mix the same ground chalk with oil to make an oil paint it turns a mucky grey colour. Animal-skin glue, also known as 'size', made a paint that worked very well upon cloth, and dried within hours, but as a protein-based medium it was no good on banners or tents that had to withstand a lot of weather, the wet encouraging mould and rot, and it never stuck well to metal surfaces. Linseed oil was the basis for oil paint. It dried very slowly over weeks or months, depending on the weather, so was useless for rush jobs, but was much more durable in the long run. Tempera was an egg-yolk paint that dried quickly but was very difficult to use to cover large areas. It was especially good at producing bright clear colour upon wooden surfaces. Glare, a paint based on egg white, was less useful, tending para-doxically to dry slightly yellower than egg yolk. Watercolour paint was produced by mixing the coloured matter with gum arabic, and was again used to cover small surface areas. If you needed to cover whole walls then lime wash provided a cheap base but was not good for precision work.

The cheapest colours were those that you could find naturally occurring in local areas and grind up to a fine powder yourself. Chalk we have already mentioned, but many areas of the country have good, strongly coloured clays (or ochres) that can be dried out and ground, giving a range of brownish-reds, yellows and of course browns. The Forest of Dean harbours a particularly good red ochre that can produce a range of colours from a dark purple to an orange-red, and Oxfordshire had particularly vibrant yellow ochres as well as brown umbers. Black could be made very successfully from soot or carefully ground charcoals. More tricky, but still producible within the painter's workshop, were the vivid greens and bluey-greens of verdigris. Sheets of copper could be suspended in a sealed jar over an inch or two of vinegar and left somewhere warm for the vinegar to begin to evaporate. As the vapours rose, they reacted with the copper to produce a copper acetate. This was the coloured verdigris that could be scraped off the copper surfaces, ground down and combined with one of the glue mediums to produce small quantities of green paint. It was also, of course, poisonous. Good ventilation and rigorous hand-washing afterwards were essential.

Far more toxic was orpiment, yet it could still be part of the home-based workshop's regular stock. A naturally occurring mineral (there is some in British rocks), orpiment contains arsenic in high concentrations but gives a strong bright yellow quite unlike the muted ochre earth shades achievable by grinding clays. The mineral was traded across the country in small amounts, almost exclusively for the use of painters. Red and white lead are also highly toxic, but they give very strong, clear colours. If you were working with oil paint, white lead was especially important, as nothing else gave a pure white when mixed with oil. It also speeds up the drying process, so a little touch of white lead within other colours can be useful. Red and white leads could also be produced within the workshop. White lead is simply a lead acetate, and was made in the same way as copper acetate (verdigris), by suspending strips of the metal over vinegar fumes. Red lead was simply white lead that was cooked to a sufficiently high temperature in the presence of plenty of air.

Red and white lead were also imported, at fairly reasonable prices, as were some ochres whose colours were often clearer and less muddy than the British versions. Roger Warfield seems to have been one merchant who ran a sideline in artists' materials. In November 1567 he imported six hundredweight of red lead and two hundredweight of white lead, in January 1568 he brought in four barrels of ochre, in February two barrels of linseed oil, and in March one hundredweight of copperas for ink production. All of these pigments, and a host of others (around forty different pigments have been found in surviving works), had to be finely ground before they were mixed with the wet medium. If they were only coarsely ground, one simply got specks of mildly coloured grit glued in place, but when ground finely enough an even layer of colour could be applied, and for most substances – although not the strong blue pigment azurite, which turned paler, greener and eventually black if you over-ground it – the finer the grind, the better the light refraction.

The grinding had to be done on a flat stone slab with a flat-bottomed grinding stone known as a muller. Naturally, you didn't want the slab or muller to grind down along with the pigments as this would add non-coloured dust, so both had to be made of the hardest of stone, polished smooth. Marble or granite was much the best. My husband has a passion for workaday sixteenth-century British art, and the shed out the back of our house is a veritable wizard's cave of pigment and paint production. I have often been pressed into service at the grinding slab. As such I have an appreciation not only of the muscles you needed to be a painter, but of the very different natures of all the pigments. No two shades behave the same. Modern painters and artists take it for granted that a tube of yellow paint will spread upon the canvas in the same way that a tube of green paint does. The real thing without the modern chemical synthesis processes, hand-made in a workshop, is a varied beast. Terre verte, for example, is a green earth that must be ground to a completely different consistency from that required by a French yellow ochre and, however hard you try, it covers the surface much less fully.

Many painters undoubtedly required their apprentices to do much of the grinding. It was a genuine part of learning the technical skills of the job, and of course it freed the master from some of the drudgery. Wives and children and paid servants could also be put to the grinding slab, and on occasion the work could be outsourced. John Cumberland, an apothecary of Ipswich whom we met before as a supplier of perfumes, was also a supplier to the painting trade. His inventory in 1590 includes '1 small stone to gryne on cullers'. Perhaps in better days he supplied ready-ground pigments to Robert Halle, the Ipswich painter who suffered so much in the crisis of 1597. Whoever did the actual grinding, however, could be sure to spend their days, from 5 a.m. to 7 p.m. in the summer, surrounded by fine dust laced with lead, mercury (from vermilion) and arsenic.

To be a successful painter you needed to know not only how to produce all these paints, but also how to use them to their best advantage. Designs often had to be planned according to the technical properties of the paint. The nature of what was actually painted in Tudor Britain is particularly interesting for its resistance to mainstream European Renaissance ideas of art. Much of the technology was identical to that being used by Italian and Dutch artists, yet mathematical exercises in perspective and the tradition of realism that characterized fifteenth- and sixteenth-century art both sides of the Alps rarely made much of a showing this side of the Channel. A few visiting foreign artists such as Holbein or Joris Hoefnagel made European-style images of British subjects, but British painters worked in a home-grown style that favoured pattern and meaning. Personally I love both the Renaissance art of Europe and the idiosyncratic art of these isles. They are very different, but I find them both beautiful and moving. By the end of the Tudor era, elements of European practice and aesthetic are moving in and influencing the home-grown style, but a certain distinctive flavour still holds.

Take, for example, the portrait of Gawen Goodman of Ruthin painted by an unknown artist and dated 1582. The Goodmans were a mercantile family who lived and worked mainly within Ruthin in North Wales, but also had some London connections (Gabriel Goodman became Dean of Westminster). The face is rendered with great competence and displays the realism of Continental practice, yet the whole feel of the piece is symbolic. The pose is a little awkward and is intended to show off a centrally placed prayer book, a death's head ring (which also appears in an earlier portrait of his father) and clothes of rich respectability. While all of these accoutrements are realistically painted, they feel like separate items offered up to scrutiny. The background is entirely emblematic, a single flat colour upon which floats a series of Latin godly phrases, the sitter's name and age (fifty-six) and a skull in a niche. Family continuity, piety and commercial success are all laid out for the viewer to read, alongside a recognizable individual. Gawen Goodman was obviously very happy with this combination of instructive, meaningful message and personal likeness, as the painting is recorded as hanging in the parlour of his family home at the time of his death in 1603. It is also an image that appeals to me. The pride, the determination to produce a statement about his position and beliefs, and the sheer force of personality that wanted a story about his life – not just a snapshot of a moment – to go down in history, give the image a real emotional resonance.

The painting could have been produced in London, perhaps during a business trip, but since Gawen was a merchant he must also have had significant dealings in the city of Chester, less than a day's ride away, so it is not totally impossible that this picture was painted by Thomas Chaloner, the Chester artist that we met earlier.

Deciding what should be contained within an image was a matter for discussion between the person paying the bill and the painter. Customers had strong ideas about what was fashionable, desirable and suitable, as well as individual requirements, and painters frequently had a number of models and suggestions to make based upon what they had seen and made before, and upon designs that circulated among craftsmen. In 1585 John Smartte of Boxted in Essex, for example, left half of his 'pattrons' to his daughter's husband-to-be (who may have been his apprentice), while in London in 1572 Richard Flint left his grindstone, brushes and patterns in his will, and in the same year Henry Eives in Norwich bequeathed 'bookes of armes and patterns of paper'. Such patterns could be either hand-drawn designs, or prints imported from the Netherlands, and particularly from Germany where the images in circulation were of the highest quality. A few pattern books, deliberately intended to act as source material for artists and craftsmen, were even published. The surviving works of painters, plasterers, woodcarvers and embroiderers all show designs taken from foreign printed works. But the surviving works always look English, Welsh or Scottish. The European aesthetic model is translated as it moves through a local lens, dropping fine perspective detail and adding in areas of flat pattern, enhancing the storytelling elements with additional symbolism. They display less fine technical modelling skill, but often add punch and impact.

If you were to look at the surviving examples of painting of all types in Britain, you would soon conclude that most painters painted interior walls with schemes that ranged from simple, often wonky, geometric designs up to elaborate scenes with multiple figures. If, however, you trawl through the documentary evidence, you would quickly conclude that the bulk of painting work was upon cloths to be hung in homes. Either way, interior decoration emerges as the bread-and-butter work of painters. From the time of Henry VII's victory at Bosworth in 1485 up to the Reformation of the 1530s, painters found a good deal of work within the Church, painting walls and rood screens, statues, religious banners and shrines for parish churches, cathedrals, monasteries and chantry chapels. The quality of work varied, of course, but much of that which survives (often only in fragmentary form) is superb and highly skilled work. Take the magnificent mural of the Last Judgement in St Thomas's church in Salisbury, for example, painted in the twenty years running up to 1500. It covers the whole surface of the chancel arch and despite some rather insensitive Victorian restoration we can still enjoy the riot of black, white, green, red and yellow, with Christ enthroned in the centre upon a rainbow, the souls of the dead rising from the grave upon the left and the descent into a fantastic hell mouth upon the right in the form of some great dragon or fish-like beast. Notable among the damned are two bishops, a miser with his money bags and a cheating ale wife, tankard in hand. Sadly there are no records to say who painted it or even how much it cost; only the cost to whitewash it over in 1593 has been recorded.

The Reformation must have been a particularly terrifying time for painters. Suddenly, almost overnight, a major group of clients, often their wealthiest clients, were gone. With Protestantism came a strong belief that paintings of religious subjects attracted idolatry. Not only did the commissions dry up, but their old work was being defaced and whitewashed over. Whatever their personal religious beliefs, the people within the painting trade were facing a crisis. When Mary took the throne in 1553 and reinstated Catholicism, there began a brief period of redecorating the remaining religious buildings (the monasteries had, of course, mostly gone). John Barber and his wife were probably very glad of the commission to paint and gild a rood screen in Leicester during this period. But when Mary died in 1558 and the country officially became Protestant once more, the new flush of clerical work was over. There was other work around during these tumultuous times, though. John Barber was employed repeatedly between 1549 and 1558 by the Leicester Guildhall producing coats of arms and municipal banners, and right at the heart of the Reformation, in 1531, Ellis Carmanelle in London was working upon the coronation pageant for Anne Boleyn, which included a trip from Greenwich to the Tower by barge, 'enlivened . . . with musicians, a dragon and terrible monsters and wylde men casting fyer', and streets hung with the stained banners, standards and pennants of all the craft guilds.

Elizabeth's reign represents the heyday of the painted cloth for interior decoration. This was termed 'staining' rather than 'painting'; in London the painters and stainers were officially two different groups who had amalgamated into one guild while attempting to maintain the division between their membership. Staining of cloth meant working upon canvas with distemper paint, the sort where the pigment was mixed with animal-skin glue. Painters were supposed to refrain from using distemper, and stainers were not supposed to use oils or paint on wood or directly upon walls. Out in the rest of the country the boundary blurred as most men needed to work in every medium possible in order to attract sufficient work. Stained cloths were cheap mass-market goods, easily affordable by tradesmen, yeoman and husbandman farmers, and even by the occasional labourer. Fifty-six per cent of the Elizabethan inventories of Nottinghamshire, for example, mention painted cloths or hangings. As a further example, take Thomas Harrys, a husbandman living on the outskirts of Banbury in Oxfordshire in the 1590s. Thomas was not unusual among husbandmen in having painted cloths within his home, but he does seem to have been particularly keen upon them. He had two in his hall and two more in his parlour, and the two best beds within the house also had testers (ceilings) of painted cloth. In the previous decade, back in Ipswich, John Kenynggale had stained cloths to the value of two shillings and eight pence, which marks them out either as a very superior set or as particularly large ones – with more in the parlour – the widow Margaret Lowe had just the one, Jacob Person the sailor had two, and so it goes on.

People were more likely to display their stained cloths in the hall, but parlours and bedchambers were also frequently decorated in this way. Most of these cloths are valued at around six pence, and they turn up all over the country, from the community of Clee in South Humberside and South Cave in Yorkshire, to Monmouthshire on the Welsh borders, Essex in the east and down to Devon and Cornwall in the south. They have only very rarely survived, despite their proliferation. The few fragments that we do have include a set from 1600 that were painted to mimic wooden panelling, and an extremely high-quality set at Hardwick Hall in Derbyshire that look at first glance to be woven tapestries. Wall painting survives the vagaries of time much more effectively, hidden for the most part beneath the paint or wooden panelling of later decorative schemes. But as they are not movable goods, wall paintings are not mentioned in people's inventories. Should we imagine, therefore, that those people who do not have painted cloths listed among their possessions had painted walls instead? The cost of wall painting was equally low, around a penny per square yard, with a complete scheme of walls and ceiling for a large reception room of the best-quality work rising to five shillings for both paint and labour. Most painters seem to have led lives that involved a lot of travelling, moving from house to house to brighten up people's interiors, with a workshop back home to make and prepare the brushes and paints.

8.   Women's Work

But huswives, that learne not to make their owne cheese;
With trusting of others, have this for their fees.
Their milke slapt in corners, their creame all so sost [soured];
Their milk panes so soltie, that their cheeses be lost.

Thomas Tusser, *A Hundreth Good Pointes of Husbandrie* (1557)

According to John Fitzherbert in his *Boke of Husbandry*, a woman's work-day began with sweeping the house, tidying the dishboard and milking the cows, checking on the calves and pouring all the morning's new milk through a series of clean cloths to ensure that no dirt or cow hair remained within it. Then she was to get the children up and dressed and make the breakfast. Later in the day she was to prepare both dinner and supper, bake bread and brew ale, make butter and cheese, feed the poultry and pigs twice a day, gather eggs, do the gardening, prepare hemp and flax and then spin it, comb and spin wool from the sheep, winnow wheat, do the laundry, make hay, take corn to and from the mill, sell her butter, eggs and cheese at market, do the family shopping, turn barley into malt and make the family's underwear. She was also to help her husband filling the muck wagon, driving the plough and shearing the corn. As he himself admits, 'thou shalt have so manye things to do, that thou shalt not well knowe where is beste to begyn.' In which case he believed that a woman should prioritize her tasks, dealing first with those that had the largest negative consequences if they were forgotten. This was the day-to-day reality of most women: the wives of farmers and the young women working as servants in husbandry. Even urban women followed much of this routine.

The dairy

Come butter come
Come butter come
Peter stands at the gate
Waiting for a buttered cake
Come butter come.

Milking, as Fitzherbert says, was an early morning job; butter, on the other hand, was best churned in the cool before dinner, and cheese making was afternoon work. Dairying was a woman's responsibility, part of the household routine, and in some areas of the country it could also be a serious income generator. The wife of Herry Beryes, for example, was obviously a very busy woman. While the plough and oxen mentioned earlier were exclusively her husband's preserve, Mrs Beryes had to deal with the milk of eighteen cows and keep an eye upon the nine young beasts who had not yet come into milk and thirteen calves who all needed weaning. Eighteen cows are too many for one woman to hand-milk twice a day, so Mrs Beryes must have had several maids to help her. The usual ratio was one dairymaid to every six cows.

Mrs Beryes would have been responsible not just for overseeing her maids, but also for their tuition. A skilled dairymaid, confident enough to take charge of a dairy, could command significantly higher wages than the ordinary run of maids, but young girls wishing to learn would often accept contracts for reduced wages if the mistress had a good reputation as a dairy woman willing to teach. Herry Beryes would not have been so inclined to sink so much of his farming capital into a milking herd if he had had any doubts about his wife's competence.

The equipment for large-scale cheese making was also a significant investment. Mrs Beryes had a lead (a built-in large boiling vessel similar to the piece of equipment that the Victorians called 'a copper', even though they were often made of iron by then) to boil water and heat milk in. She also had two cheese presses, two long shelves for maturing cheeses, a butter churn, an array of cheese vats to make the cheese in, and milking bowls to settle out the cream. Altogether it was valued at twenty shillings, more than many male craftsmen had invested in the tools of their trade. And in store sitting on the shelves in August 1557, when her husband died halfway through the cheese-making season, were twenty stone of cheeses. This was a big operation by Tudor standards, as most milking herds at that time numbered less than a dozen cows. Living in the parish of Clee on the south shore of the river Humber, the Beryeses were in a good position to supply the small but thriving town of Grimsby. Cheese keeps well, so it is an ideal product for market in a world where transport can be slow.

Mrs Hacket senior must also have been a very fine dairy woman. Her son Thomas certainly thought that everything she had done when he was growing up in Suffolk was infinitely superior to the practices of the women he encountered in south Hampshire. His *Dairie Book for Good Huswives* (the earliest text to focus exclusively upon dairying), published in 1588, is full of comparisons between the two. As a man writing about an essentially feminine craft, he must have paid close attention to his mother. He begins by describing his idea of the ideal dairy building, with large windows all along the north and eastern walls to ensure a strong airflow and broad wooden shelves, three feet deep, running around the walls inside at chest height. This is indeed good advice. Successful dairying is reliant upon scrupulous cleanliness and accurate temperature control. A strong airflow means that surfaces and vessels dry quickly, inhibiting bacterial growth once they have been scrubbed down, and by having openings only on these two faces of the building you exclude the sun, keeping temperatures more even.

Temperature management can be further aided by a number of simple practices that Thomas Hacket doesn't mention. One is damping down. If your dairy had a stone, tiled or brick floor, then a bucket of water sloshed over the surface would sink in and slowly evaporate during the day in the cool crossflow of air from your windows. This can reduce summer temperatures by four or five degrees. Standing a bowl of milk on a wet stone floor or shelf can likewise provide effective cooling. The other method of temperature control is to use a mixture of different substances for shelving. When you need to warm your milk and cheese during a cold snap, wooden shelves and vessels hold their heat better, and large shallow vessels of hot water can be used to stand churns, jugs and bowls within.

Pendean Cottage at the Weald and Downland Open Air Museum in West Sussex, although early seventeenth century, provides an almost perfect example of a period dairy. Its unglazed tile floor, its correctly placed windows, its wooden shelves and stone shallow tray all allow precision cheese making and it is one of my favourite places to work. It stands on the northern side of the house, which means that the summer sun does not even fall on its external walls, and the parlour next door has a chimney that allows one to heat the milk to help it turn, and boil water to scald all the equipment in order to clean it.

Thomas Hacket gives what he considers to be the perfect recipe for cheese making. He tells the housewife to combine the milk from the previous evening's milking with that of the next morning while the morning milk is still warm from the cow. Rennet (juices from the stomach of a calf that has not been weaned), which turns milk into curds and whey, requires warmth, ideally the same temperature that is found in a calf's stomach. Thomas Hacket was concerned that some people heated the previous night's milk to achieve this warmth, accidentally overheating it and ruining the eventual flavour of the cheese. He forgets to mention that the rennet has to be added and the vat of milk left undisturbed in a warm place for an hour to set, but does remind his readers to drain off the whey and break the curd into very small pieces before it is salted and packed into the cheese mould: 'The Curdes being so well and small broked, presse them downe often with your hands holden a crosse.' Apparently the custom in south Hampshire was to leave the broken curd sitting in the whey until it was stone-cold, a practice that he really didn't approve of. He didn't much like the cheese moulds in local use either, and admitted to having gone as far as taking an example of the Suffolk version to a woodturner to show him what he wanted, but still been disappointed with the result.

With the curd packed into the cheese mould it was ready for pressing. Thomas advocated the use of a wooden press, believing that it made more evenly shaped cheeses than simple stone weights. Two wooden uprights were fixed in place with matching slots running through much of their length. A third piece of timber, narrow at the ends and broad in the middle, was inserted across, with its two ends lying in the upright slots. It could be moved up and down and secured in place with iron pins and wooden wedges. 'In this kind of presse, ye may well presse four or five cheeses at once.' It is a direct wooden forerunner of the iron screw press that took over in the mid nineteenth century. Once pressed, the cheeses received a salting, sitting in a pile of pure salt that gradually melted into brine as more liquid was drawn out of the cheese. Finally they were wiped over with warm brine, dried, and laid upon wooden shelves to be turned over every day. If you follow these instructions, remembering to add the rennet and also to wrap the cheese in cloth as soon as it comes from its first pressing, another detail that Thomas Hacket overlooks, you end up with a cheese that is somewhere between a Single Gloucester and a Caerphilly, or at least I do.

Christabel Allman made cheese in Nottinghamshire for the Willoughby family at Wollaton Hall. In 1566 she had three women under her: Elizabeth Hayes, Elizabeth Ranfield and Margery Clarke. Christabel was paid twenty shillings for half a year's work, very good money indeed for a woman. Her three members of staff were paid half the amount she was, but even so these were well-paid jobs. Undoubtedly the women earned their money, producing around twenty-six to twenty-eight cheeses a week from June to mid August, and tailing off a little in September with just sixteen to eighteen cheeses per week. June to September were the classic cheese-producing months, following closely the seasonal cycle of grass growth. As anyone with a lawn to care for knows, grass doesn't grow much in the winter, but as the weather warms in the spring it shoots up with lush green blades. By high summer it looks a bit dry and grows rather more slowly, producing thinner, greyish-green blades. By the end of September, growth is slowing down rapidly. Tudor cows were very reliant upon grass, and the milk that they produced closely reflected what they were eating. Spring grass made for rich, creamy milk, ideal for making butter, but as summer approached and the grass changed, milk became less creamy but much richer in caseins, a form of protein. The higher the casein content, the higher the cheese yield. So while both butter and cheese production could be undertaken throughout the milking season, good dairy women prioritized butter in the spring and cheese in the summer.

All dairy work required rigorous hygiene. Salt, elbow grease and boiling water were the main tools in the war against unwanted bacteria. The business of scrubbing, scouring and scalding every utensil and work surface took as long as the actual cheese making. Of course, no Tudor dairy woman thought in terms of bacteria, but it was clear to everyone that without scrupulous cleanliness, milk soured and produce rotted. The greasiness of butter might tempt you to use detergent when it came to washing up, but if you used soap or lye on wooden dairy vessels the residue they left would taint the next batch of milk. Both substances also caused the wood to dry out too much and made it split. Instead it was necessary to begin with scraping out as much of the remaining butter as possible, then a splash or two of boiling water could be swilled around to melt the fat and scrubbing began. Several rounds of boiling water, scrubbing and emptying out eventually rendered everything clean. Particularly difficult jobs could be made easier by vigorous scrubbing with a handful of coarse salt and a damp cloth. The salt acted firstly as a scouring agent and then as a sterilizing one, getting deep into the grain of the wood. Any salt residues – unlike soap residues – could only benefit the next batch of butter or cheese. The final rinse was always a thorough one with boiling water. Everything then had to be dried as quickly as possible. Damp dairy vessels soon begin to smell sour and moulds quickly develop, so once they had been wiped with a clean dry cloth they were propped up somewhere draughty, and preferably in full sunshine. Once again the Tudor dairy woman knew by experience that sunlight kept her vessels 'sweet', unaware of the scientific explanation that points to ultraviolet light as an antibacterial agent.

Silk women

Not every woman's life was lived on the farm. Just as for men, a minority of Tudor women derived their livelihood from trade and manufacture.

In 1485 Alice Claver sold the new king six ounces of red silk ribbon. She had also sold goods to his predecessor, Richard III, and Edward IV before him. Alice traded in her own right; as a widow, this was fairly normal. Single and married women were legally under the authority of fathers and husbands, and were not permitted to hold public office, make any sort of legal contract or head up a business. But when a woman was widowed, she became independent. Widows ran all sorts of businesses, from tailor's shops to smithies, often with the assistance of their former husband's apprentices. Yet within the city of London in the fifteenth and early sixteenth centuries, silk women like Alice Claver could take female apprentices and run independent businesses even as married women. They had no guild of their own, but indentures of apprenticeship were enrolled by the chamberlain of the city. This autonomy makes them and their businesses much more visible in the historical record. Many women must have acquired craft skills as daughters or servants, found husbands within that craft for whom a skilled wife was an attractive proposition, and continued to exercise those skills on and off within the family business.

But with all legal references appearing in the father's or husband's name, their skill and daily work is overlooked. It is easy to assume that craft skills were a male preserve, that wives and daughters were kept out of the workshops at the back of houses. Yet that need not have been the case. Silk women operating as wives and mothers, with all the usual responsibilities of the household, were also practising their craft, and it was one that involved good negotiation skills and business acumen as well as very specialized technical know-how. When Alice died in 1489 she left her business to her apprentice, Katherine Champion. Under Alice's tutelage Katherine would have learnt to 'throw', or spin raw silk into thread, to manufacture a range of braids, ribbons, cords and tassels, and to make up small articles of dress that utilized these products, such as coifs and partlets. In addition to manufacturing, it is clear that many silk women also acted as middlemen or traders in small luxury goods, selling on silk ribbons from Tours in France, black cypress silk, fine lawn and packets of pins. The equipment was fairly simple: 'coffyns, focer and frames' are specified in Maud Muschamp's will of 1498 ('coffyns' may have been boxes, or possibly box looms, and 'focer' was possibly something to do with the production of silk floss), and just 'frames' in Margaret Reynolds' of 1528. Ribbons could be worked upon box looms – small wooden boxes with a roller front and back to wind on the warp, and a rigid heddle – or the ribbons could be simply imported from Tours or Venice and sold on.

Ribbons were employed most frequently for 'points', the short lengths used to tie articles of dress together – functionally on men and more decoratively on women – such as the two gross and nine dozen 'venice rebande pointes of sundry colours' that were sold to Queen Elizabeth in 1576. Tablet-woven braids were less fashionable than they had been, but the technique offered a way of making very intricately woven patterns. The finest surviving examples have words and pictures woven into them as well as repeating geometric designs. Tablet weaving can be done with no more than a single anchor point – something tied around a table leg, for example, and a set of small wooden or bone tablets pierced with between four and twelve holes – although the more elaborate designs are easier to work if you string your warp threads between two points held firmly apart to create a simple frame. The signature product of the silk woman, however, was the finger-loop braid, which needed nothing but a single anchor point. Either a double-length piece of thread is tied into a loop or, for more intricate patterns, two pieces of different-coloured thread of the same length are tied together to form a loop, one end of which is attached at the anchor point and the other slipped on to one of your fingers. The simplest of these braids used five such loops; complex ones used up to forty loops which several people worked on at once. The loops were manipulated through, over and under each other in a vast variety of patterns to create flat braids, round strings, hollow laces, laces that split and rejoined, fat and thin laces, and any number of colour patterns as threads picked out stripes, checks, waves, herringbones and dog-tooth forms.

Several manuscripts detailing how to make these braids have survived, including one in the Victoria and Albert Museum dated around 1600 which has worked samples attached to the page, with each 'recipe' worked in red and white silk threads. A fairly simple example tells you: 'To make this flat string warpt 3 bows of red and 2 of white place red on the one hand and white on the other, then work through double boes takinyge the up side of the boe of the left hand and the lower on the right.' The length of sample braid is narrow, with a white ground upon which the red silk forms a series of hollow diamonds. It is not exactly a 'how to' manual for beginners but rather an aide-memoire for an experienced worker. The six dozen and seven pieces of 'hollowe lace of silk of sundry colours' that appear in Queen Elizabeth's wardrobe accounts for the year 1576 were made following a much more elaborate set of instructions. A hollow lace could have another cord or wire threaded through its centre, or if used empty acted as an especially soft and flexible trimming or lace.

When my daughter was eight years old she learnt to make a

simple finger-loop braid. As many young girls take to friendship braids and loom bands, she took to finger looping and within a year she had her first professional commission for fifteen yards of a two-colour flat braid to decorate the doublet of a character onstage at the Globe Theatre. It took her about a month to make, putting in the odd half-hour of an evening, but off it went on time, all neat and finished, and she has not looked back since. These days her work graces television productions, museum displays and opera stars at the New York Metropolitan, as well as theatre. Watching her work is an interesting experience. When most of us take up a craft as adults, for all that we practise and master techniques, we rarely approach the work rates of our ancestors. She does. Her hands fly so fast that when she was employed recently on the BBC production of *Wolf Hall* to be the hand double and weave some finger-loop braid, they had to ask her to slow it right down so that they could see what she was doing. It's not just the sheer speed, though: her hands can make movements that no one else can manage, having developed the flexibility and myriad tiny muscles from childhood. Someone who takes up the violin or ballet or hurdling in their thirties knows full well that they stand little chance of competing with those who trained their bodies from childhood. It is the same with craft skills.

Plaited braids using between three and eleven bundles of threads formed another string to the silk woman's bow. These also came in numerous designs and could be flat or circular in profile. I have seen linen-plaited four-strand braid preserved in abundance upon decorated saddles. Mistress Vaughan, working in the 1540s, supplied goods to the value of £128 13s 6d to Queen Catherine Parr's stable, presumably for a similar purpose. While my attempts at finger-loop braid are frankly terrible, I do have the knack for plaiting and rather enjoy experimenting with the different designs and textures that can be created by mixing different twists, tensions and thicknesses of thread with the various techniques.

Silk women had to master all of these skills: surviving clothing regularly displays several different types of braid upon the same garment in the same matching threads and patterns. This provided a visual consistency for the different braiding techniques that were required for specific functions – from braids used to fasten buttons to braids used to strengthen cut edges and others to cover seams.

Like most aspects of Tudor life, success and advancement depended heavily upon family connections. The raw materials of the silk woman's trade were expensive, so a certain amount of capital had to accompany the skill. Many of the silk women that we can identify in the historical record were married to mercers, merchants trading in just such raw materials. Young men apprenticed to mercers often grew up in the same household as young women training to be silk women; the two trades were highly compatible, each probably contributing to the success of the other. Stephen Vaughan was very keen to promote his wife's career, writing first to Thomas Cromwell to suggest that Anne Boleyn should employ her, sending samples of her work, and then writing again to complain that he hadn't heard anything back. He was quite sure that 'she can serve her better than any other woman in the realm'. Mistress Vaughan did, however, manage a little while later to convince Anne of Cleves to buy her wares, and subsequently Catherine Parr, who in addition to the braids for the stable purchased £186 12s 5d of braids for use on clothing, and much more modest amounts for the coffer maker to use in trimming chests and the embroiderer to use upon the articles that he supplied to the queen.

Away from the court, and indeed London, the work of the silk woman was much less exalted and involved cheaper materials. Mistress Sheale lived in Tamworth in the late 1550s and early

1560s. We know of her work simply because her husband was a minstrel who wrote a song about their life together:

> My wyff in dede ys a sylke woman be her occupacion,
> And lynen clothe moste cheffly was here greatyste trayd,
> And at fearis and merkyttes she solde sale-war that she made,
> As sherttes, smockys, partlyttes, hede clotthes, and other thingges,
> As sylke threde, and eggynges, shurte banddes, and strings.

Mistress Sheale was mostly working as a fine seamstress making ready-to-wear, one-size-fits-all items of linen apparel. She was, however, also making shirt strings – linen finger-loop braids, often with small tassels on the ends, used to tie up collars and cuffs – and selling silk thread, both of which were seen as work of the silk woman. With no permanent shop, she took her easily transportable wares around a circuit of markets and fairs.

It was at about this time, the middle of Elizabeth's reign, that the silk woman's unique position began to slip away. Alice Montague, who had been doing a roaring trade selling her wares to the queen, expanding her lines to include network, bobbin lace, cutwork and embroidered smocks, sleeves and ruffs, and undertaking the most specialized laundry tasks, began to hand her business over to her husband, Roger. From then on fewer and fewer women appear as independent operators. William Harrison, in his *Description of England* (1587), was able to write: 'And until the tenth or twelfth yeere of Queene Elizabeth there were but few silke shoppes in London, and those few were only kept by women, and maide servants, and not by men, so now they are.' As the nation's prosperity rose in the latter half of the sixteenth century and technological leaps in ship design promoted trade, the market grew. Those who could command the capital for larger-scale investment had new opportunities, and this primarily meant men. They were importing a much wider range of goods and they were increasingly taking charge of the silk shops. The women did not all disappear overnight, however. Susan More is still discernible in 1599, giving evidence in the Chancery Court. She worked for Mistress Berk, making points for five shillings and four pence the gross. Mistress Berk was obviously still holding out as an independent silk woman with her own business to run, as her husband, Randall, was described as a bookseller.

The work of a silk woman appears at first glance to be a gentle, ladylike pursuit, but as with all jobs there is a harder side to it. Recently my daughter had a large order to fulfil for an international production. Some of the silks took a little longer to get to her than they should have, and of course the tailors were keen to get their hands on braid that needed sewing on. First her fingers started to bleed and she had to strap them up; then the gold thread stripped through the strappings, but there was no time for her hands to heal: strapping went on over the top of strappings, eighteen-hour days became the norm and the RSI began to bite. The order was completed on time, but she couldn't do any further silk work for a couple of months afterwards. Her forebears will have faced similar problems, as indeed did tailors, embroiderers, painters and a host of other craftspeople whose businesses relied upon keeping a few wealthy, time-sensitive customers happy. The royal court was as demanding as any modern opening night.

9. A Time to Play

... above all earthly things, mirthe is moste excellent, and the best
companion of life ... Company, musicke, honest gaming or any
other virtuous exercise doeth helpe against heavinesse of mind.

William Bullein, *The Government of Health* (1558)

Sunday afternoons were the traditional time for leisure activities. The more puritanically minded clergy of Elizabeth's reign
kept up a steady stream of complaint about the fact that 'the
multitude call it their revelling day', as one moaned in 1571. But
at the top of the list of Sunday afternoon activities – at least so
the political elite hoped – was archery. Richard III's administra-
tion in the 1480s was already complaining that the skill of
archery was in decline and that a major shortage of bows was
encouraging a rise in other, unlawful, pursuits. Henry VII's
officials worried in equally lamenting tones about the 'enfeeb-
ling of this Realm', but blamed the perceived decline in Sunday
afternoon practice sessions upon crossbows. Henry VIII, determined to stop the rot, demanded, by Act of Parliament, that all
men under the age of sixty, with the exception of clergymen
and judges, should 'use and exercise shooting in longbows'. His
laws set out the stipulation that boys between seven and seventeen years of age were to have a minimum of two arrows as well
as a bow provided for them by their fathers or guardians and be
taught to use them. From the age of seventeen a man had to
provide himself with a bow and four arrows or face a fine of a
shilling a month until he sorted out the deficiency. All the Tudor

monarchs agreed that archery practice after church on a Sunday afternoon was a man's patriotic duty.

The official concern stemmed from a need for trained archers in warfare. The longbow had brought military success at Agincourt and many other battles, and while gunpowder was gradually eroding the archer's position of military supremacy, few were willing to countenance its abandonment. Developing the skill and the muscles required for effective use of the long-bow, however, took many years of training. Ideally, that training should cover the period of a person's skeletal growth and development, hence the insistence upon boys joining their fathers each week, equipped and ready to learn. Regular practice for the adult men kept muscles and technique honed, ready at need to defend the country or fight the king's battles.

Evidence of the ordinary Englishman's and Welshman's willingness to spend his Sunday afternoons practising his archery is still to be found in and around many of our towns and villages in the form of road and place names. Butts Close or The Butts denote an area set aside, generally close to the churchyard, with permanent archery butts. These were raised banks of earth and clay against which a target could be set up. Men didn't just turn up out of patriotic duty or simply in obedience to the law of the land. Sunday afternoon archery was truly embedded in popular culture as a sport and pastime, enjoyed for its own sake. Ale-houses overlooking the butts did very good business as men got together to practise and compete.

Roving, as well as stationary, target practice had many adherents. It has left us with little or no physical evidence but plenty of documentary references. Small groups of men would set off across the fields with their bows and arrows. A mark would be chosen, such as the branch of a particular tree, a clump of grass, or a gatepost. Everyone would stand and shoot at the mark, then the whole group would amble over to retrieve their arrows, see who had got nearest and choose a new mark. It bears a striking resemblance to a round of golf. The woodcut map of London produced in around 1559 (often referred to as the Agas map) shows the fields around the city heavily populated with women doing the laundry, groups of people out walking and picnicking, and many small companies of men with their bows, walking and shooting. Court records are also littered with references to men being out, bow in hand. Sometimes we hear about such social groups through tragedies, such as the death of Jerome Boswell in 1564, shot accidentally by a shooting party on Finsbury Fields, and John Philippes, who was too close to the 'twelve skore pryckes' that Henry Grynsted was aiming at in Kirdford, Sussex. Sometimes the archery is just a stray mention, explaining why men were out and about when thieves struck or brawls took place.

The use of weaponry does not appeal to me in the same way as, say, the making of cheese, but I have shot Tudor-style bows, made bowstrings and arrows and spent a good deal of time listening with half an ear to groups of men and women in earnest archery discussion. There is certainly an aesthetic appeal in the bows and arrows themselves. Tudor bows are fashioned from a single piece of wood, carefully selected for its straight grain and cut to include both heartwood and sapwood from the tree. The heartwood is older and denser and lies towards the centre of the living tree. It is strong in compression. The sapwood lying close under the bark is much newer wood, more supple and springy. The heartwood is positioned facing towards the archer so that when the bow is pulled it is this part of the weapon that is compressed, while the sapwood is on the outside, facing away from the archer, and is stretched as the string is pulled. Careful shaping controls how much and where the bow bends in action and how much force it can release. A heavy, chunky bow can throw a larger arrow further and with more force, but it will require strength to pull and there may be a lessening of accuracy. A lighter, thinner bow can be used with great precision at slightly shorter distances with finer, slighter arrows. Both can be deadly. In the main heat of battle, massed ranks of archers could be used to fill the skies with a rain of arrows. In such cases, accuracy was unnecessary.

Cheap bows were made from elm, hazel and ash. English yew wood made more expensive bows, but the best, and most pricey, were made from imported yew, particularly Spanish yew, which grew straighter and with fewer knots. They are remarkably beautiful things; strung, they seem to come alive in your hands, each one subtly different from the next. I can also see why many people become quite addicted to them as a sporting activity. A traditional longbow requires skill as well as strength. Brute force will indeed pull back a strong heavyweight bow, but without skill and control much of that force will be squandered, as well as compromising accuracy. Many a small, thin, wiry bloke has outshot a great bear of a man, a truth that is also found in the old stories of Robin Hood and Little John. I need something pretty light indeed if I am to have any accuracy at all. I did not train from childhood and have never had much upper body strength, but I am accustomed to reasonably fine control of my muscles, a legacy of childhood ballet lessons and a lifetime of craft activities. That control certainly helps make the most of the frankly feeble amount of force that I can put into a bow. I would like to be much better at it, and I know that there is still time left. My godmother, way back in the late 1950s, took up field archery in her fifties (her sons badgered her into it), and within four years she was competing internationally. So I have no excuse.

The most famous writings about archery at the time are those contained in Roger Ascham's little book *Toxophilus*. Written when he was just twenty-nine years old and presented to Henry VIII in 1545, it extols the virtues of archery for martial purposes and for health and exercise of both body and mind. If archery were simply practised to prepare men for war, argued the character Philologus in Ascham's book, then surely they would go out into the fields alone and let loose as many arrows as possible with a good strong bow, building strength and speed. And yet we see instead, he says, men going in groups to shoot at targets, favouring accuracy and chat over rigorous shooting. Ascham's hero, Toxophilus, is quick to point out, however, that it is because men set off in groups and turn it into a competition among themselves that they are eager to take out their bows. Without sociability and play, few would heed the exhortations of concerned governments. Competition and rivalry, a variety of different shots and locations, combined with convivial company, made for a pleasant afternoon, not a chore, and provided men with a welcome break from their weekday activities.

If archery was a pastime that came with firm official approval, what were the 'unlawful' games that successive governments feared were drawing men away from their bows? Henry VIII's officials thought it might be 'slidethrift, otherwise shovegroat', a game that comes down to us under the name of 'shove-ha'penny', where small coins are slid across a table in an attempt to finish their slide on a number of marked targets and to knock other players' coins away from those same targets, rather like the modern Winter Olympic sport of curling in miniature.

Queen Elizabeth's lawmakers blamed afternoons of 'bear baiting, unchaste interludes' and 'bargains of incontinence' for drawing men away from archery. Roger Ascham, meanwhile, considered bowls, skittles, card and dice games to be the culprits. Bowling had a bit of a mixed press, condemned by some but promoted as healthy exercise by others (Sir Thomas Elyot, for example). It was a game mentioned in descriptions of village alehouses as well as the country seats of gentlemen. Bowling alleys became a fashionable garden feature, their outline frequently still discernible beneath later plantings at the stately homes of Britain. Trerice in Cornwall not only has its bowling alley still, but an original Tudor set of kayles, which are rather fat-bellied skittles, or bowling pins, to play with. And whether it really happened or not, Sir Francis Drake is reputedly said to have refused to break off his game of bowls when the Spanish Armada was finally sighted, a story that gains its credibility from the popularity of the game among gentlemen. The city of London had public bowling alleys, both indoor and outdoor. In 1580 the Lord Mayor wrote to the Privy Council, urging the government to take action against them. They were much too popular in his opinion: large numbers of labouring people were drawn to them when they should have been working, gambling away their wages and 'even their household goods' and leaving their families in desperate poverty. To make matters worse, he complained, drink was served at these venues, and cards and dice and 'table' games were also commonly played there, all of which contributed to daily scenes of drunkenness, blaspheming, picking (by which he meant pickpockets), cozening (confidence tricksters) and all kinds of disorder. His letter seems to have had little effect. The bowling and the gambling continued.

Gambling in all its forms was very much a part of aristocratic and gentlemanly behaviour. Heavy betting upon sporting out-comes promoted a form of social double standard, with approval for those who were seen to be able to afford the stakes and censure of those who were not. Robert Dudley, 1st Earl of Leicester, for example, leaves us a record of his gambling expenses in his household accounts. On 13 December 1586 he had £20 in his purse to play Tantos (a card game) with Sir William Russell, a sum that it would take a skilled craftsman around eighteen months to earn. New Year's Day saw a game of Double Hand Lodam, for which another £10 was set aside to play with Sir William, Count Morris and the Earl of Essex. He lost another fourteen shillings playing the same game three nights later. It was a pattern that repeated itself throughout the year, with the household setting aside sums of money to be gambled, and various pages and other members of staff needing to be reimbursed after the earl had borrowed more money from them for gambling. The game in question is sometimes mentioned – generally a card game – and those he plays with are his social peers. Several hundred pounds a year was spent in 'play'. Robert Dudley's winnings are much more elusive: no one had to account for those.

The sums involved in Dudley's gambling are, however, chicken feed in comparison to those of Henry VIII fifty years earlier. January 1530 saw an entry in the privy purse records of £450 lost playing dominoes, and another £100 went on card games with the gentlemen of the privy chamber. Two years later he managed to lose £45 playing shovelboard – the very game that his officials were concerned was the cause of a decline in archery practice among his subjects. The risk involved in gambling and the ability to face that risk with equanimity and self-control had more than a whiff of martial masculinity about it to Tudor sensibilities. Right down the years, the image of the suave gambler has held on to a certain social cachet.

It is no surprise that those further down the social scale also liked to gamble, to present themselves as sophisticated men of the world, steeped in masculine bravura. In 1495 Henry VII issued an edict that banned servants and apprentices from playing card games except at Christmas. Worries about aping one's betters, time wasting and potential impoverishment were already warring with a strong cultural enjoyment of and approval for the manliness of gambling. But it is clear from the elaborate books of household rules governing servant life within the great aristocratic houses that cards and dice and other forms of gambling were an everyday experience, not only for the masters but also for the ushers, grooms and waiting gentlemen who populated these buildings. So commonplace and regular was gambling that particular officers were responsible not only for keeping dice and cards on hand, but also for looking after the profits that were generated – one officer for the gambling that took place in the great hall, and another for that of the bed-chamber or adjoining waiting rooms.

'Even if gambling were an evil, still, on account of the very large number of people who play, it would seem to be a neces-sary evil,' or so said the Italian Girolamo Cardano in his 1564 book *Liber de ludo aleae*. He was an enthusiastic player and apologist for all types of card game, arguing that most of the games in general use were not pure luck, but based upon a degree of mathematically determined outcomes, or what Blaise Pascal a century later would call 'probabilities'. The gambling, therefore, was in part redeemed by its relationship with the exercise of skill and intellectual excellence. Reginald Scot was an English gen-tleman with wide-ranging interests, from the growing of hops, about which he wrote the seminal work *A Perfite Platforme of a Hoppe Garden* (1576), to the impossibility of magic and witch-craft, the subject of his *Discoverie of Witchcraft* (1584). His attempts to debunk the popular superstitions of his day also led him to describe the tricks and sleight of hand that could be employed in card games. He begins with explaining how to shuffle while keeping track of a particular card, and gives several variations upon the classic trick where the conjuror tells someone, 'Pick a card, any card,' shuffles the pack and then reveals the chosen card, something that still forms the basis of a modern illusion-ist's stock-in-trade:

> When you have seene a card privilie, or as though you marked it not, laie the same undermost, and shuffle the cards as before you are taught, till your card lie againe below the bottome.

Then shew the same to the beholders, willing them to remember it: then shuffle the cards, or let anie other shuffle them; for you know the card alreadie, and therefore may at anie time tell them what card they saw: which nevertheless would be done with great circumstance and shew of difficultie.

With large sums of money changing hands rapidly and frequently, gambling attracted crooks and cheats. Reginald Scot cautions his readers, 'If you plaie among strangers, beware of him that seems simple or drunken.' Acting either alone or with accomplices, there were plenty of card sharps practised in the very sleight-of-hand tricks that Reginald describes, armed with loaded dice and brimming with distraction techniques and secret signals between themselves. From the 1550s onwards a steady stream of literature warns of the numerous cons that could be practised upon the unwary. Apparently a small industry making loaded dice existed within the King's Bench and Marshalsea prisons, but the master of the craft was a man named Bird who lived in Holborn and produced fourteen different types of loaded dice to suit different types of game and methods of cheating.

Henry VIII's favourite afternoon pastime for much of his youth was tennis. His father, Henry VII, was also a tennis fan and had had new courts built at the royal residences. He also employed a couple of professional players, perhaps to act as coaches and teachers to his sons. It was a style of tennis now known as real tennis to differentiate it from the more common lawn tennis that was not invented until the Victorian era. The Tudor game has several elements that are reminiscent of the modern game of squash, since it was played in an enclosed court with balls being bounced off walls. The Venetian ambassador wrote that Henry VIII was 'extremely fond of tennis, at which game it is the prettiest thing in the world to see him play, his fair skin glowing through a shirt of the finest texture'. The king didn't always strip down to his shirt, however, as in 1517 his wardrobe accounts list a black and blue velvet coat made of six yards of cloth. Velvet was woven in narrow widths, generally only eighteen inches wide, so a coat of six yards was probably quite close fitting to the body and arms, with a fuller skirt around the hips. In the 1520s he dispensed with the coat and played in one of his two crimson satin tennis doublets. As well as special clothes the king also had tennis shoes, six pairs of which had felt soles attached by the Great Wardrobe – the part of the royal household that acquired, stored and maintained the king's clothing – in 1536. When the playwright William Shakespeare wrote *Henry V* (*c.*1599), he placed a scene about tennis at its start. The French ambassador makes a gift of tennis balls on behalf of the French dauphin to the young English king in a mocking gesture designed to point out the king's youth and former playboy ways, implying as he does so that a king so enamoured of play was no statesman and no threat to the French monarchy. Henry responds in aggressive tones, equating sporting prowess with vigour, strength and martial prowess:

> When we have matched our rackets to these balls,
> We will in France by God's grace, play a set
> Shall strike his father's crown into the hazard.

It is a scene that will have conjured up strong memories for the audience – especially for the queen and her court – not of Henry V but of Henry VIII.

In the 1530s, Sir Thomas Elyot, a notch or two down the social scale, advocated tennis as a good pastime for young gentlemen 'now and againe'. Roger Ascham, the champion of archery, also approved of tennis, writing that it was 'not only comely and decent, but also very necessary, for a courtly gentleman to use'. A full tennis court was of course an expensive luxury, confined largely to royal palaces and great houses, so you might think that ordinary folk had little chance of playing this game. But that was not the whole picture. Tennis had begun life without rackets as a game of handball in French courtyards, and an entire French industry had built up that was involved in making tennis balls and rackets. The London port books record the importation of very large numbers of tennis balls. George Collimor, for example, brought in 4,000 tennis balls on board the *Prym Rose* in October 1567 and another 8,000 in the same month aboard the *John*. Not all tennis balls were imported, however: there was a home-grown industry too. The royal balls were made in London by the Ironworkers' Company. This, then, was a popular game, not one restricted by a lack of suitable places to play. Even among royalty, tennis courts had not become fully standardized. Overall, sizes varied, as did their internal architecture, with galleries and windows for spectators punctuating the walls. For the rest of society, any convenient courtyard or even street could be pressed into service, with scoring systems adapted to match.

The tennis balls that found their way into the country in such large numbers were quite unlike the bouncy modern versions – rubber was not yet available in Tudor Britain. The Tudor tennis ball was harder and a little heavier, made from tightly packed wool bound with tape and then covered in a tight coat of wool, giving it a strong tendency to spin and ricochet off walls. In 1461 the French king Louis XI had had to intervene to stop unscrupulous tennis-ball makers from filling them with cheaper chalk, sand, ash or sawdust, stuffings that made them punishingly hard and heavy. Shakespeare makes a joke in *Much Ado about Nothing* (1598–9) that refers to tennis balls stuffed with human hair: ' . . . the barber's man hath been seen with him, and the old ornament of his cheek hath already stuffed tennis balls'. In 1920 one leather ball stuffed with dog hair was found lodged in the roof of Westminster Hall, proving that, even at court, tennis was not restricted to formal tennis courts. Rackets were not imported in anything like the numbers that tennis balls were, so it seems likely that on English streets it was the older handball games that were being played. Formal tennis courts may have been the preserve of the wealthy, but ball games were much more widespread in a free-form fashion.

Football was described by Sir Thomas Elyot in his *Boke Named the Governour* (1531) as unsuitable for gentlemen: 'wherein is nothing but beastly fury and extreme violence, whereof proceedeth hurt'. It continues to be denounced throughout the century, particularly when played on a Sunday, and is often linked with drinking and dancing as a festive activity. Shrovetide football seems to have been a long-standing tradition in many parts of the country, but had to be banned in Chester in 1540 because of the 'great inconvenience', a problem that was put down to a minority of badly behaved thugs who were spoiling it for the rest. Rules were conspicuous only by their absence. The elite did not turn their backs entirely upon the more popular ball games, however: Henry VIII had one pair of shoes 'for football', and under its alternative name of 'camping' it earned the approval of Thomas Tusser in his *Five Hundreth Pointes of Good Husbandrie* (1573) as an excellent improver of grass:

> In meadow or pasture, to grow the more fine,
> Let campers be camping in any of thine;
> Which if ye do suffer when low in the spring,
> You gain to yourself a commodious thing.

Stoolball, probably utilizing those same Tudor tennis balls, was a bit like rounders or cricket, with two teams, a stool, a ball and sometimes a bat. It was thought of more as a sport for women, while tennis and other ball games had a more masculine edge. In *A Dialogue between Two Shepherds* (c.1580), Sir Philip Sidney writes:

A time there is for all, my mother often says,
When she, with skirts tucked very high,
With girls at stool ball plays.

Dancing

Perhaps more popular than tennis, stoolball and football combined, however, was dancing. Much of what we know about
popular dancing comes from complaints about raucous, unruly
dances at alehouses, and youngsters dancing on Sundays during
service time – a particular problem during evening prayer, or
evensong, which took place in the late afternoon. Dancing was
something that crossed social and sexual boundaries, bringing
together groups of people in both public and private spaces. It
was a very cheap form of entertainment, with a strong bias
towards the young. In June 1606, one alehouse keeper in Yorkshire got into trouble for holding Sunday dances that were
attracting over a hundred young people to dance to the music of
the piper and drummer he had laid on. Churchyards were
well-tended, open public spaces, unencumbered at that time by
gravestones, and they also lent themselves very well to dancing
and were regularly used for this purpose. Their proximity to the
church, however, heightened sensibilities about profaning the
Sabbath among some parishioners, leading to conflicts that
ended up in the court records. Such conflicts often centred upon
the fact that the dances were held during church services, rather
than on the fact that young people were dancing at all. Many of
those who were pressing for reform were clearly quite comfortable with dancing per se, and even with dancing in the
churchyards at appropriate times.

To judge by the number of concerns raised by writers of
'godly' literature in the later Elizabethan era, when puritanical

Protestant thought was building, large groups of energetic youngsters of both sexes were enthusiastic proponents of the art of dance. While the disapproving 'godly' literature mostly emerged from London, dancing was recorded everywhere across England and Wales. Outdoor public dancing was inevitably a summer activity, and much mentioned among the activities of Whitsun and 'May games', which took place right through both May and June. Maypoles seem to have been perfect venues, with people dancing both around them and next to them, although there is no indication that anyone danced while holding ribbons attached to the top of the maypole – that seems to be a Victorian invention for use within a school context. Thoinot Arbeau's *Orchesographie*, a dance manual published in France in 1589, includes a number of fairly simple dances that were performed in a ring, holding hands. These dances would have translated to encircling a maypole with ease, and were simple enough for anyone to pick up quickly and have fun with, regardless of heavy agricultural footwear. Bagpipes are frequently mentioned as the musical accompaniment to dancing – not the Highland pipes of modern Scottish fame, but a simple pan-European version with a single drone pipe to make the accompanying buzz, a bag to supply the air pressure, and a chanter pipe with finger holes to play the tune upon, loud enough for the sound to carry among a large crowd outdoors. Stephen Gosson made a rather exaggerated moan about music and dance in his *Schoole of Abuse* of 1579: 'London is so full of unprofitable Pipers and Fidlers, that a man can no sooner enter a tavern, but two or three caste of them hang at his heeles, to give him a dance before he departe.'

The majority of the outdoor dancing was social in its nature, but there is also plenty of reference to morris dancing and to solo jigs and dance competitions: dancing that was less about dancing together and more about display and attempts to impress the opposite sex with one's vigour and virility. Philip Stubbes's description of morris dancing is just one of numerous rants against all types of fun in his *Anatomie of Abuses* (1583), but it gives a fantastic glimpse of a Sunday afternoon. Once the gathering had chosen and crowned a summer Lord of Misrule, or king of the revels, his group of retainers were appointed. They dressed in the brightest coats they could find:

> This done, they tie about either leg 20 or 40 bells, with rich handkerchiefs in their hands, and sometimes laid across over their shoulders and necks, borrowed for the most part of their pretty Mopsies and loving Bessies, for bussing [kissing] them in the dark.
>
> Thus all things set in order, then they have their hobby horses, dragons and other antiques, together with their bawdy pipers and thundering drummers to strike up the Devil's Dance withall. Then march these heathen company towards the church and churchyard, their pipers piping, drummers thundering, their stumps dancing, their bells jingling, their handkerchiefs swinging about their heads like madmen, their hobby horses and other monsters skirmishing amongst the throng.

It is the young, the fit and the vigorous who are implicated in this, not the more mature, stouter-bellied gents who populate the modern perception of morris dancing. This was a far less-tamed beast.

It wasn't exclusively male, either. When William Kempe, the country's most famous comic actor, undertook to dance cross-country in early 1600 in a sort of publicity stunt, he encountered many people who danced along with him, including a fourteen-year-old girl who kept pace with his jig (a very energetic style of dance that has much in common with both the Highland fling and the Irish step dancing of *Riverdance*) for over an hour, leading Kempe to declare that he might 'have challenged the strongest man in Chelmsford, and amongst many I think few would have done as much'. In Suffolk a butcher was trying to keep pace and failing miserably when 'a lusty country lass' laughed and said, 'If I had begun to dance, I would have held out one mile though it had cost my life.' When the crowd dared her to do so, she hitched her skirts, tied on some bells and danced all the way beside him to the next town. Both young women were obviously familiar with the steps involved. Beyond what contemporaries called morris dancing (apparently anything with bells, energetic leaps and flamboyant clothing counted, sometimes solo, sometimes in groups), there were other styles with which you could show off. In his *Survey of London* (1598), the historian and antiquarian John Stow recalled seeing dance competitions between young women in the streets of London during Henry VIII's reign, where they would 'dance for garlands hung athwart the street'. Joris Hoefnagel's painting *A Marriage Feast at Bermondsey* (c.1569) has a group of five young people dancing. Two men and three women are dancing, to the music of a couple of fiddlers, in poses very reminiscent of the type of dance wherein participants dance singly and take it in turns to display their moves (in a similar way to break-dancing and hip hop today), copying and competing with one another in a display of virtuosity and stamina. Towards the end of the sixteenth century, puritanical hostility towards such dancing was growing. There had always been an undercurrent of hostility among certain sections of the more ostentatiously devout, but what had been odd mumblings and occasional outrage at some example of misbehaviour at dances became more open and widespread. Londoners and those of a more Calvinistic bent became especially vocal and indeed strident. All but the most extreme, however, continued to approve of dancing at court.

Ambassadors at the courts of both Henry VIII and Elizabeth I were generally impressed by both the quantity and the quality of the dancing. According to the Milanese ambassador in 1515, Henry 'exercised himself daily in dancing'. Elizabeth did too, generally as part of her morning routine before breakfast. She continued dancing both privately and publicly, almost to the last. In 1599, when she was in her mid sixties, the Spanish ambassador was writing home that 'the head of the Church of England and Ireland was to be seen in her old age dancing three or four galliards', and in April 1602, the year before her death, she danced two galliards with the Duke of Nevers. Although Spanish ambassadors had a history of scathing comments about dancing at the English court, with one describing Henry VIII's efforts as 'prancing', they seem to have been a lone voice. The Venetian ambassador considered Henry to have 'acquitted himself divinely', while the Milanese representative reported that 'he does wonders and leaps like a stag'. Henry was generally partnered in these early years by his sister Mary, whose 'deportment in dancing is as pleasing as you would desire'. Henry's first wife, the Spanish Catherine of Aragon, also enjoyed a dance, but generally did so in her rooms with her ladies; she was, after all, almost permanently pregnant. Her absence from the public ballroom may well give a gloss to the Spanish ambassador's attitude.

Sometime around 1500 John Banys opened his commonplace book and picked up his quill to add notes upon twenty-six dances, along with thirteen pieces of music to dance to, eight of which are matched with particular dances. The dance notes appear along with Latin prayers, a treatise on chiromancy and another upon physiognomy. We don't know anything about John Banys beyond his name and the contents of his book, which was unusual only in containing such fulsome dance notes. The book spent many years among the papers of the Gresley family in Drakelow and is now kept in the Derbyshire record office. He was not then a member of the royal court, but he was well educated and had ties to Derbyshire. All the dances are for two or three people, never specifying sex – or rather calling every dancer a man, as in the first man, the second man or the third man. Presumably he is using the term 'man' to mean person, rather as we use the word 'mankind' to mean humankind, as all the images of social dance we have are mixed sex and many of the more vociferous puritanical objections are based upon the close mixing of young men and women when dancing. He gives very little attention to the steps that you use or where your arms should be, concentrating instead upon the shape of the dances – the patterns that the protagonists make upon the dance floor, something that already feels distinctly English rather than Continental.

Esperanse de tribus

TRACE

Al the vi singles with a trett / then the ffyrst man goo compass till he come behind whil the medyll retrett thre and the last iij [three] singles and the medil iij singles levyng the last on the left hand and the last iij retrettes thus the medill endyth before the last in the middist and the ferst behind thus daunce iij tymes calling every man as he standdith / After the end of the trace the ferst iij furth outward turning ayen his face / Then the last con-tur hym and the medill to the fyrste and then the first to his place / the first and the last chance place whil the medyll torneth / Al at onys retrett iij bake / bak al at ons / Then the first torne whill the last torne in his own place / Then al togeder thre furth.

I am particularly fond of John Banys's dance notes, not least because of his creative spelling. In this dance, for example, he spells the word 'first' in four different ways: ffyrst, ferst, fyrste and first. You have to read through his notes a number of times quite slowly to understand them, but then the choreography begins to emerge: clear rhythmic patterns that have a certain grace and flow. The Esperanse de tribus above (or Spanish dance for three people) begins with three people in a line, one behind the other. Everyone moves forward with six 'singles' steps. At the next phrase of the music, the man in front dances round to the back of the line while the other two dancers swap places and then swap back again. The music repeats and the same steps are repeated twice more, so that each man has a turn at the head of the line. The next move turns the line through ninety degrees. The first man dances out round to the left in three-quarters of a circle so that he ends up alongside the middle man but facing him. The last man in the line then executes a similar move so that he ends up on the other side of the middle man, facing him; the middle man, meanwhile, simply turns to face the first man in his new position. John Banys doesn't mention it, but if I was dancing this dance as the middle man I would probably turn twice on the spot while men one and two were doing their thing. A degree of improvisation was expected in performers of both music and dance of this period. Now the line returns to its original orientation as the first man dances to his starting position, the middle man moves to the last position and the last man steps into the middle. At the next musical change the two men at the ends of the line change places while the middle man turns on the spot, thus changing everyone's position within the line-up. All in unison they dance backwards, turn on the spot and then dance forward to mark a sort of punctuation in the dance before it all begins again with a new leader.

Three different steps are mentioned: the 'singles', the 'trett' and the 'retrett', the last of which appears to be a trett going backwards. There is one English text that gives some indication of what these step terms might mean, but it's not a dance manual. In his *Boke Named the Governour*, Sir Thomas Elyot chose to use dance as a means to teach moral virtue, describing how each step both reflected and encouraged particular 'noble qualities' in the performer. Every dance, according to Sir Thomas, began with an 'honour which is a reverant inclination or curtesie with a long deliberation or pause and is but one motion comprehending the tyme of thre other motions or setting forth of the foot'. This is never mentioned in John Banys's notes, probably because it was not part of the differing choreography of each dance but a general introductory movement so universal and well known that it went without saying. Singles he described as 'of two unities separate in passing forwarde', and the retrett 'is one moving only, putting backe the right fote to his felowe'. Even with these descriptions it is still not easy to see what was meant. The retrett seems fairly clear, and presumably a trett is therefore simply a step to bring both feet together. But whether it is done on the flat foot or on the toes is still open to question. As for the singles, does he mean two walking steps forward, or like the French form of the step, which is described as a single step forward and then the other foot joining it? Both forms would fit the shape of the dance and indeed the music. If we want to dance like a Tudor we are therefore back to improvisation, interpretation and variation. The music is quite lively, in a 6/8 time for the most part, not the more ponderous 4/4 of modern country dance.

There is a hint that such dances may have been 'called', with someone shouting out the steps, in a song of the 1550s collected by the Tudor minstrel Richard Sheale, and again in an anonymous ballad of 1569. Richard Sheale's song is about a country wedding between Jocke and Jone:

> Halfe torne Jone, haffe nowe, Jocke!
> Well dansyde, be sent Dennye!

And he that breakys the firste stroke,
Sall gyve the pyper a pennye.
In with fut, Robson! Owt with fut, Byllynge!
Here wyll be good daunsynge believe . . .

The 1569 ballad also features dancing at a country wedding, with a slight sneer at country people who ape the latest fashions from France. A 'brall', by the way, is a word for a type of dance:

Good fellows must go to learne to daunce
Thy brydeal is full nere a
There is a brall come out of France,
The tryxt ye harde this yeare a
For I must leape, and thou must hoppe
And we must turne all three a
The fourth must bounce it lyke a toppe,
And so we shall agree a
I praye thee, mynstrall, make no stoppe
For we wyll merye be a.

With brisk rhythms, patterns traced out upon the floor, simple steps and a caller, we have a picture of English dance that is very familiar and distinctive, one that may well have crossed the Atlantic with the very first settlers.

In 1521 Robert Copeland included at the back of his book on the French language a brief primer on basse dances (low dances) as danced in Burgundy and France. Only a year before, much of England's elite had been in France at the Field of the Cloth of Gold where such dancing had been part of the festivities. He, too, describes singles and retretts (the latter under the name 'reprise') and his timing and style notes are interesting. Were they included because they were different from the English approach? In his description, two singles were to take the same time as one reprise or one honour, and in performing singles, 'ye must reyse your body'. Basse dances were noted for their formality, with less room for improvisation than other forms, and were performed as a procession, with couple following couple. There were no figures or patterns on the dance floor, just different combinations of the four steps, made while slowly progressing around the room. Dance notation was therefore a much simpler discipline. Once you knew that *R* stood for the initial reverence or honour, that *s* stood for single, *d* for double (three steps forward upon the toes with a pause on the fourth beat), *b* for branle (a step sideways away from your partner and then back towards them) and an *r* for reprise, whole dances could be written out in one line. This can be seen in the 'Filles à Marier' dance, which fell into four discernible parts, or measures, and was written in Copeland's version as: 'R.b.ss.ddd. rrr.b.ss.d.rrr.b.ss.ddd.ss.rrr.b.ss.d.ss.rrr.b.' Every basse dance began with the reverence and ended with a branle. The reprises divided the dance into the separate measures, which followed musical phrasing.

There was a strong international currency in dance, with ideas, music, steps, style and choreographies eagerly sought out and copied across national and social boundaries. Indeed, the basse dance itself, though it might appear to be the epitome of stately aristocratic dancing, began as a country or peasant dance that was taken up by the court. The basse dance also made its way into common English practice, at least at court.

Alongside the pattern dancing of John Banys, and the formal basse dance of Copeland, Henry VIII partook of other styles. He was, after all, praised by the Milanese ambassador for leaping 'like a stag', movements that don't fit either of these two forms. The tordion may well have been the dance that required those leaps. Sir Thomas Elyot mentions it as a 'turgion' in his fashionable dance list, alongside the basse dance and others. The tordion step was four hops and a cadence where the dancer landed on both feet, the cadence taking the same time as two of the hops. It was a rhythm that was often voiced as 'one, two, three, four and five'. There is no pause for breath, as sprung step follows sprung step, and dancers were required to leap high, keep perfect time and look elegant as they did so.

The English dance record goes a little quiet during the reigns of Edward VI and Mary I, but in Elizabeth's era we again find ourselves with dance notes in a commonplace book. This one belonged to Elinor Gunter and is full of poems and songs. The dance notes, however, may have been by her brother Edward, who went to Lincoln's Inn to study law in February 1563. These are the first of a series of dance notes spanning the next hundred years, all by trainee lawyers at the Inns of Court, all describing the same dances – more or less. An annual ball with a fixed dance list formed one of the compulsory elements for prospective lawyers, and each generation had to learn that suite of dances. There is no accompanying music this time and certainly no descriptions of steps or styles, but armed with knowledge of all that went before, here and on the Continent, and with a good list of contemporary popular tunes, you can make a stab at a performance. As Elinor Gunter's book informs us, the festivities began with a pavan, a slow and stately dance suitable for aged gown-clad senior lawyers. The three dances that followed are all recognizably in the basse dance tradition; the first even uses the title 'Turquylonye le basse':

A duble forward reprynce back iiij [four] times
ij [two] Singles side a duble forward reprynce backe twyse

Then follows a set of 'Allemayne' dances, incorporating a German-style hopped double and some of the floor patterns that we remember from John Banys's work. A coranto comes towards the end of the evening. This was certainly a more vigorous dance and very popular, with lots of fast and bouncy music written for it. Edward Gunter's description is somewhat breathless and complicated. He gives no such indication, but it is possible to interpret the dance as being for a line of men facing a line of women, a formation that later country dances of the seventeenth and eighteenth centuries termed 'a longways set for as many as will'. The section that tells you to dance 'iiij dubles to and fro betwyne your women & when you be all past them come side longe to them with iij traverse & honour everye man to hys woman' seems particularly to fit. Sir John Davies, in his poem *Orchestra, or a Poem of Dancing* (1594), described the coranto as a chaotic winding dance performed at speed to a triple dactyl rhythm (6/8 time signature) with sections of sliding steps (the traverses):

What shall I call those current traverses,
That on a triple dactyl foot do run
Close by the ground with sliding passages?
Wherein that dancer greatest praise hath won
Which with best order can all order shun;
For everywhere he wantonly must range
And turn and wind with unexpected change.

The evening began, then, slow and orderly, became more vigorous in the middle of the evening and ended fast and furious as the older members of the gathering retired to let the young have their fun. A couple of years after Queen Elizabeth died the lawyers had finally updated their list of dances to incorporate the especially vigorous and flamboyant galliards and voltas that had been popular at court and out and about among the young for twenty or thirty years. John Ramsey was at the Middle Temple around 1605–6, and after the sedate 'Turkeyloney' and other basse-style dances and almains, he struggles to find a way of noting down the 'half capers, traverses, round turns & such like, learned onlye by practise'. The galliard was danced to the same beat as the tordion – one, two, three, four and five, but to a slower, stronger beat to give the dancer time to leap much higher on every step. And height was expected, especially of male dancers. If you watch a modern ballet dancer performing one of the jumped solos of the classical tradition, with entrechats, where he beats his feet rapidly back and forth mid-jump, and performing huge travelling *jetés* and spins in the air, you will have some idea of the athleticism and moves of the Elizabethan courtly dance floor, all performed to the 'one, two, three, four and five' rhythm. The French dancing master Arbeau particularly disapproved of performance wherein 'damsels are made to bounce about in such a fashion that more often than not they show their bare knees unless they keep one hand on their skirts to prevent it'. He thought it neither beautiful nor honourable, 'unless one is dancing with some strapping hussy from the servants' hall'.

I like to think of myself as a strapping hussy from the servants' hall. Perhaps you have gathered that I am a big fan of dancing, and Tudor dancing especially. That which you see enacted in film and television dramas is of necessity the rather tame, simple stuff that actors can learn within rehearsal times. The impression that many people get, therefore, is that all historical dancing was the calm and stately stuff that opened an evening's entertainment, the pavans and basse dances suitable for serious and senior people. The fun stuff that followed, danced by the young and fit, who competitively practised their moves, rarely makes a modern appearance. But let me assure you that being thrown five feet into the air by your partner when you are dancing the volta is exhilarating. Galliards leave you seriously out of breath, sweaty and laughing. And determined to master the next trick, so you can really show off next time.

Blood sports and the theatre

An afternoon off for a Londoner also held out the possibility of a trip to the south side of the Thames with its bear-baiting arenas and, in the late Elizabethan era, theatres. Other towns and cities also had their bear baitings and occasionally a travelling troupe of actors, but only London had permanent structures dedicated to both forms of entertainment.

Blood sports in general were popular in both town and country, not only for the spectacle but also for the gambling opportunities. They were even seen as having a practical and healthy purpose, whereby tough, difficult-to-digest meat could be made fit for human consumption. The understanding of the natural world was still heavily based upon the theories of the ancient Greeks, with all flesh, both human and animal, and indeed vegetables, thought to be composed of the four humours: blood, phlegm, yellow bile and black bile, each with its hot, cold, wet, dry balance. Young adult male animals (just like humans) were believed to be dominated by the blood humour, which was hot and wet in nature, but as they matured flesh cooled, dried and hardened. Such flesh, it was believed, would yield up very little of its nutritional value to those who ate it, but would instead sit in a heavy lump in the stomach. Only the strongest and hottest constitutions would be able to process it into the good 'chile', or juice, that nourished the body. An ox or cockerel slaughtered at the end of its useful life was thus thought to be indigestible unless in the frenzy of fury the blood were to once again rush around its body, softening and moistening its flesh. By baiting an old beast, people believed themselves to be making the most of the resources God had given them. There was even a system of fines that had to be paid by butchers upon any oxen that were slaughtered unbaited.

In their simplest form, blood sports were often sponsored by the parish as money-raising events. A cockerel was tied by the leg with a six-foot length of string to a post set in the ground, for example. Contestants retired behind a line scratched in the dirt and took turns to throw stones. He who killed the jumping, squawking, frantic cock could claim the carcass for his prize.

When Gervase Markham published his book *The English Husbandman* in 1613, he left out the viniculture that had played such a dominant part in the French book that had inspired his own work, but took great pains to point out to his readers that he had added a chapter upon one essentially English element of rural life: cockfighting, 'Since there is no pleasure more noble, delightsome, or voyde of couzonage, and deceipt'. He makes no pretence here that cockfighting was to prepare birds for table; what he describes is purely for 'sport'. The cocks were specially bred to be small and fierce, with strong beaks and legs, small heads and large heel spurs. At two years old the most aggressive were prepared for battle. Each had its separate pen, made of wood two feet square and three feet high with a slatted front, a water trough and a feed tray, 'the models whereof you may behold in every Cockemasters or Inn keepers house'. A feeding regime of white bread and water was interspersed with practice bouts, during which the deadly spurs were carefully sheathed in 'hots' to prevent injury. As the cockfight approached, plain bread was replaced with a rich, brioche-like mixture of wheat flour, oat flour, eggs and butter worked to a dough and baked. His feathers were clipped away from his head, neck and rump, and his wing feathers trimmed to dangerous sharp points. His beak and spurs were sharpened with a knife, and his bared head was moistened with spittle before he was turned into the ring to do battle. Fights were short but bloody, and bout followed bout in rapid succession as different pairs were matched against each other. Henry VIII had a purpose-built cockfighting ring at

Whitehall Palace, while John Stow noted that Londoners could sit in the gallery of the Smithfield cockpit for a penny to watch the sport or shell out a little more for a ringside seat among the gambling action.

Bull-baiting drew larger crowds but was more expensive to stage. Although the bulls were ultimately sold to butchers, there were dogs to be bred and trained, and bulls who put up a particularly strong fight might be kept to return to the ring time and again. Sir William Faunte was involved in breeding and keeping dedicated fighting bulls. In the 1590s he wrote to Edward Alleyn in London that he had three bulls available: one a cunning, well-shaped four-year-old; another that had lost an eye in a previous baiting but was still good for the fight; and a third, called 'Star of the West', that was an older beast who had recently lost his horn right down to the quick and that he thought would never fight again.

The 1574 plan of Bankside in London shows two separate baiting arenas side by side, one for bulls and one for bears. Unlike the Spanish form of bullfighting, where a bull is free to move about the arena and is fought by armed men on foot or horseback, bull-baiting in Tudor England pit a tethered bull against a pack of large dogs. The bull had little room for manoeuvre, just a rope 'two paces long' according to the Italian ambassador Alessandro Magno, who watched the proceedings at the London Bankside bull-baiting pit in 1562. But if the bull could not run or charge, he did have full use of his horns to gore the dogs, and feet to kick them. The dogs were mastiffs. Numerous skulls have been found on the site of London's baiting pits which show these mastiffs to have been a very different-shaped animal from the modern breeds that bear the name 'bulldog'. These were large and powerful dogs, both tall and heavily built, with none of the foreshortening of the snout that selective breeding has more recently led to in the bulldogs of dog-show fame. Fights could go either way, and both dogs and bulls were in danger of injury and death. Animals that had proved themselves in previous bouts became favourites with crowds, and matches were often set up in such a way as to prejudice the outcome, with experienced 'celebrity' bulls matched with dogs who, due to age, health or inexperience, were unlikely to kill a crowd-pleaser. Unsurprisingly, the heavy betting that accompanied these bouts encouraged a range of bull- and dog-nobbling activities in an attempt to change the odds in favour of one gambler over another.

Bear-baiting closely resembled bull-baiting, but without the excuse of tenderizing the meat for human consumption. The exoticism provided as much of a draw as the blood-sport element. Bears were expensive beasts, and their owners were not keen to lose them. The baiting therefore, though violent, was rarely permitted to result in fatalities for the bears – dogs were a little more expendable. Once again the spectacle consisted of a tethered animal set upon by dogs. Unlike the bull-baiting, however, where the fight was the whole show, there was more of a circus element to bear-baiting, with bears being led out on a chain by their keepers and paraded around for everyone to see. The bears were sometimes trained to 'dance'. Harry Hunks the famous blind bear was whipped as he tried to swat his tormentor and evade the unseen whip. It was considered to be a very 'comic' turn. An inventory of the bear garden in London in 1590 listed five 'great bears' and four others. The great bears will have been the performing animals who had to stand their turn in the ring; the 'others' may well have been female breeding stock, as Jacob Meade the keeper sold on bear cubs to other 'bear keepers', including Sir William Faunte, who specifically requested a pair of black male cubs.

The crowds who flocked of an afternoon to the bear gardens on the edge of the city were large, boisterous and very socially mixed. The £4 that was taken as gate money upon St Stephen's Day (26 December) in 1608 represented a crowd of around 1,000 people. The next day, St John's Day, saw an even bigger gathering of 1,500 people, and on Christmas Day itself 1,000 people enjoyed a day out at the bear-baiting. Large crowds always made the authorities nervous, but the social mixing of these gatherings created even more tension in official minds, and for the crowds themselves probably added an extra frisson of excitement. Bear-baiting was popular with noble lords and humble carters alike. Visiting ambassadors were as likely to be among the throng as visiting sailors from the port of London. Prostitutes, con men, pickpockets and fast-food sellers all congregated to seek their respective customers, rubbing shoulders with, if not the actual noblemen themselves, then at least with their bodyguard of menservants around them. If scanning the crowd for celebrities lost its appeal, then a visitor could always go and look at the animals in their pens or watch the dog training while waiting for the main event.

Right next door to the bear gardens on the south bank of the Thames in the last years of Elizabeth's reign sat the main theatres of the day. Permanent theatres were brand spanking new, the very first not appearing until 1576. Throughout the reigns of Henry VII, Henry VIII, Edward VI and Mary I, theatre had been a mobile activity, and a largely amateur one. During the years of Henry VII's reign, many of the larger towns and cities of Britain had their own version of mystery plays performed by the townspeople on a yearly cycle. Forty-eight related playlets or pageants survive from York, thirty-two from Wakefield and twenty-four from Chester. Another group of texts is generally known as the 'N Town' cycle, as no one is certain of their geographical home. Just two out of Coventry's cycle remain, and one each from Norwich, Newcastle upon Tyne, Northampton, and Brome in Suffolk. There are also references to similar playlet cycles existing in Aberdeen, Bath, Beverley, Bristol, Canterbury, Dublin, Ipswich, Leicester and Worcester, although none of the words from these playlets has made it down through the centuries. The surviving playlets show every sign of having been originally composed by learned churchmen and subsequently adapted piecemeal by others, presumably by the layfolk who performed them. Scenes from the Bible formed the subject matter of each separate pageant, fairly loosely interpreted with additional rustic characters. Elements of slapstick and pathos combined with portrayals of moral virtues and vices. Each pageant was the responsibility of one guild of townspeople. They had to supply costumes, props, sets, actors and musicians and, in the case of York and Chester (but not the N Town cycle), wagons to perform upon and horses to move their scene from venue to venue.

For residents of these towns, the mystery play season – Corpus Christi in June, which celebrated the presence of the blood and body of Christ within the Eucharist – must have been a fairly all-encompassing experience. The sheer expense could be a problem for some of the smaller guilds. The cappers (makers of knitted caps) of Chester, for example, petitioned the Lord Mayor in 1523–4 to be excused. They were supposed to put on a 'playe concernynge the storie of kynge Balak & Balam the proffet', but simply could not afford to do so. They declared themselves more than willing to go ahead with the play should the mayor be able to find any monetary solution to their problems, which stemmed, they claimed, from the poaching of their trade by other retailers. In 1577 the expenses incurred by the coopers' guild at Chester of £2 13s 2d for their play indicate that the cappers, a poorly remunerated trade at the best of times, may well have had real difficulties in finding that sort of additional money on a yearly basis among a small membership. A high proportion of the coopers' money was spent on their wagon, both repairing it and building the set upon it. In 1577 it required a pair of wheels, a wooden board, several separate batches of nails, 'clapes' of iron, hinges, two sets of cords, 'dressing' and a new 'housing'. The hinges and cords are suggestive of movable elements of scenery worked by pulleys. Much of the work was carried out by the members of the guild, who as coopers had a range of tools and skills at their disposal, but they also called upon the craft skills and labour of other Chester residents. An unnamed 'wright', presumably a cartwright, was paid to set up and take down the set. The guild also paid someone to paint the costumes. Painted cloths were common for banners and represented a cheap way of producing elaborate-seeming costumes quickly and cheaply out of simple coarse tabard- or tunic-like overgarments.

The expenses also mentioned items for four separate rehearsals: three fairly low-cost events, perhaps just with the main protagonists in the play, and one 'general' rehearsal, later on, which was a much more pricey affair. With twenty-four such plays being staged simultaneously in a town of scarcely 6,000 inhabitants, there can have been few who were purely spectators. A large proportion of the population must have had a hand in the proceedings somewhere, hammering nails, painting cloths, learning lines, supplying drink, writing out the parts, making visors and other props, practising musical instruments and looking after the horses. When the big day came, everyone assembled at the appointed starting places with a boy on horseback to lead, trumpeters next, and then the wagon lumbering behind, piled high with its finery, complete with guildsmen in their costumes ready to play their parts. Those standing in the street to watch could nudge their neighbours and point out their sons, fathers and husbands, or the hat they had made, or moan about how much work it had taken to repair those axles. They could compare this year's version of the play with those they had seen in the past, denigrate the efforts of rival guilds and heckle the unpopular characters. Whether they watched all of the plays or just a select few, whether they held their place all day or wandered about the city to catch different performances, or followed their own guild as it moved about and repeated the play in several locations, the streets were full and noisy.

The city of Chester, in common with other towns, also used its repertoire of amateur plays as civic-sponsored displays that could be called upon to entertain visiting dignitaries. The young Prince Arthur, eldest son of Henry VII and elder brother to Henry VIII, visited in 1498–9 and was treated to a rendition of *The Storie of the Assumption of our Ladye* in front of the abbey gates. More private theatrical experiences were to be had within the houses of the nobility, royalty and in schools. Schoolmasters found that the performance of excerpts of Greek play texts was an excellent device for engaging their young pupils in Greek language and literature lessons. Whole generations of educated men grew up with their own amateur theatrical experiences, just as did hundreds, perhaps thousands, of urban craftsmen. What is generally taken to be the first out-and-out secular comedy written in the English language, *Ralph Roister Doister*, was the 1550s work of Nicholas Udall, a former headmaster of Eton and later headmaster of Westminster School, for the boys to perform. Interludes, sometimes with a moral message and sometimes not, became regular parts of the entertainments of court life, with increasing pressure for novelty and high-quality performance. Henry VIII started keeping four professional actors and their boy apprentice as part of his household just as the townsmen's mystery plays were beginning to fade away under the eye of the Reformed Church.

Biblical or secular, out in the street, in the courtyard of an inn or within the halls of a great man's house, right across the period and across the social class boundaries, the theatre had certain basic qualities, foremost among which was spectacle. People expected costumes, easily discernible characters, music, showmanship, theatrical tricks and props; they also expected to watch and listen as part of a crowd, and they expected to enjoy themselves.

Elizabeth's reign saw the nobility involved as patrons of troupes of professional players. Over twenty such patrons are recorded, from Robert Dudley, the Earl of Leicester, whose troupe performed at court in front of the queen as well as for audiences in both London and the provinces, to Lord Beauchamp, whose much smaller group of men is recorded as playing in Southampton but never seems to make an appearance in London. Earls were especially prone to lending their names and protection to a troupe, with the Earls of Oxford, Warwick, Worcester, Hartford, Pembroke and Sussex all getting in on the act. But however enthusiastic a nobleman was for the new complex dramas, and however much the patronage of such a troupe added to one's social prestige, no one wanted to watch a play every day. Over the Christmas period, presenting a series of such fashionable entertainments for one's family and friends was becoming de rigueur and of course a nobleman hoped to be able to stage them again when important visitors came, but acting was not an everyday necessity. The actors had become largely free agents who needed to make their living where they could. When their patron did not require (and pay for) their performances, they sought out other, less exalted, audiences.

The first permanent theatre was built in 1576, in Shoreditch, by James Burbage and four of his fellow actors from the Earl of Leicester's professional acting troupe. Players on tour had previously used a series of London inns – the Cross Keys, the Bull, the Bel Savage, the Red Lion and the Bell – to elicit gate money. Outside of London, players used a host of venues, including market halls and open spaces. The Dolphin Inn in Southampton was one temporary theatre used by several companies over many years, Exeter's Market Hall another, and in Chester the

High Cross was mentioned as one location for visiting players. When one traces the journeys of the different companies it is hard to find any town with more than a few thousand inhabitants that was not graced with a play now and again. But in addition to all this touring the Earl of Leicester's Men now had a permanent base just outside the city boundary in their Shoreditch theatre, within easy distance of both the citizens of the capital and the court. They called it 'The Theatre', and so successful was the enterprise that only a year later a second, called 'The Curtain', was built nearby (the remains of which were uncovered in 2012). People clearly liked going to a play, and they especially liked going to a new play. The pressure was on for anyone who had the skills to write new material as fast as they could.

For those who had an afternoon to spare, a penny in their pocket and an inclination to see a play, Shoreditch – or, from 1587 onwards, Bankside, where the new Rose Theatre and later the Globe Theatre were located – proved a busy destination, with Edward Alleyn topping the bill with the Admiral's Men at the Rose, and Burbage leading the Lord Chamberlain's Men at the Globe. Contemporaries claimed that a full house accommodated as many as 3,000 people – if so, they must have been packed in like sardines. The archaeological remains of the Rose show that at a push around 2,000 people could have fitted within in its first incarnation and around 2,500 after it was expanded, so long as those people were both slim and not fussy about personal space. Philip Henslowe was the main force behind the building of the Rose Theatre, and in his diary, or commonplace book, he records his takings. Theatregoers who stood in the yard paid just a penny, and this money went to the actors; those who sat in the galleries paid two pence, half of which went to Henslowe and half to his business partner. Henslowe's methods of recording his takings are not quite as clear-cut as they first appear, but nonetheless it is possible to get an idea of audience sizes, how much money was being generated and at which plays. The popularity of a new play is easy to see. Opening nights almost invariably brought in much bigger takings. *Galiaso*, for example (a play now completely lost to us), opened on 26 June 1594 and brought Henslowe £3 4s that night. Its next performance, on 12 July, produced £2 6s, and the third performance, on 23 July, garnered £1 11s. This was a common pattern. A new play filled the theatre, but thereafter its takings tailed off, some more quickly than others. Holiday crowds were bigger than workday crowds, and although the players often moved indoors to perform for the court over the Christmas season, New Year's Eve takings for the year 1599 at the Rose were particularly buoyant. *Galiaso* did not prove to have long-term popularity. It played just nine times, the last occasion being on 25 October, when Henslowe received just eleven shillings.

Some plays, however, were firm favourites, commanding solid audiences for years; these were often rested for a while and successfully revived for further long runs. Chief among these at the Rose Theatre were Christopher Marlowe's *The Jew of Malta* and *Doctor Faustus* and Thomas Kyd's *The Spanish Tragedy*. The Rose Theatre was, when plague and government restrictions allowed, putting on around six different plays every week, adding a new play into the mix at fortnightly intervals. The most popular plays were carefully spaced out. Henslowe and his troupe of actors, the Admiral's Men, were clearly encouraging repeat business from their audiences, expecting the same people to return time and time again. There was a mass market for drama, but not an unlimited pool of potential customers. The population of London was still below 200,000, so with at least two competing theatres for most of the period, each holding 2,000 customers, the figures point to a sizeable proportion of Londoners making regular visits.

JOHN HEYWOOD
Unknown artist, 1556

A man of some sartorial pretensions, with his full-length gown over his coat and trunk hose, a coif as well as a cap, and cross-gartered at the knee. He presents himself as a young (the gartering), up-and-coming professional (the gown and coif).

MONKEYS

Pieter van der Borcht, *c*.1562

Aping the fashions of your superiors is the satirical
point of this engraving, but the details it reveals about
the practicalities of laundering ruffs are superb. Look
out for the starch-bearing roots on the surface on the
right-hand side of the picture, the wonderful wooden
setting stand, and the careful working of damp
starched ruffs through the fingers.

1520S FASHION

Unknown artist, *c*.1528

This is a study not just of the most elegant clothing
of the 1520s but of elegant fashionable posture.
Note how the lady stands with her shoulders behind
the level of her hips and tucks in her chin. The
gentleman, meanwhile, sits full square with firmly
planted feet set apart. They both use a series of
props, not just for their symbolism but also to
show elegant arm and hand positions.

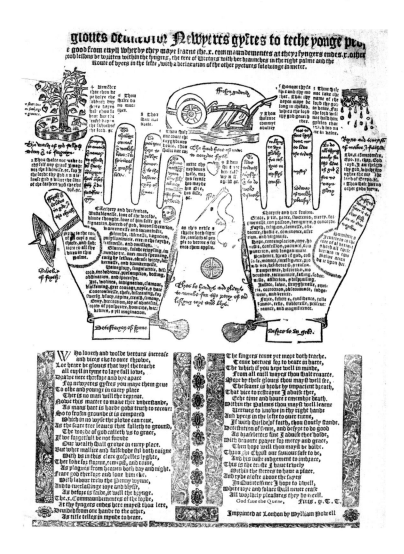

SOME FYNE GLOVES

Unknown artist, 1560s

This is a cheap moral teaching aid laid out in the form
of a pair of gloves (a common gift item) that could be
pinned or pasted up on the wall. Such woodcuts sold
for a penny a piece, so were affordable even to a
labourer in work as long as he was willing to go
without a few pints of beer.

THE COOK

Unknown artist, 1495

Pottage could come in every imaginable flavour and
was a staple for both rich and poor. Here a male
professional cook has a rabbit (or coney) hanging
up ready. Coneys were farmed and something
of a luxury meat; they had yet to become
common as a wild animal.

THE PLOUGHMAN
Unknown artist, *c.*1525
Ploughing was the work of men, and most men at
that. Here we see a sophisticated two-wheeled plough
suitable for heavy soil being pulled by two oxen.

THE DAIRY WOMAN
Unknown artist, 1526

Mrs Beryes's spring morning routine would have
looked something like this. A rural wife in the village
of Clee on Humberside, she was responsible for the
dairy. With an apron on and her veil pinned up out of
the way, she is churning butter. It's a big churn, but
she did have the milk of eighteen cows to process.

BEAR-BAITING

Unknown artist, 1521

A tethered bear set upon by six large dogs. The
British bear-baiting tradition was one that drew a lot
of people together for the 'sport' and the gambling.

Large crowds of people, eager to see something new, were crushed into a brightly painted space open to the elements in the centre and roofed in the seated gallery area around. The sounds of the city outside fell away as music sounded and the first actors walked out onstage. The backdrop was fixed and there would be few props, but the clothes were spectacular. The clothes used by the actors at the Rose were valued as highly as the building itself. When Francis Langley built the rival Swan Theatre on Bankside in 1595, he also spent £300 on clothes for the players to use onstage. An Elizabethan audience was quite prepared to simply imagine 'the vasty fields of France', but they expected Henry V to be dressed like a king in silks and velvets, gold lace and elaborate ruffs (historical accuracy was not a priority). In his inventory of the Admiral's Men's possessions in 1598, Henslowe lists cloth-of-gold gowns, coats, venetians, and hose; a cloth-of-silver coat, jerkin, pair of venetians and pair of hose; and a scarlet cloak with two broad gold laces and gold buttons. Since cloth of gold and cloth of silver could only be made with long thin strips of the actual precious metals themselves, woven with silk, it is easy to see how valuable such costumes were and what a spectacle they made onstage. Few people outside of court circles had any chance of seeing such fabrics and such clothes in any other context. You could quite reasonably visit the theatre simply to gawk at the costumes. According to Thomas Platter, a Swiss gentleman who was in London in 1599, 'The actors are most expensively and elaborately costumed; for it is the English usage for eminent lords or Knights at their decease to bequeath and leave almost the best of their clothes to their serving men, which it is unseemly for the latter to wear, so that they offer them then for sale for a small sum to the actors.' Certainly the theatre was buying aristocratic garments which sumptuary laws forbade anyone else to wear. Along with the cloth of gold and silver, which was supposed to be restricted to members of the royal family, the Rose also owned a scarlet gown furred with ermine, a garment that was supposed to be worn only by members of the House of Lords.

Not all clothing had to wait for its aristocratic owner's demise to be sold on to playhouses. Fashion at court changed rapidly, and that which had cost the equivalent of a large town house to buy could appear upon the back of the most ambitious only a handful of times before appearing passé. For those like Robert Dudley, patron of one of the acting companies, handing on such clothes could form part of his financial support package, perhaps in lieu of cash for private performances. It was also possible for such public display of his recently worn clothing to be seen as advertising and promoting his standing among the populace. The stage was a fashion show and a window on to the rarefied world of court and courtiers. It held much the same appeal as the Hollywood glamour films of the 1930s and the more modern celebrity lifestyle shows.

The fashion wasn't restricted to the stage, either: while doublets and gowns of Italian velvet mingled with cardboard crowns and false beards upon the boards, the audience, bathed in full daylight, was just as visible in their finery. The enclosed space of the theatre allowed eyes to rove, and the open yard gave ample opportunity for peacocks to strut. This is demonstrated in Ben Jonson's introduction to the printed version of his play *The New Inn* (1631), which offered the following rebuttal to those who had criticized it: 'What did they come for, then? thou wilt ask me. I will as punctually answer: To see, and to bee seene. To make generall muster of themselves in their clothes of credit: and possesse the Stage, against the Play.' Jonson's choice of the phrase 'clothes of credit' is an interesting one here. He could have been referring to their 'best' or most worthy clothes, but he could equally, and perhaps simultaneously, have been calling them borrowed or rented clothes. The renting of finery for special occasions was a common practice. Other people moved their most showy clothes in and out of pawn, using them as a form of storable, negotiable wealth. Philip Henslowe's accounts include large sections of such transactions, as he acted through a number of different agents as a pawnbroker. Clothes for the theatre also moved regularly through his hands – lent, rented, bought, altered, made and sold on as the needs of the company and its repertoire changed. Variety, novelty and spectacle were essential parts of the theatre's appeal; the same clothes could not be recycled endlessly, no matter how expensive.

While contemporary fashion was a draw, so too was a taste of the exotic. The *Tale of the Two Brothers*, which opened in 1602, was enhanced by the work put in by the 'tyre' man (or wardrobe master), who made two devil's suits and a gown for the witch. Shakespeare's *Titus Andronicus*, set in the ancient world, offered the chance to use the 'Antik sutes' listed in an inventory of 1602; these are plainly Elizabethan clothes with a Roman flavour, sumptuously refashioned from crimson velvet and cloth of gold, reminiscent, I think, of the costumes of the Hollywood epic *Cleopatra* starring Elizabeth Taylor, where contemporary fashion and ancient Egyptian elements collide.

It is hard for us as modern theatregoers to understand the excitement and thrill that such clothes added to the drama, to see a Roman general in a 'cote of crimson velvet cut in payns and embryderd in gould' and know that it was worth more than your house and several years' income combined, to feel that you were seeing something rare and strange, even the fabrics usually reserved for aristocratic eyes, as the words rolled richly about you. The words mattered too, of course: the theatre was about a lot more than the visual display. Elizabethan audiences enjoyed novelty, but they came back again and again for high-quality words. Henslowe's bestsellers – *The Jew of Malta*, *Doctor Faustus* and *The Spanish Tragedy* – the plays that filled the theatre most reliably, are also among those that modern literary scholars pick out as the 'best' and most accomplished of that period, while *Henry IV* and *Titus Andronicus* by the new lad on the block William Shakespeare also proved their worth as far as the Rose Theatre's clientele were concerned.

Strong dramatic plots that chart the highs and lows of human emotion feature in all of the more successful Elizabethan plays. Edward Alleyn, probably the most famous actor of the day, and his arch-rival Richard Burbage were both renowned and admired for their powerful performances, playing intense characters caught up in the depths of tragedy. Comedy also played well: even the most violent and tragic of Shakespeare's plays contain comic scenes to provide light against the shade. Indeed, if the most famous thespians were specialists in high tragedy, the second most famous were two comedians: first Richard Tarlton, whose career stretched right back at least to the 1560s, then William Kempe (we met him earlier, jigging his way across the country with bells and handkerchief). Shakespeare worked briefly with Edward Alleyn at the Rose Theatre, but later he was to work extensively at the Globe with both Richard Burbage, who played his Hamlet and Lear, and William Kempe, writing for him a series of comic rustic and bumbling characters who wittily play the fool, often hitting upon the meat of the subject as if accidentally.

There are those, of course, who find it hard now to follow the comedy, to find it truly funny. This, I think, is entirely down to problems of translation. As people who have spent many years deep in experiments recreating Tudor life, who cook the food, make the clothes and drink the beer, my friends, family and I have, without any conscious effort or thought, acquired a fairly Tudor vocabulary. I am regularly surprised when people treat words that I consider perfectly normal as arcane and mysterious. Surely everyone knows the difference between peascods, a peascod, codpieces and pieces of cod (pea pods, a fashionable doublet shape, the covering of a man's 'fly' area, and a bit of fish, respectively). When my friends and I go to the Globe to see a performance, it is very obvious that we are laughing at least twice as often as the rest of the audience, and not just at the more slapstick elements. Shakespeare really is very funny.

Something else that was exceedingly popular with Elizabethan audiences were the individual words, almost for their own sake. We know because they took so many away with them. Shakespeare made up thousands of words, over 1,700 of which are still with us. Both *moonbeams* and *mountaineers* are his, and if you were to sit in your *bedroom* and *submerge* yourself in *lacklustre* chat as you *hobnob* with those you have *friended*, you would still be talking his language. His phrases, too, fall from the mouths of people who might claim to hate his work: to be *as dead as a doornail* or *up in arms*, to come upon something *all of a sudden* and decide that *it's a foregone conclusion*. These are everyday idioms that pepper our common tongue. When people went and heard a play, it often made such an impression that they came out quoting it, gradually incorporating the words into their everyday speech and passing them down to their children.

An afternoon at the playhouse had many attractions.

10. Supper

To-night, grave sir, both my poore house, and I
Doe equally desire your companie:
[. . .]
Yet shall you have, to rectifie your palate,
An olive, capers, or some better sallade
Ushring the mutton; with a short-leg'd hen,
If we can get her, full of eggs, and then,
Limons, and wine for sauce; to these, a coney
Is not to be despair'd of, for our money . . .'

Ben Jonson, 'Inviting a Friend to Supper', *c*.1605–15

At the end of the afternoon's pleasures or the day's work came supper. The ideal time for this was 5 p.m., around five hours after
dinner, when the physicians were happy that ample time had been
allowed for healthy digestion but before a hungry stomach could
injure itself from lying empty too long. At five o'clock there was
still time for a meal to be eaten in daylight and, more practically, for
the washing-up to be done in natural light. Animals and poultry
had still to be bedded down for the night in their pens, stables and
coops, so a little twilight was still needed once all was eaten and
cleared away. A single fixed hour for supper was, of course, a rather
artificial concept. In the depths of January, supper might well have
to be at 4 p.m. to fit with the early hour of dusk, and in August,
when the harvest was in full swing, supper would be an early evening break within the work routine rather than at its finish, as people
used every scrap of light to keep working out in the fields.

There was one group of people, however, who were supposed to go without supper for a large section of the year. Monastic rules dictated the times of meals, together with the quantity and type of food and drink on offer to those following the enclosed religious life, as well as outlining a calendar of feast and fast that formed the ritual year. Monks and nuns had dinner every day, but supper was only served between Easter and 13 September, when the days were long, and even then was not served on Wednesdays and Fridays. The actual contents of supper on the days when it was allowed were unspecified in the Benedictine Rule (the most commonly followed), but practice at Westminster Abbey in the early Tudor period, for example, involved bread, ale and one meaty pottage or dish if monks ate in the main refectory or up to three pounds of cooked meat with bread and ale if they ate in the misericord. Surviving on just one meal per day was a part of the Benedictine idea of religious sacrifice and discipline. With the Reformation and the Dissolution of the Monasteries, however, the idea of going supperless lost its appeal as a mark of piety. Medical men of the Elizabethan period emphasized the importance of regular, moderate-sized meals for health and, rather pointedly, as a way to ensure high-quality studying and thinking, the implication being that good Protestants ate supper.

So what constituted a good supper for most people? In Lancashire it was what we might call porridge. In addition to making their bread from oats – the large sourdough-raised jannocks we mentioned before – working Lancastrians ate oats for supper too, often in the form of water pottage, milk pottage or whey pottage. Water pottage, made simply from oatmeal and water, could be served with salt and a handful of herbs or, in season, a large knob of butter could be stirred in. Milk pottage was just oats and milk; a little honey to go with it was something of a treat. Whey pottage, made with the whey left over from cheese making, was more economical than milk pottage, but again seasonal. These simple oat pottages are easy and quick to cook, and work beautifully over the slow peat fires that many people in upland regions depended on. They are also hearty and filling, if a little dull.

In milder climes with richer soils, similar pottages were made with other grains, often under the name of frumenty. The wholegrain versions are closer to risotto than porridge, although the ingredients are very similar. Whole wheat, rye or barley grains are put into a pan over the heat and broth is added little by little as the grains swell and absorb the liquid. As with the Lancashire oat version, handfuls of herbs can be thrown in towards the end of the cooking process, and a final knob of butter gives the dish a rich, creamy texture. A milk version calls for the whole grains to be steeped for a few hours in the milk before the pan is put on to a gentle heat and brought up to simmer. When the grains are cooked through and soft, the frumenty can be eaten as it is or thickened by stirring in cream, butter or eggs. Partially crushed or cracked grains cook more quickly and give a more porridge-like texture than that of risotto. The season, the soil types and the weather all influenced the final supper dish, therefore. Local custom and individual skills and tastes must have also played their part, but essentially a mess of softened cooked grains provided calories cheaply and easily for rural labouring households.

Townspeople also had the option of a takeaway for supper. Then, as now, people had to balance the economics of stopping work in order to cook, together with the price of fuel, against the greater cash outlay of buying a ready-made meal. Pre-cooked food was available for sale from bakers, hot meat shops and ale-houses. London had a row of all-night hot meat shops on the south side of London Bridge from at least the thirteenth century ready to serve travellers, those heading for the capital's markets and locals alike. Most towns boasted a baker or two who sold pies as well as bread, available hot at mealtimes; and villages, particularly those on major roads, frequently had alehouses, inns and ordinaries that served basic food along with drink, both on the premises and to take away. Many craftspeople in the larger urban areas were heavily reliant upon takeaways. Their lodgings were small and didn't always include a fireplace. The ideal of a stable family unit wherein the men and their male apprentices worked in the shop, and the women and their maidservants kept house, was just that, an ideal. The wealthier craftsman with a retail shop at the front, a workshop behind, and a hall and rooms over, could look forward to home-cooked meals while he had a healthy wife, sister or daughter at home, but not everyone was so lucky. Takeaways filled a gap when facilities were scarce or when a rush of work required all hands to the pumps, when sickness or death depleted the family unit or just occasionally when everyone fancied a night off.

For those, rural or urban, for whom resources were plentiful – perhaps 5 per cent of the population – supper could be a full repeat of dinner, with soups and pottage, boiled and roasted meats, tarts and custards, fruit, cheese and nuts all taking their turn upon the table. And this was the order it was supposed to be eaten in. You might not have noticed that it was listed in any specific order as this is very much the order of a modern meal too, and it's easy not to notice the familiar; however, the Tudor (and therefore modern) tradition was based upon ancient medical theory. Tudor medicine was heavily influenced by the Galenic understandings of the body which held that the stomach was like a cauldron, acted on by the natural heat of the body. Within this cauldron food was believed to be 'concocted', or broken down, and changed into chile, or juice. This juice then passed to the liver, where it was concocted a second time and converted into blood. The blood went forth from the liver to the right-hand chamber of the heart, where it mixed with vital spirits before being drawn away by the veins for its third and final concoction, turning into matter that could be assimilated by the body. Digestion was only complete when this invigorated, concocted blood was taken up by the various components of the body and changed into flesh, sinew, bone and skin.

Food was central to good health since it became the blood and ultimately flesh of man, but there was a lot that could go wrong during the process of digestion. Eating well was a central tenet of period medicine. It required a knowledge of the basic nature of all edible things. Such knowledge had been circulating around Europe for centuries from writers such as the Islamic philosopher Avicenna (Ibn Sina, *c.* 980–1037) and Hildegard of Bingen (1098–1179), as well as translations of the ancient Greek physician Galen's works, all of which assigned living things to a place upon the scale of humoral balance. It had long been possible for the literate to look up detailed descriptions of plants and animals which delineated their properties, how they should be cooked and eaten and in what circumstances. Over time, much of this information had percolated down into popular oral culture. Avoiding bad digestion and subsequent sickness required careful attention not just to what you put into your stomach, but also how and when you did so, something that shaped social practice.

According to physicians, the natural cauldron of the stomach was useless without the heat of the body to cook the food. Food put into a cold dead stomach just sat there and eventually rotted, but the action of the natural fire in the belly in a living person broke down, softened and changed food, and hopefully did so before that food had time to decay. Not everyone, however, had the same metabolism, the same basic nature. Some were hotter, others cooler, some drier in their basic nature and some moist. Each of us was formed from the same basic humours – blood, phlegm, yellow bile and black bile – but the exact balance varied from person to person. Men, in general, had more of the blood humour, which was hot and wet in nature, making them strong and virile, while women were formed more of phlegm, which was cool and moist, rendering them weaker both physically and mentally. Older people were much drier-fleshed than the young, and certain personalities reflected different balances. I, as a redhead, clearly exhibit an imbalance biased towards the yellow bile or choleric humour, which is both hot and dry in nature, and this gives me, I am still to this day regularly informed, a hot temper. Those with a dark, sallow complexion are prone to introspection and sadness, being dominated by the black bile – the cold, dry, melancholic humour, according to these ideas. One's lifestyle could also alter the balance of humours within one's body. Those who engaged in heavy exercise stoked up the fire of the body, increasing natural heat, making men more manly as it boosted the levels of blood within their system. Ploughmen, with their tough outdoor life, would have strong, hot fires in their bellies. Those who sat quietly over their books in contemplation were tipping their personal balance towards the cool humours – melancholic for men and increasingly phlegmatic for women (although obviously too much female thinking could lead to an overheated brain and madness). Their natural fires would be cool and slow.

All of these differences had a profound effect upon digestion. Those with hot fires in their bellies could clearly break down or 'concoct' lots of strong and heavy food, while light foods would be consumed in an instant. Those whose fires burnt slowly and coolly would be unable to cope with rich and heavy food; it would putrefy before it had a chance to be digested. Instead, such people needed light foods that would break down easily. The fire that did this cooking within the belly was thought to be located under the base of the stomach, so it made sense that it was to the bottom of the stomach that those foods needing the longest and hottest concocting should be placed, whereas those that needed less heat and less time should lie on top, where they could be more gently cooked. This formed the basis of the thinking behind the culinary order of dishes. Soups and pottages needed to be eaten first at any meal. They frequently contained ingredients such as beef, oatmeal and peas that required long concocting, but they were also wet, which prevented them from 'catching' on the bottom of the stomach where the heat was at its strongest. Had you begun with something like a biscuit, it would simply get burnt without being broken down. Juice could not be made purely from dry ingredients. Soups and pottages were ideal as a cooking medium for the food that was to follow. Bread ought, according to these theories, to accompany this soup or pottage. Bread was a highly nutritious but strong food that needed good heat, but it also permitted 'aglutination' of the pottage, aiding its breakdown and conversion into juice. Once you had eaten your bread and pottage, you could feel comfortable that you had lined your stomach properly and were now ready for the next foodstuff.

During Lent, or upon the weekly fasting days of Wednesday, Friday and Saturday, the next foods would be fish. The medical profession, acknowledging that this was both your Christian and patriotic duty, grudgingly accepted that fish had to be eaten at this point, but grumbled that it was not as healthy as meat – the medical ideas, after all, pre-dated Christianity, having been formulated in ancient Greece. Fish, they said, was formed of pure phlegm, and too much of it made you effeminate. Fish that swam in the sea were to be preferred to freshwater fish, as their salty nature somewhat mitigated the extreme wateriness of fish flesh. Meat was made, not of the phlegm humour, but of pure blood humour, and was closer to the flesh of people. This meant not only that meat would make excellent quality blood within the body, but that it would do so with far less effort or need for change. There was more goodness to be derived from that which was already body-like. It also clearly followed from this belief that those who were weak or in need of additional strength, such as pregnant women or men going into battle, should ignore the fast days and eat as much meat as possible. Pig meat was considered to be the most nutritious of all by the Greeks, but English physicians were keen to argue that if those ancient authors had ever visited England, seen the climate and eaten the beef there, they would have praised the healthiness of beef above that of pork. Beef, they felt, created the purest form of blood in the body, and if it proved too much for Greek constitutions that was because the hot climate of Greece encouraged more sluggish internal fires.

If you were lucky enough to have several dishes of meat upon your supper table, then the boiled meats were to be eaten before the roasted meats. Again, this was down to the relative cooking times and heats of the meat within the stomach. Roast meat had been subject to more intense heat in its first cooking and was thus more ready for digestion within the stomach. Boiled meat needed more time in concoction. Roast beef, therefore, was always a main course, never a starter. After the fish or meat, the lighter, gentler foods could be eaten. Indeed, if you were still hungry it was good to make the most of these at this stage of the meal. If you simply carried on with more and more of the heavy, hard-to-digest foods, you would overload your stomach, and while it might be able to concoct that which lay towards the bottom of the stomach, heavy foods near the top would remain underdone. This was also a good moment to take a long drink of wine or ale. With all that solid food upon the top of the pottage it was a good idea to moisten the contents again. If you had taken a long drink immediately after the pottage, there was a danger that you would drown the stomach, cooling it so severely that the concoction would slow to an unhealthy crawl, but with a good layer of boiled and roasted meats inside you, drink was a good thing. Ale was the most cooling of alcoholic drinks, so was ideal for labourers with hot stomachs. If, however, you were intending to indulge in salads after the meat it would be a sensible precaution to drink wine, as wine was a heating liquid and salads could be very cooling.

Wine was also a sensible precaution if you intended to eat fruit. Salads and fruit alike were very watery in their nature, containing little that made good blood in the body. Root vegetables were more substantial, but in general all vegetable matter other than peas and beans was seen as a very poor source of nutrition. You could eat a bellyful and gain very little from it. Fruit was very tasty of course, and many people chose it for pleasure, but health required it to be eaten with caution lest its watery nature thin the blood too much, causing vapours to rise within and putrefaction and hence sickness to ensue. It was a common saying, for example, that 'pears were poison without wine'. A pear poached in wine was a very different beast from a raw pear. The wine, with its natural warm and drying nature, along with the cooking process, which drove out water from the pear, made a dish of poached pears perfectly acceptable.

At the very end of the meal came cheese. This was a food that was slower to concoct, but it had the advantage of closing the stomach, sealing in all the other foods, particularly the more watery fruits that might otherwise rise up, sending vapours towards the brain. The Italians today claim this advantage for coffee.

So, to sum up, a healthy supper was one that began with soup followed by boiled and then roasted meats and a large glass of wine. Then you moved on to vegetables, small pies and fritters, then tarts and custards with fruit, nuts, and finally cheese and another glass of wine to finish. It may be that unbeknownst to you, you have been following Tudor, and indeed ancient Greek, dietary advice for years.

Since wealth and literacy generally went together, those within Tudor society who were able to afford to pick and choose among foods were also those who had the most access to medical thinking about healthy eating. And with that education, wealth and healthy eating went an obligation to exhibit the very best of table manners.

When we sit down to eat today, we each expect to have our own plate or bowl, and to have our food served on to that receptacle, each of us eating solely and directly from it. This was not the Tudor way. Sixteenth-century eating was a much more communal affair and involved a lot less cutlery and crockery. Each person brought their own knife and spoon to the table, except in the very grandest of houses, where some spoons and occasionally knives were kept for guests. In front of you, as you sat down in 1485 in a more prosperous household, was a four-inch square of dry bread, called a trencher, and either a separate linen napkin or a long additional cloth upon your side of the table that served as a napkin for all those seated with you, called a surnap. The food arrived on the table carefully cut into bite-size pieces, served in portions for four or six people, called messes, which were repeated along the length of the board. The group of three or five people with whom you shared these dishes were your mess mates. Each different dish was laid out thus.

Around you, therefore, were several dishes of food in easy reach to be shared with the same few people. Given this arrangement, the temptation for those of us schooled in modern manners is to spend a few moments piling food from the serving dishes on to our trenchers, from which we then eat. But no, that's not how it was done. The trencher was used only as a small staging post if a morsel should need to be cut up further: ideally, the bite-size food was taken directly from the mess to your mouth.

Period instructions to children speak of helping yourself only from the side of the dish nearest to you, not to go fishing around for the good bits. It was important, of course, to keep your spoon and your mouth as clean as possible, wiping yourself upon the napkin and your spoon upon a piece of bread. When you wished to take a drink, you called for the cup. This was also a communal vessel, so it was polite to first wipe your lips. When the cup was brought you drank heartily and handed it back, no hanging on and tippling from it during the meal, thank you very much.

A hundred years later and a few changes have crept in. By 1585 bread trenchers had largely been replaced by wooden ones, and the very wealthy were just beginning to use small personal plates of pewter and silver (but not pottery: the surviving pottery plates seen in museums were serving platters for the mess of food). Surnaps had also gone out of fashion, and individual napkins were much more common. Some people were also providing individual drinking vessels, but this was by no means universal. The essentials, however, remained: people still ate in messes with their spoons and knives. Small sweetmeat forks were making an appearance for nibbling on candied fruits at separate banqueting courses but were not used at table. (A banquet by the way, as we mentioned earlier, was not the word for a large meal – that word is 'feast' – but rather was the word for an additional course of sweets, nuts, fruit and cheese taken in a separate location while wandering around admiring the view.) It would not be until the 1670s that London merchants, always at the forefront of fashionable living, began to list sets of knives and forks among their inventories.

The communal nature of the meal was further emphasized by the polite convention of offering food to your fellows. If you did fish out a particularly good morsel, or the dish was so orientated that all of one thing was at your side, then you were expected to offer it to those dining with you, handing over your spoon with the tasty bit on it.

Within a great household, where you sat determined what you ate. Each person had an assigned spot. Every mess got the basics: bread, pottage and a dish of boiled meat usually. Imagine an aristocratic great hall where a hundred people, mostly men, sit down to eat each day. Divided into messes of four, that means that twenty-five dishes of pottage and boiled beef came out of the kitchen. However, there might only be fifteen dishes of stewed lamb, ten dishes of fried pork and two each of chicken, custard, veal and grouse. The lord and his family, dining in the adjoining parlour, had some of everything, the chief household staff had the boiled beef, fried pork and stewed lamb, the yeomen servants had both beef and lamb, and the grooms just had the beef as well as the pottage and bread that everyone else had too. Knowing your place had a very practical meaning.

As Erasmus had pointed out at the beginning of the Tudor era, everyone was expected to wash their hands before eating, and to refrain from belching or speaking with their mouth full, but educated diners were also supposed to keep up a stream of suitable polite conversation – something that could be tricky for the socially awkward.

My favourite book of dietary advice is Henry Buttes' *Diets Drie Dinner* of 1599, which treats each edible plant, fish or meat to a two-page spread. Upon the left-hand page he gives the usual medical advice found in dozens of other texts, here helpfully divided into sections of which foodstuffs you should choose, their usefulness, the hurt that could be done if taken by the wrong people at the wrong time, the corrections that could be applied to mitigate problems, their degree of heat and moisture according to humoral theory, and finally their seasonality. Take strawberries, for example. Under the heading 'Choice' he recommends that strawberries should be red, ripe,

fair, fragrant and garden grown, all of which seems entirely reasonable. Their usefulness medically was their ability to 'asswage
the boiling heate and acrimony of blood and choler: coole the
liver: quench thirst: provoke urine and appetite'; they are also,
he notes, 'passing grateful to the palate'. Under the 'Hurts' section he notes that strawberries should never be eaten by those
with palsy, diseased sinews or weak stomachs, and that the wild
strawberries that grow in the woods are much too sharp. To correct their faults he recommends rinsing them in wine and eating
them with plenty of sugar, dietary advice that I am happy to
follow. He assigns them to the melancholic humour, saying that
they are cold and dry in the first degree. So far this is all conventional stuff, but on the facing page Mr Buttes gives us his 'story
for table talk', a series of interesting facts suitable for conversation at the supper table:

> They were utterly unknown to antique leeches, and are indeed
> yet more beholding to poets than phisitians. They have named
> them fraga: neither have they any other name, as farre as I
> know. The English name importeth their manner of setting in
> beds, not cast upon heapes, but (as it were) strawed here and
> there with manifest distance. Conradus Gesner reporteth, he
> knew a woman that was cured of the pimples on her face, only
> by washing it with strawberrie water: and yet it was very
> homely and rudely distilled, betwixt two platters, and not in a
> limbeck.

Oh dear! Poor Mr Buttes. One can just imagine him trying to
keep up his end of the conversation at some awkward meal, just
a bit too pedantic. He gives a similar story for every single foodstuff. 'The spinny artichoak differes only from the common
artichoak in the having of spines'!

With food came drink, and the drink of Englishmen was ale
and, towards the end of the period, beer – taken both with

supper and on into the evening afterwards. Unclean water was obviously a bringer of sickness, and even where pure clean water from springs and streams was available it was not considered to be the ideal healthy drink. Medical men considered pure water to be fine for those who were used to it or had never drunk anything else — as the physician Thomas Cogan believed to be the case for Cornishmen — but those who were accustomed to ale or beer would find water too watery, too apt to chill and drown the internal fires. Ale and beer, on the other hand, had some heating properties — beer more so than ale — that counteracted the very watery nature of the drinks, making them more humorally balanced beverages. Moreover, they contained nourishment. Whether people took on board the medical opinions of the physicians or not, most preferred ale and beer to water.

Brewing ale was a regular part of the domestic cycle, one of the universal female skills, alongside baking, dairy work and laundry. Ale, made from malted grain and water, has a very short shelf life, souring after a week or two, so it needed to be made regularly in smallish batches, just sufficient to take the family through to the next brew. If ale formed the complete liquid intake of a family, these 'small batches' would consist of around twelve to twenty gallons per week. Brewing was therefore a considerable operation in any household.

First, the grain had to be malted. Some people specialized in malting and supplied their neighbours; others made their own at home. Malt is grain that has begun to sprout, but not yet put forth its first leaf. The malting process is all about capturing the moment when the grain has turned most of its stored starch into sugars, ready to power the spring growth of the plant. These sugars will feed the yeasts that make the alcohol. You begin by soaking your grains in clean cold water for a day or two until they have swollen and are ready to split. The water is then drained off and the grain turned out on to a clean indoor surface – a wooden boarded floor is best – and spread out into a thick and even heap. Within the heap, warmth begins to generate. The heap has to be turned regularly so that no grain sits too long on the surface, far from the warmth of the centre, and dries out. Over the next few days the heap is gradually spread out more thinly so that the temperature is managed, maintaining just enough warmth to keep the processes going but not so much that the grain is damaged. The grain must stay above fifteen degrees Centigrade, but not exceed twenty-five degrees. The heap must always be of an even thickness so that it all develops at once, as you have no way of separating out the grain that is ready from the grain that is not. Four or five sessions with the malt shovel are needed each day to turn, mix and spread the grain sufficiently. The length of time it takes to turn grain into malt is dependent on the weather. In cold weather you have to keep your heaps deeper than usual, and in hot weather you must spread them more thinly. Rain can make a big difference too, affecting the humidity levels within the malting shed.

The longer and slower the malting process, the more complete will be the conversion from starch to sugars within the grain. William Harrison, in his *Description of England*, thought it should take at least twenty-one days. At last all your grains will display a small pale nib of shoot. Now you need to stop them developing any further so that they can't use up your precious sugars. This is done by spreading the malt out upon a gently heated surface in order to dry it. It is important at this stage to avoid smoke, which could affect the final flavour of the ale. Straw fires were thought best, although gorse and heather also burnt with a good clear flame. If you had to use wood, it was best to remove the bark and chop it into fine sticks so that it burnt as cleanly as possible. Using peat or, worst of all, coal produced very nasty-tasting ale. Although a slow and gentle heat is better than fast and furious, particularly at the outset when the enzymes can easily be destroyed, as the moisture level reduces you can apply a bit more heat in safety. The best malt was hard and a clear yellow colour; when you broke it open, according to Harrison, it would 'write like a piece of chalk'.

I have only once tried to produce a large batch of malt, but it went fairly well. First I had to clean my grain, all four sacks of it. The barley had to be carefully winnowed to remove weed seeds and stray husks. This takes a lot of labour, but it's worth doing thoroughly as some of the weeds can be detrimental to health. Next I spread the grain out to about an inch deep on a wooden floor and watered it in situ. I just didn't have a big enough vessel to soak that much grain in one go. An hour later I returned and my colleague (we were making a TV programme at the time) helped me stir the malt, then spread it out and water it once more. It took two more sessions before the grain had all swelled sufficiently, then we heaped it up to an eight-inch depth to warm the mass. Seven days in I got a little worried when the centre began to sprout with no sign of any action at the edges – we had had to go away for a day to film some eel fishing and the heap had been neglected. Emergency remedial mixing more or less solved the problem, and fourteen days after the initial water-ing the malt was ready for the drying to begin. Very large establishments had specific kilns for this purpose, a low brick or stone floor supported on arches beneath which a fire could be lit. I, like many people in the period, did not have such a structure, so I dried my malt out on the floor of my oven. Small batches could also be done on a bakestone, or even in a pan over the fire. It was a slow process, but in common with many of the domestic processes of the Tudor household it was a matter of putting in a few minutes' work, leaving it for a period and then returning for a few more minutes' work, and so on. Eventually you can build up a routine combining a myriad of small jobs, doing one while you wait for the next stage of another. The batch came out a little weak, due probably to that mid-malting neglect, but was very palatable.

Barley was the most common grain to be used for malting and brewing, but in Cornwall and in the north of England oats were used. Rye and dredge also occurred occasionally as grains for ale. Wheat was even rarer. Brewing began with grinding the malt into a coarse meal, boiling the water and then ladling that hot water over malt placed in the bottom of a large wooden tub. One bushel of malt could yield ten gallons of ordinary household ale. The recipe for strong 'March' beer (traditionally brewed in that month, but which had now become simply a description of strong beer) in Gervase Markham's *The English Huswife* called for a higher proportion of malt to water, more like one bushel to eight gallons.

By ladling the boiling water bit by bit on to the malt, a good housewife could ensure that the water was fractionally below boiling point, something that maximized the extraction of sugars from the malt. It now had to stand for about an hour and a half. Large batches held their heat well and needed no special care at this stage, but a small, family-sized batch of ale could easily cool too quickly in the winter so a lid and a wrap of straw around the tub to insulate it was a good idea. While this 'mash' occurred, a second batch of water could be heated. The finished liquid (called 'wort') was strained off and returned to the heat to boil, leaving the malt behind, and a second batch of water was ladled on to the used malt and allowed to mash. The first batch of wort, now heating up in the kettle, the lead or a pan, could be flavoured with a variety of plants. Some, such as alecost (*Tanacetum balsamita*, or costmary), make reference to their traditional usage. A huge range of plants were liked by different people, often following regional traditions. Broom, gorse flowers and heather were popular wherever heathlands were to be found, ground dried berries of the bay tree were liked by some

Londoners, and elderflowers were another seasonal favourite across much of the country.

The second heating of the wort stabilized it, killing the enzymes and sterilizing the liquid. A long boil evaporated some of the water, strengthening the mix. Once boiled, the wort was poured into an open tub to cool. A successful brewer tried to cool the wort as quickly as possible to minimize the opportunity for new infections to arrive. From the cooling vat, the wort was dripped slowly into the fermenting vat, where the 'balm' was waiting. This balm was the yeast, a batch of active liquor from the previous brew. It was gathered from the top of the vat, where the fast-acting yeasts that work well within the usual temperature range of British brewhouses can be found. The Pilsner-style brews that are so predominant among modern commercial brands utilize instead the yeasts from the bottom of the vat, which ferment more slowly at lower temperatures and frequently require some element of refrigeration, a difference that has a big impact upon flavour and clarity and marks a major divide between the modern and Tudor experience of ale and beer drinking. When it was clear to the Tudor brewer that fermentation was well under way, a portion of the wort was taken off and put aside to act as the balm for the next brewing, and the rest of the wort could be poured into clean, well-scrubbed barrels, leaving the bung off. The first day of fermentation was the most rapid, which was why you didn't seal it at this stage. Twenty-four hours later the main bung went in, leaving only a small vent, and this too was sealed two days after that. The ale was ready to drink from this point on.

Dealing with the quantities of liquid needed by the average family was heavy work and required either a big investment in vessels, or efficiency and ingenuity. Mrs Beryes, our dairy woman from the parish of Clee, was lucky enough to have a lead in her house. It would have been invaluable for boiling all the scalding water she needed to keep her commercial dairy operation spotlessly clean, but it could also double as her brewing vessel. A large lead had a capacity of around twenty to thirty gallons, so she could have made enough for the family in one boiling. However, if she had to supply the drink for all her dairy-maids and her husband's labourers and servants in husbandry as well – which is quite likely as the provision of drink was often part of the employment agreement – then she would have needed to boil two lots of water and found enough barrels to store it all while it fermented and while the finished ale was waiting to be drunk, as well as a couple of open wooden vats to mash the wort and cool it.

The rural parish of Clee has a particularly rich historical record, with ninety-three surviving probate inventories between 1536 and the end of Elizabeth's reign in 1603. Legally only adult men and single or widowed adult women could make wills that needed a probate inventory, and those with very little to leave rarely bothered with a will, so the ninety-three inventories are dominated by the more substantial settled households of the parish. Many parishioners and their modes of life are missing from the record, but you can still get a feel for the brewing and drinking of rural Humberside. Thirty-three of these snapshots of household possessions include brewing equipment, while in a further fourteen everything is lumped together in phrases such as 'all the howshold stuff'.

John Awdman, for example, had a lead together with a mash vat and a 'gylyng' vat (a gyle vat was the name given to the vat where the wort cooled and the balm was introduced), together with several other smaller tubs, and Thomas Yates had a lead, a pair of querns to grind malt, and 'other bruynge vessels'. John Awdman was in much the same financial bracket as the Beryes family, with a pair of oxen, two mares, six milking cows and another half-dozen cattle, sixty sheep and a few pigs and chickens. Brewing and dairying went on within his home, a home that is likely to have included some employees and concentrated on livestock farming. The spent malt at the end of the brewing made excellent animal feed, a useful bonus for someone like John Awdman. There was a considerable arable-farming element to Thomas Yates's livelihood, and a similar list of livestock and the ten mattresses listed among his household goods add to the picture of a man employing a much larger labour force, either as live-in servants or as day labourers, all of whom will have needed ale to drink.

When you move a little lower down the scale of resources – those with fewer livestock and less arable acreage – many people had to do their brewing using the pots, pans and kettles that were also used for cooking. One way to manage this smaller hot water capacity was to put all of your malt into the mash tub, boil as much water as you could and pour it in, making an extremely thick first mash. The second boil made a medium-strength batch and the third boil was weaker again. All the finished worts could be mixed together in the gyle vat before the balm was added.

Jennott Ranneor was another of Mrs Beryes's neighbours. She was a widow and at her death in 1546 owned five cows and the contents of a small one-room, perhaps two-room, house. Among her household goods are listed a great pan, a gyle vat, two boards, four ale pots and 'other bruyeng vessell'. This is a suggestive list. Jennott had no built-in lead, yet the brewing equipment was still substantial, and while those ale pots could have been storage vessels, they are more likely to have been large jugs for serving ale. Many widows turned to brewing as a way of making a living. You really didn't need very much to set yourself up as an alehouse. A bench outside provided the only customer accommodation necessary. When the night watch in Shakespeare's play *Much Ado about Nothing* say that they will 'sit

upon the bench til two', they are referring to just such an establishment: a bench against the outside wall of a small alehouse
where pots brimful of ale could be handed out of the window.
Customers for the main part didn't even need the bench: many
alehouses functioned more as takeaway suppliers, allowing
other local families to buy in their ale rather than have to brew
it themselves – for if thirty-three of our inventoried parishioners of Clee had brewing equipment listed and we are unsure
about another fourteen, forty-six did not. Those who brewed
were for the most part fairly well-equipped farmers, owners of
ploughs, dairying or spinning equipment alongside the vats and
leads. They were more likely to be employers who not only had
more people to supply, but also had access to more labour to do
the brewing.

The most handsomely equipped brewing family was that of
Robert Howldsworth, who had a dedicated kiln to prepare malt
from barley in its own house or shed. Alongside the kiln sat a
large vat to steep the barley and a set of 'pare cloths' that were
spread over the surface of the kiln and underneath the malt during the drying process. Four-and-a-half quarters of finished
malt was stored in the chamber next to the best chamber – that's
nine large sackfuls. In the kitchen sat a quern to grind the malt
and a chest to store it until the family was ready to brew. A lead
also stood in the kitchen next to a mash vat and three other tubs,
allowing several large batches to be processed at once. But the
process did not finish within the kitchen. The buttery housed
the gyle vat where the yeasty balm was added and fermentation
began, and two firkins with 'gantries' sat alongside, ready to
receive the ale from the vat. This is surely the equipment of a
commercial operation on a much larger scale than that which
Jennott Ranneor could have managed. Up and down the country, rural communities followed similar patterns, with the better
off brewing at home, the poorer sort buying their ale, and two

separate groups of commercial suppliers: the prosperous, large-scale, well-equipped producer generally headed up by a male businessman; and the poor, small-scale, ad hoc producer who was frequently female. In an urban setting, commercial production was more important. Fewer people had the space and facilities for home brewing and were therefore reliant upon alehouses for their daily supplies.

So far we have been largely talking about ale, the traditional drink of Britain, but during the Tudor period ale was being gradually ousted by beer. Beer was ale that was flavoured with hops. In modern Britain the word 'ale' is often used for a style of hop-flavoured beer, and no one commercially produces true ale, so the chances are that whatever the name upon the bottle you have never actually tasted Tudor ale. It is remarkably sweet and thick in comparison to modern brews, but not terribly alcoholic. There is huge variety from one brew to the next, of course, depending upon the type and quality of the grain, the effectiveness of the malting process, the amount and type of smoke that surrounded the malt in the kiln, the quality of the water, the proportions of the brew, the timings of the boil, the flavouring herbs employed, the strain of yeast, and the strength and speed of the ferment, not to mention any flavour that was picked up from the brewing vessels and storage casks. The environment in, and equipment with which brewers worked meant that there was little chance of complete consistency between batches within one household, let alone across different parts of the country. People had their own personal favourites and local reputations. My own experiments have been very varied. I have had batches which barely fermented at all, I have made alegar (like vinegar, but ale-based rather than wine-based) by accident, and I have also produced a series of very drinkable brews, all different from the one before. Such huge variation stems in part from the fact that I don't have one stable environment in which to brew, and have instead brewed at several different museums, houses, sheds and yards, but it also reflects something of the Tudor experience. Bad brewing or just bad batches could and did happen. Margery Kempe's disasters are recorded in the fifteenth century, before our period begins, in her religious writings. She writes of her attempts to brew commercially being dogged by brews that failed to ferment at all and brews that soured in the making, before finally deciding that God didn't want her to brew. Such problems, allied with the central importance of ale within daily life, prompted early attempts at consumer protection and quality control. From the fourteenth century, anyone who wished to offer ale or beer for sale had to have each brewing tested and approved by a local official known as the aletaster, or aleconner. This person was on the very lowest rung on the ladder of officialdom, and was chosen at parish level from the adult male householders. If they found the ale or beer to be too weak or otherwise deficient, they were empowered to set a lower price.

Beer acquired its first foothold in Britain in London, where it was produced primarily by immigrants from the Low Countries. Even as late as 1574 over half of the capital's beer breweries were owned and run by those classified in the official records as 'aliens'. Beer had been produced in London since at least 1390, and beer dominated the market for provisioning the ships that sailed in and out of this, the most important port in the country. It also became a major export, back to the Low Countries, where it soon acquired a reputation as a quality product.

Beer's eventual predominance stems from the preservative effect of hops. Ale, whatever its strength or herb flavour, has a short shelf life, a couple of weeks at best, and much less if the weather is hot. Beer will keep successfully for many months, however. From a commercial point of view this is clearly a major benefit, allowing large-scale production, storage, and transport to new markets. An ale brewer could only supply his immediate neighbourhood, whereas a beer brewer could be supplying a host of alehouses a cart-ride away. Beer would last throughout a sea voyage or could be bought by a household in bulk. As towns grew and long-distance sea voyages became more common, the demand for beer rose.

The earliest beer recipe in English lies within a real hotch-potch of a book written in 1503 by Richard Arnold. In among lists of the parish churches of London, sample letters for businessmen to employ, and lists of customs duties at the port of London, lies a simple five-line instruction 'To Brewe Beere'. It calls for ten quarters of malt (presumably barley malt), two quarters of wheat, two quarters of oats and forty pounds of hops to make sixty barrels of beer. These are very large quantities: there are thirty-six gallons in each barrel, enough for several busy alehouses or a long sea voyage with a full ship's company.

Londoners themselves gradually acquired a taste for hopped beer in preference to ale, William Harrison deriding ale as 'an old and sick man's drink'. His wife's recipe for beer in the 1570s bears a number of similarities to that of Richard Arnold seventy years previously. She began with eight bushels of malt, which she ground herself with a quern to avoid the miller's fee. To this she added half a bushel of ground wheat and another half a bushel of ground oats. She then heated eighty gallons of water and poured it upon the mash in two batches due to the restrictions enforced by the size of her lead. Three and a half pounds of hops were added in total when she boiled the wort. She mixed her balm with half an ounce of orris root to act as a clarifying agent and an eighth of an ounce of bay berries for flavour, before it was put to the cooled wort. The rough proportions and main ingredients of both Mrs Harrison's and Richard Arnold's recipes remain the same across the years. Beer took much longer to catch on in the rest of the country, with the two drinks running alongside each other for many years. Ale was primarily home-brewed and produced on a small scale, while beer was primarily made by larger commercial businesses able to make the capital investment in bigger vessels and bigger batches of raw ingredients, particularly in an urban context. Larger concerns were able to dominate larger areas at more competitive prices, encouraging alehouses and inns to buy in their beer rather than brew their own. As a result a rough gender split developed, not only between who was brewing ale and beer, but who was drinking it, with ale remaining a feminine beverage drunk within a domestic setting, and beer acquiring a more masculine clientele, especially away from the home.

If a large jug of ale stood upon the supper table as part of the meal, drinking could, and often did, continue on into the evening. Merchants were renowned for holding supper parties that went on into the night, with people sitting up until midnight, a truly late hour in a world where most people were up and busy at around 4 a.m. William Harrison describes craftsmen and their wives – slightly lower down the social scale – each bringing a dish of food to share the costs of conviviality when visiting one another. Supper parties provided a social life for respectable householders within their own social circles, accompanied by a jug of ale.

For those whose homes offered less space, facilities or cheer, an evening at the alehouse was often very welcome. In 1577 a nationwide survey of drinking establishments recorded 24,000 such premises, roughly one per 142 inhabitants. Inns provided overnight accommodation for travellers, stabling for horses, food and of course drink. The tavern was a more urban phenomenon, catering to a middle-class customer base and serving food and wine, as well as ale and beer. An ordinary was a humbler establishment, offering both food and drink. Alehouses were primarily purveyors of drink. At the beginning of the

Tudor era, alehouses generally brewed their own ale and sold it by the jugful to customers who remained outside the building. As time moved on, alehouses slowly moved towards a format that we would recognize as a pub – an indoor space for drinking whose ale and beer may have been brewed upon the premises but were often bought in in bulk from larger commercial producers. In 1495 an Act of Parliament granted Justices of the Peace authority over ale-selling, allowing them to shut down any alehouse that they thought surplus to requirements, unruly or likely to corrupt local morals. And from 1552 onwards, individuals selling ale or beer had to be licensed.

As alehouses became more social spaces, the authorities became more nervous of them. Even the most puritanical and fun-hating writer of tracts conceded that alehouses were necessary for the provision of ale and beer to those who had no brewing facilities of their own, but their use for 'tippling' (or continuous drinking in order to get drunk), for gambling, or as locations for large raucous gatherings, was deeply worrying to such people. In Basingstoke in 1516 the local authorities specified that no alehouse keeper was to serve apprentices after 7 p.m., or servants after 9 p.m., in response to worries about young people being fit for work and wasting all of their money, possibly in the presence of bad company. In 1563 Leicester sought to control social drinking by introducing a bylaw that forbade any townsman or woman from sitting drinking for more than an hour. The town tried to gain further control in 1574, when it forbade those selling ale or beer retail from brewing, and those who brewed from selling retail, with the brewers all belonging compulsorily to a guild. The strength of brews could thus be regulated and it would be much easier to shut down alehouses that stepped out of line, or so it was thought.

Alehouse accommodation was basic – just the bench against the wall outside for many. If there was room inside, the furniture was still likely to consist of no more than benches and stools, perhaps a table. These were not purpose-built premises as an inn might be, but rather people's homes adapted for use. Most of those who turned to keeping an alehouse for a living were not prosperous, so the homes that were adapted were fairly simple to begin with. Earthen floors were commonplace. There was no bar, of course: drink was brought straight from the barrel in jugs or ale pots by the alehouse keeper, their family or servants. Drinking vessels were supplied by some establishments, but many customers will have brought their own. A good cheerful fire made all the difference to the atmosphere, encouraging people in from their own, possibly unheated, homes.

'Do ye make an alehouse of my lady's house, that ye squeak out your coziers' catches,' demands Malvolio of Sir Toby, Sir Andrew and Feste in Shakespeare's play *Twelfth Night*. The three reprobates have been singing popular songs, 'Three merry men we be', 'There dwelt a man in Babylon' and 'O' the twelfth day of December'. This was indeed alehouse behaviour. Dancing at the alehouse, as we have seen, was an afternoon activity when there was light to see by, but in the evening music and singing took over. Musicians were sometimes paid by the landlord or a whip-round among the customers. Singing, being free, was probably more common. A whole industry writing, printing and selling ballad sheets for people to learn and sing developed in the latter half of the sixteenth century as literacy levels rose and the printing industry geared up. It was a form of literature frequently sneered at by the more educated members of society. As William Webbe writes in his *Discourse of English Poetrie* (1586):

> For though many such can frame an Alehouse song of five or six score verses, hobbling upon some tune of a Northern Jigge, or Robyn hoode, or La Lubber etc . . . we shall shortly have whole swarms of Poets: and every one that can frame a Booke

in Ryme, though for want of matter, it be but in commenda-
tions of Copper noses or Bottle Ale, wyll catch at the Garlande
due to Poets: whose potticall, poeticall (I should say), heades, I
would wyshe, at their worshipfull comencements might in
steede of Lawrell, be gorgiously garnished with fayre greene
Barley, in token of their good affection to our Englishe Malt.

Writing songs in praise of beer and ale to be sung by those
consuming it made good commercial sense, even if it wasn't
going to win you any poet's laurel crown. Thousands upon
thousands of ballad sheets were being produced and circulated
by the end of our period, and many of them appear to have
ended up pasted to the walls of alehouses for customers to enjoy
and sing.

Drinking and singing were closely entwined in the Tudor
mind. In his *Anatomy of Absurdity* (1589), Thomas Nashe, a poet
of strong opinions, described such ballads as 'our new found
songs and sonnets, which every rednose Fidler hath at his fingers
end, and every ignorant Ale knight will breath foorthe over the
potte, as soone as his braine waxeth hote'. The songs that survive are a varied bunch, from triumphal celebrations of English
military victories, such as the 1597 sack of Cadiz led by the Earl
of Essex, to news of local disasters, such as the fire at Beccles in
Suffolk in the 1580s that destroyed half the town, or comic songs
about marriage, and moral reminders about the inevitability of
death. All are characterized by a good strong rhyme and metre,
and many reuse tunes that were already well known. Their sentiments are painted with broad brushstrokes to appeal to a mass,
probably tipsy, audience. Take the patriotic, if not exactly politically correct, triumphalism of the song about the sack of Cadiz:

Long the proud Spaniard advanced to conquer us
Thretening our Country with fire and sworde
Often preparing their nay most sumptuous

> With all provision that Spain could afford
> Dub, a dub, dub, dub, thus spake our drums
> Tan tara, tan tara the Englishman comes . . .

Off sails the earl at the head of a small fleet to catch the Spanish in port and burn their supplies:

> Now quoth the noble Earl, Courage my souldiers all
> Fight and be valiant and spoyle you shall have . . .

The capture of booty gets several verses of its own, interspersed with comments about how the townsfolk ran away.

> Entering the houses then of the richest men
> For gold and treasure we search'd each day
> Dub, a dub, dub, dub, thus spake our drums
> Tan tara, tan tara the Englishman comes.

The chorus is particularly fine for belting out at volume as part of a crowd with a pot of ale in one hand. Other songs are more suitable for one singer and a group of amused listeners, like that about the woes of a man with a jealous wife:

> When I was a Batchelour
> I live'd a merry life;
> But now I am a married man,
> And troubled with a wife,
> I cannot doe as I have done,
> Because I live in feare;
> If I goe to Islington,
> My wife is watching there.

He longs for the days when he wore yellow hose and flirted with all the girls. A hundred lines later he concludes that he is 'weary of my life'.

Alehouse customers were predominantly, but not exclusively,

male, and tended to be drawn from the poorer end of society, but some more prosperous people joined them. The historian Amanda Flather's analysis of the alehouse visits that appear within the court records of Essex suggests that a third of alehouse customers were female and two-thirds male, while husbandmen, servants and labourers at the lower end of the social spectrum made up over half of the customers, about a third being drawn from the more comfortably-off groups of artisans and yeomen, with even the occasional scattering of professionals and members of the gentry in attendance. Women tended to go to the alehouse, when they were not simply collecting a jug of ale to be drunk at home, in family groups with husbands and friends. Men went both as part of a couple or family and solo to meet with friends. People went to the alehouse for refreshment at the end of a long day at market, or to celebrate family events or seal business contracts, or even just to have a pleasant evening out. Alehouses were perfectly respectable places for both men and women to go for a quiet evening's drink and talk with friends, neighbours and family, and reasonably respectable places to go for a more boisterous song and even a dance. Young courting couples might meet there in company with others, but they were not quite respectable enough places for women to frequent alone.

The alehouse became a place of great concern to those in authority, however, and to those who worried about living a godly life, if the drunkenness got out of hand, if gambling was rife, if people indulged in openly sexual behaviour, if the talk turned seditious, if fights broke out or if the noise levels disturbed others nearby. Outright drunkenness was an evil decried by all levels of society, even many enthusiastic alehouse patrons, for while 'goodfellows' were praised in song and literature for their ability to drink deeply in a social context, those who lost control – those who passed out, were unable to walk home, or vomited or otherwise soiled themselves – were called drunken sots, fools and 'no true men'. Drunkenness swallowed a family's money, comfort and hope. The drunkard was a slack worker and frequently failed to support his, or her, family, not just causing misery for his dependants but laying an additional financial burden upon his fellow parishioners, who had to provide funds for the poor. Those trapped within the family of a drunkard – generally among the poorest of society, with the least likelihood of literacy – rarely get to tell us of their plight directly, but those in authority who had to try and sort out the mess leave us in no doubt that excessive drinking meant the sharp pinch of hunger, clothes sold or pawned off people's backs, explosions of domestic violence and public shame. Nonetheless, ale and alehouses remained both important and popular parts of working Tudor life.

11.   And so to Bed

As the stable door was bolted, the chickens settled down inside
their coops and darkness fell, men and women retired to bed and
said their prayers: 'O everlasting light whose brightnesse is never
darkned; looke favourablie upon me thy poore and sinfull servant . . .' The day both began and ended with Christian worship,
a quickly mumbled formula for some and a deep introspective
journey for others. Pleas for safety through the night and for
forgiveness of the day's sins were the most generally used themes:
'And now I bow the knees of my hart unto thee most mercifull
and heavenlie father, beseeching thee for Jesus Christ his sake, to
forgive me all my sinnes, negligences and ignorances.' And
many published prayers also spoke of handing oneself over into
God's care: 'For I commit my bodie and soule, this night and
evermore, unto his most holie hands.' These words quite consciously echo those of last wills and testaments and the service
for the dead. This was considered to be a good time of day to
contemplate one's own mortality; a strong connection was made
between the small oblivion of sleep and the larger one of death,
in the hope of rising again – to a new day or to the joys of
heaven. The evening prayer was a good time to set your spiritual affairs in order, to beg forgiveness, to put aside arguments
and bad feelings, and to clear the slate ready for a new beginning, rather like balancing the books daily, before the big audit
at the end of the year.

Once again it was a very personal form of prayer, one engaged
in alone even if you were in the same room as other people, who
would be saying their own prayers. Images abound of people

already dressed in their nightclothes (a shirt or smock and a linen nightcap), kneeling by the side of the bed. Parents might well guide the youngest children through their prayers, but the ideal was for children to have their own spiritual conversations with God as soon as possible.

Sex

> And this appetite or lust, was given by God to mankind from the beginning, as appeareth in Genesis. So that none, neither male nor female is cleane without, although it burne more in some than others, according to age and complexion . . .
>
> Thomas Cogan, *The Haven of Health* (1577)

The Tudor attitude to sex was as contradictory and complicated as our own. Some held that sex was essential for health, while others argued for the moral value of celibacy. Women were perceived as sexually voracious and uncontrolled, yet many thought that men were more likely to stray. A celibate life was a pure life, but sex itself had the power to drive away lecherous thoughts and polluting dreams.

At the heart of the matter lay a tension within Christianity between the original promotion of family within the texts of the Bible, drawing upon the Jewish tradition, and the preference among early Church leaders in the following generations for sexual abstinence, in response to ancient Greek and Eastern spiritual influences. Reading the Bible, one is faced with both these viewpoints. Christ is recorded as attending weddings, and his teachings take sex and marriage largely for granted. St Paul (who as an educated man of the Roman Empire had more exposure to certain Greek schools of thought) advocated celibacy, however, and taught that while the unmarried cared for the things of the Lord, the married cared for the things of the world, eroding their spiritual life. In addition to these written religious attitudes, a person at the outset of the Tudor era was also presented with a 500-year-old legacy of communal celibacy within the monasteries and nunneries that dotted the countryside. Monastic ideals, which initially grew out of Eastern mysticism from the Hindu tradition of holy men living apart from society, had swept with great vigour right across Europe. Within this monastic culture, celibacy was seen as a spiritual tool that brought people closer to God by removing the distractions of bodily and social life and channelling all of a person's energies into contemplation and worship. But in the sixteenth century Martin Luther, unable to find such ideas in the Bible itself, turned his back on them and championed marriage for the godly, including the clergy. Marriage, he argued, was the proper way for a person to live a holy life. Sexual relations within the marriage, and the procreation of children, were godly works; the bringing up of children within such a household was a Christian duty. Sex was thus at the heart of the great religious debate of the era. For the Catholic Church, celibacy was the favoured state and marriage only ever a second best. For the new Protestant faith, marriage and married sex represented a more biblically pure life for adults.

Within the British experience of the Reformation, however, there was no clear-cut switch from the lauding of celibacy within the Catholic era to an acceptance of married sex in the Protestant; the tension remained. Handbooks on Protestant marriage continued to uphold the sanctity of virginity and chastity. In 1568, Edmund Tilney began his treatise, for example, with the words 'the virtues of the matrimonial estate, which (setting virginitie aside as the purest state) is both holy and most necessary'. And while the religious messages about sex pulled this way and that, the increasingly influential texts of the ancient

Greeks added further layers of complexity, claiming that regular sex was essential for male health but warning of dire consequences for those who overindulged. Good sex, they said, promoted good digestion and appetite, it made the body light and nimble, opened the pores and purged the phlegm. Minds became quicker when sex was properly partaken of; sadness, madness and melancholy were driven away. Yet bad sex brought terrible weakness of both body and mind, sapping the strength and dragging a man down to the level of common beasts. Meanwhile, women, as creatures dominated by the cold, wet, phlegmatic humour, were possessed of a great hunger for sex, an uncontrollable urge for the hot essence of a man. However lusty a man was, he had the strength of mind to control his appetites, but women were weak.

Such ideas were not just a matter for debate, but influenced the sexual behaviours, as well as the thoughts, of the whole population in one form or another. Most people married. Even in the late fifteenth century when Catholic opinions about the value of celibacy were still unchallenged, the number of people who followed the rule – clergy, scholars and members of religious orders – was fairly small, numbering in the thousands in a population of around 2.5 million. Indeed, marriage was often seen as essential for full adulthood and a public place in society. The unmarried man of fifty was as much a spare part and slight embarrassment as the unmarried woman of the same age. Neither could head up a household. On a purely practical basis, a lone man or woman suffered from a simple labour-and-skills shortage, unable to carry out both male and female roles. Men needed a woman to cook, brew, manage the dairy, the poultry and the laundry, and tend the garden, regardless of any childcare that may have been needed. Women needed a man to plough and tend the fields, take care of the sheep or ply a trade. No single man could take on an apprentice to his trade or stand for local public office. The unmarried were considered to be foot-loose; with few responsibilities or ties, they lived in a half-world as temporary members of other people's households. Their lack of sexual experience, although seen as eminently respectable, was nonetheless often a cause for amused glances.

Sex was central to marriage: without consummation a union could be annulled; within a successful marriage sex was a glue that bound a couple together, smoothed over arguments and fostered love and patience. 'The wise man maye not be contented with his Spouse's virginitie,' wrote Edmund Tilney, 'but little and little must presently procure that he maye also steale away hir private will, and appetite, so that two bodies there maye be made one onely heart.' Marriage, said Tilney and a host of other authors of advice books, could be difficult and had to weather many storms. It needed to be strong if the health, wealth and happiness of not only the two partners but their children, servants and wider families were to be maintained. The pleasures of the marriage bed could help to create deep feelings of love and respect that could be drawn upon when the going got tough. When rifts occurred, the same physical closeness helped to re-establish a cooperative and supportive environment. The anonymous *Tales and Quick Answers, Very Mery, and Pleasant to Rede* (1567), for example, tells of the widow who wanted a husband, 'not for the nice play' but more as a business partner to protect her in a world of men, but when her friend found a suitable but impotent candidate she rejected him: 'yet I will that my husband shall have that, where with we may be reconciled, if we fall at variance.'

Sex within marriage was viewed across society as a positive experience – a private act, but one with a public function as it benefited the whole of society by promoting harmony and marital stability. Within this notion lay the assumption that both partners would find pleasure. The Tudors did not imagine that one partner in bed at night would take the active role and the other simply lie back and 'think of England'. Sex was enjoyable, something to be looked forward to by the young and as yet unmarried, and something that both men and women had a right to expect. Young couples were advised not to short-change their partners in this aspect of married life. As *The Art of Love* (1598) recommends: 'chuse not a man either too yong, or over wearied with yeres: for no age can be more successful in loving, than when a man is in the state of firme strength and abilitie: which being already spent and gone in old men, makes them unapt or incapable of those sweet pastimes the case of love requires.' Satisfying your spouse sexually was a marital duty. The dangers associated with failing in your sexual duties were the stuff of popular farce. The somewhat misogynistic anony-mous text entitled *The Deceyte of Women* (1557) is a collection of tales very much in the popular tradition about women lying and cheating and frequently taking lovers behind their husbands' backs. But although it returns again and again to the theme of women as being morally corrupt, men who are deceived by them are treated with little sympathy. 'And if my lorde had biden at home peradventure the woman had never fallen to that' is one conclusion: a wife left with no one to fill her bed would find another to do his duty. Another of the tales describes how 'the two lovers gon to bed together and lovingly have helsed and kissed eche other laborynge so sore that they both did swete in obtaining thyr lovely purpose': a vigorous mutual enjoyment of an illicit liaison. Many of the tales in this and similar collections feature old men and young wives, a shorthand perhaps for sexu-ally inactive husbands. The man whose wife took a lover was a 'cuckold', a laughing stock, a weak and ineffectual figure whose lack of sexual activity within the marital bed was seen as a major factor in leading his wife to stray. Those ancient Greek ideas about the sexual appetites of cold, wet, phlegmatic women desirous of men's hot seed are being played out within these tales.

Medically, sex was understood in terms of the four humours. A man's seed, it was thought, arose within his body as a natural result of the digestive process. At the third concoction a portion of blood, unnecessary for other bodily health and functions, was set aside and changed within his testicles from blood to semen. Medical opinion varied about the equivalent for women. Some believed that within women blood from the third concoction was held in the womb in order to nourish any child that might be conceived, naturally flowing away monthly if not required. Others believed that while some blood from the second concoction undertook this function, a few precious drops from the third concoction went to the female testicles inside the body and formed female semen. In all versions sexual appetite was therefore closely connected with an appetite for food and especially with red meat, sugar and wine, which were considered to be the richest and most nutritious foodstuffs. Those whose humoral balance was most inclined towards the sanguine, or blood humour, were likely to have the most sexual appetite, a belief that put the focus of attention upon young men, especially those with brown hair and ruddy complexions. The seasons could also exert an influence upon desire. During the colder months of the year, people dressed warmly and the body naturally closed up the pores of the skin, holding in the heat of the body, which led in turn to a better, fuller process of digestion. Better digestion produced more blood, giving the testicles more to work on and more reason to seek an outlet for the resultant sperm. Those wishing to damp down the fires of lust were advised to eat sparingly, avoid red meat and not bundle themselves up too much, but rather throw off the bedcovers and encourage a bit of shivering. Hard physical labour, which drew blood away from the testicles in order to fuel the muscles, could be useful, and there was always prayer to aid chaste living.

Physicians fell into two rough camps in their views on sexual anatomy: those who held that a woman's womb was simply the field into which the man's seed fell, nurturing the growing child but not providing any original part of it; and those who thought that conception required the mingling of two seeds, one male and one female. They all agreed that male sexual organs consisted of his yard (penis) and testicles. The change within the testes of blood into semen could be promoted by 'chafing', and when they were full and a man's thoughts were turned to lust by the company of women his yard would be inflated by the wind within (wind-inducing foods such as beans are often at the centre of ribald humour). Eight or nine inches was considered to be a healthy size. The foreskin, described as 'double' and 'moveable' in Thomas Vicary's *The Englishman's Treasurie* (1587), was believed to help the semen gather together and be 'cast forth by the testicles; for by him is had the more delectation in the doing'. Pleasure was understood to be fundamental to the ability of a man to procreate, and the foreskin heightened that pleasure, ensuring prompt and full ejaculation. Circumcision would have been an anathema to the Tudor mind.

The way in which sexual anatomy was believed to work could alter sexual behaviour, too. Perhaps most important to many people was the idea that the right and left testicles could produce different seed. It was believed that the right-hand testicle received blood more directly from the heart, so this was more likely to produce male seed, while the left-hand testicle, with a weaker blood supply, was more likely to produce female seed. A couple wishing to conceive a boy child could therefore imagine that their chances would be improved if a ribbon was tied around the left testicle during intercourse, preventing female seed from entering the fray.

The confusion surrounding female anatomy meant that some people could interpret the feminine role within intercourse as essentially passive, with the woman's enjoyment of the act simply preparing the ground within her womb for the male seed to fall on; or if it was held that her seed was required, her pleasure had to be sufficient to stimulate the release of that seed. For those who considered a woman to have seed, the female genitals were believed to mimic the male's in shape, the vagina taking the same form as a man's penis and two testicles nestling at the top of the vagina near the mouth of the womb, as if a man's genitals had been simply popped up inside, rather than hanging down on the outside of the body. Whereas a man's seed was observed to be hot, white and thick, that of a woman was described as thinner, colder and feebler.

The Church's position on marriage laid strong emphasis upon the role of sex for purposes of procreation. The godly and moral were encouraged to use sexual practices that promoted conception, and if conception required a female orgasm then a couple who dedicated time and attention to the pleasure of both were able to feel that they were carrying out God's work. Sexual positions could also be influenced by medical theory. Just as the right testicle, receiving the purer blood, was believed to produce male sperm, the right side of the womb was considered to be more receptive to the male seed, and maintaining a suitable position during intercourse so that the seed would naturally fall to this side of the womb was seen as another determining factor in fixing the sex of any potential child. If, however, a couple had intercourse while standing upright, the seed would surely simply fall to the base of the womb and drain out as the man withdrew. Naturally, upright sex was therefore deemed morally reprehensible, but it also appears to have made it popular among those partaking of illicit couplings, who thought that it would prevent unwanted pregnancies. Rather depressingly, a belief that you are unable to get pregnant if you have intercourse standing up is still erroneously repeated among young people today. Moreover, there was one extremely negative consequence of the medical orthodoxies of the day: if a woman was pregnant, the sex that led to conception must have been consensual, indeed pleasurable for the woman; no rape charge could stand.

Sexual language had a strong place within both popular and elite culture, although there were those whose sensibilities led them to silence. Christopher Langton, in his 1545 guide to human anatomy, stated that he was not going to mention the generative organs at all, since he had no wish to inflame 'wanton youth'. Others writing for publication chose their words with care and used a range of euphemisms, but it's clear from slander cases that the language on the street was far less restrained and the poems that circulated in private manuscripts among men at court were frequently heavily and openly sexual. Thomas Nashe, for example, in a handwritten manuscript that circulated among educated gentlemen for several years before 1598, writes:

Softlie my fingers, up theis curtaine, heave
And make me happie stealing by degreese.
First bare hir legs, then creepe up to hir kneese.
From thence ascend unto her mannerly thigh.
(a pox on lingering when I am so nighe)
Smock climbe a-pace, that I may see my joyes.
[. . .]
I kisse, I clap, I feele, I view at will
Yet dead he lyes not thinking good or ill.
Unhappie me, quoth she, and wilt' not stand?
Com, let me rub and chafe it with my hand.
[. . .]
Not ceasing till she rais'd it from his swoune.
And then he flue on hir as he were wood,

And on hir breech did thack, and foyne a-good;
He rubd', and prickt, and pierst hir to the bones,
Digging as farre as eath he might for stones.
[. . .]
With Oh, and Oh, she itching moves hir hipps
And to and fro, full lightlie starts and skips.
She jerks hir legs, and sprauleth with hir heeles . . .

Though this is describing an encounter with a prostitute, it is a tale of mutual energetic pleasure, replete with graphic description.

Less literary, but just as explicit, were the words of Ann Symes in 1586 when she stood up in church and proclaimed that the parson, Mr Lisbye:

hast most shamefully committed carnall copulation with me and hast occupied me dyvers and sundrye tymes as namely twise in one Treales house a cook by Pye Corner and there thow gavest money to the mayd to kepe the dore whilst thow didst occupye me and another tyme at the sign of the black lyon without bishoppsgate and divers other tymes since thow hast had thy pleasure in use of me and in occupying me thow didst use me more ruffianlike than honstlye.

While openly and publicly describing her sex life – much more publicly than Thomas Nashe – Ann Symes uses much less positive language. The descriptions she gives of their intercourse all imply a very male agency and a very passive female involvement. He 'occupies', 'uses' and 'takes his pleasure' of her. Whatever the truth of the dynamic of their relationship, this particular piece of public talk about sex reveals a social pressure upon women to present illicit sex as being an unequal activity. Since this is not a sanctioned series of sexual encounters, as procreation was not the primary purpose, mutual sexual pleasure loses its moral standing. Here we are hearing people speaking of shameful sex, and it is a story constructed in terms of weak women giving way, of an inability to control themselves in the face of male desire.

The consequences of being exposed as an indulger in unauthorized sex were considerably worse for women than for men. Punishments meted out by the courts focused heavily upon the women, and the public shame was longer lasting and more severe. We can see, therefore, a certain defensiveness in the presentation of Ann's experiences for a public hearing. If society generally believed that both sexes derived pleasure from sex, they also considered sexual misbehaviour to be very much worse when committed by women than by men. A double standard was firmly in place. A man describing his own misconduct could be boastful about his prowess and appetite; a woman sought to find extenuating circumstances and to downplay the element of choice in her actions.

Various sexual insults were bandied about the streets, insults that landed their speakers in court precisely because they caused so much private hurt and public damage: 'whore' and 'harlot', for example, meaning a female prostitute; 'jade', 'strumpet' and 'queane', which generally applied to a woman who had sex outside marriage but not necessarily for money; 'cuckold', the husband of an unfaithful wife; 'bawd', a pimp arranging paid sexual liaisons; and 'knave', a man with no morals. These insults were a public performance of sexual language in an arena of conflict and aggression. Less fraught discussions of sex made fun of 'smellsmocks', who sniffed after ladies' underwear, and used words like 'trulls' and 'Jills' as less loaded terms for prostitutes. Descriptions of sex as 'bed sports' and 'tilling the fields of Venus', and the phrase 'nice play' we met earlier, offer a more positive view of sex and a view that encompasses both male and female enthusiasm.

People talked about sex in a wide variety of ways and in many different contexts. Jokes and popular ballads employed a range of slang terms and euphemisms such as 'secret parts', 'pie', 'corner', 'case', 'flower', 'plum', 'hole' or 'pond' for a vagina, and 'shaft', 'tool', 'cock', 'prick' or 'horn' for a penis. Many of these have continued in use down to the present day. Prostitutes, in addition to being whores, harlots, trulls and Jills, could be described as geese, mackerel and drabs, and 'to make a fist' could mean to masturbate as well as to punch someone. Such talk could even be employed in highly respectable and respectful contexts, such as the 1554 ballad in celebration of Queen Mary's announcement of pregnancy, 'The Ballad of Joy', which includes the line 'And that noble blossome, that is planted to springe'.

Not everyone was delighted with the widespread use of explicit or suggestive language, however. In 1570 Thomas Brice wrote a ballad decrying the fact, using the same medium – the cheap, popular, printed ballad sheet – as the literature that he sought to censure: 'What means the rimes that run thus large in every shop to sell? With wanton sound and filthie sense.' A wanton sound with a filthy sense was indeed to be found in the plentiful cheap print of the age. Take, for example, the ballad 'How a Bruer Meant to Make a Cooper Cuckold'. The brewer and the cooper's wife are caught when the cooper returns home early. The wife hides her lover beneath an upturned tub and tries to disguise the noise and prevent her husband from looking beneath it by claiming to have a pig trapped there. After several verses about different types of pig and what to do with them, all punning on the idea of a pig as a sexually overactive animal that wallows in filth, the brewer is finally discovered and a financial solution is negotiated: 'The bruer shall pay for using my vat.' The ballad is all innuendo, allowing it to be enjoyed in mixed company.

274 How to Be a Tudor

Far more open in its intent is the extremely popular ballad 'Watkins Ale', referred to in many other works of literature:

There was a maid this other day
And she woulds need go forth to play
And as she walked she sithd and said
I am afraid to die a maid.
[. . .]
For I will, without faile
Mayden, give you Watkins Ale
Watkins Ale, good sir quoth she
What is that I pray you tel me?
Tis sweeter farre than sugar fine
And pleasanter than muskadine.
[. . .]
He took this mayden then aside
And led her where she was not spyde
And told her many a pretty tale
And gave her well of Watkins Ale.

Much of the enduring appeal of this ballad stems from its gradual exposure of the true nature of 'Watkins Ale', a brew that eventually leads the maiden, nine months later, to motherhood. Much less appealing to modern sensibilities is the ballad 'Pinning the Basket', wherein a bossy wife is forced to have sex by her husband, with subsequent verses describing the same outcome for further reluctant wives. 'Basket' is yet another term for a vagina, and the introduction of a pin hardly needs any explanation:

The basket, Dame;
Goe, gossip, give it hym, and see
You pinne the same
Tantara, tara, tantara

Now doth the sport beginner,
Knowe thou, quoth she, sir, knave that I
The basket will not pinne!
[. . .]
Then with a bastian that stood by
Which he did smell
At her he freely did let flie
And bumde her well
Tantara, tara, tantara
Unguentum bakaline
Did make the housewife quickly pinne
The basket passing fine.

The tune that this ballad was set to was one generally used for martial themes emphasizing the aggression and combative sexual victory of husband over wife.

A society-wide approval for mutually enjoyable sex within marriage, and a robust tradition of songs, jokes, stories and poems about sex, did not, however, translate into unrestrained sexual activity. Illegitimacy rates throughout the period and across the nation remained low. The accusations of whoredom and harlotry that brought so many people to court on charges of slander were effective insults because the behaviour they described was so strongly disapproved of. Those convicted by the Church courts of adultery and other sexual transgressions were forced to undergo very public shaming rituals, kneeling week after week in front of the whole community during church services wearing nothing but their underwear and holding a lighted taper, in addition frequently to corporal punishment.

Illicit sex offended against the Tudor idea of society in two major ways, one religious and one practical. Those whose transgression involved both could expect the severest response. All sexual activity outside marriage was condemned by the Church.

Even thoughts and dreams were branded 'unclean' and were to be striven against. Thomas Becon's *Homilies against Whoredom* (1560), for example, exhorts people to turn to prayer and fasting to clean their minds of thoughts offensive to God. It calls upon multiple biblical examples of the punishment of the sexually lax and on the frequent praise heaped in Scripture upon chastity and purity. Nor, he says, is it enough to guard against sexual misdemeanours individually: since God punishes whole communities for moral failings, it is therefore the duty of Christians to guard the morals of their family and neighbours. As far as the Church was concerned, all sexual misbehaviour was lumped together as an evil. There was no scale of wickedness, with one illicit practice being better or worse than another. Instead moral failure was graded upon the frequency of transgression. A person who sinned once and repented was in a different category from one who sinned repeatedly. However, once you had stepped over the boundary of chastity (married sex counted as chaste), one practice or behaviour was deemed to merge into another. Such views were clearly in operation when a woman who took a lover was called a whore. If she had stepped beyond chastity for one, then she would clearly have no qualms about having sex with all and sundry for financial gain. The man who took a mistress would not restrain himself from taking male lovers too.

Upon the practical side of the equation was both the spread of venereal disease and, more important to the authorities, children born out of wedlock. Children without legal fathers were a drain upon the communities' resources. The structure of Tudor society, which concentrated resources in male hands, made it virtually impossible for a woman to bring up a child without the financial support of a man, or, in his absence, the support of the parish. Parish rates (local taxation) were very visibly tied to the number of poor people within the parish requiring assistance, a fact that made the rate payers extremely keen to prevent

the birth of illegitimate children. Responsible community leaders were thus being told both by the Church and by their
neighbours that sexual transgression within the community was
a major problem on several levels. The well-run community
needed to educate its members upon their moral sexual duties,
and to police and to punish those who failed to meet the prescribed levels of chastity. Social supervision of an individual's
sex life was the norm.

Prostitution was perceived as an urban phenomenon. Within
the countryside there were of course women who were willing
through choice or desperation to grant sexual favours in
exchange for goods or cash, but there was little chance for such
activities to support even the most meagre of lifestyles. Too few
clients and plenty of watchful neighbours made the villages of
Britain the venue for only occasional transgression, places of
adulterous lovers and the hurried marriage of maidens, rather
than sustained economic activity. London, however, had a large
and shifting population that drew in a continuous supply of
young people far from their families. It was easier to fall between
the cracks, to find yourself alone and friendless. Judith Taylor,
for example, had come up to London from Essex looking for
opportunities, as many did. In 1575 she found herself lame, out
of work and homeless, sleeping under a market stall in
Shoreditch. It was in desperation, she said to the overseers at
Bridewell, that she had gone with Thomas Smith. The fluidity
of the London population also made it easier to cover your
tracks, to escape at least some of the shame. Alice Partridge was
told to change her name by the bawd who arranged liaisons for
her, 'saying else it would be a discredit unto her'. London was
also where the wealthiest clients were to be found. In 1598 Alice
was sent to Mr Brooke, along with another woman, Barbara
Allen, who earned thirty shillings from the encounter. The
bawd took half, but that still left Barbara with more money than

some maidservants earned in a year (although they did get board and lodgings as well as the cash). Mr Brooke was a rich and powerful man, brother to Lord Cobham, and the prospect of such partners could be a draw. Alice, who had been dismissed from the eminently respectable Lady Margaret Hoby's service for the poor standard of her work, had actively sought the bawd out, and her mother had accompanied her. This, then, if not her first choice of lifestyle, was not the last-ditch desperation of Judith Taylor.

The authorities ran periodic crackdowns upon prostitution. According to *A Chronicle* (1503), written by Richard Arnold, in 1474 the Lord Mayor 'dyd diligent & sharp correccion upon Venus' servauntys, and cawsid theym to be garnyssheid & theyr mynstralsy before them'. London had its own public shaming rituals for dealing with prostitution, which involved the wearing of distinctive clothing (for more on which see below) and a parade through the streets while speeches were made to explain their moral failings, something that continued to be part of the official response to moral transgressions for the whole of the Tudor period. The crackdown of 1474 seems to have caught at least sixty people in its net, many of whom were also banished from the city at the end of the shaming ritual. The punishment of five women in 1529 is described in more detail:

> The said persones shalbe conveyd from the Countor to Newgate wt mynstralsye that ys to say wt panes & basones ryngynge before theym and they to were ray hod & to have in their hand whyte roddes in tokyn of comyn bawd, strumpet & harlot; and so from thens to be conveyed to the Standerd in Chepe and there this proclamacon to be made, and so to be conveyd through Chepe into Cornehill and there to stoned under the pyllarye duryng this proclamacon, and from thens to be conveyd to Algate and there to be banished the citie for ev.

Dressed in striped hoods, they were to tour the city preceded by people banging on saucepans to draw attention. At each stop on the route they had to stand in the pillory, where citizens were encouraged to throw things at them – often stones – while a list of their crimes was read out. Finally, bloodied, with insults ringing in their ears, they were thrown out of the city, homeless. By the time Judith Taylor was prosecuted for prostitution in 1575 the striped hoods had gone and the pillory had been replaced with a whipping, but there was still a procession through the streets tied to the back of a cart.

Not all prostitution received this type of treatment. For the first half of the Tudor era, licensed brothels operated at Southwark under the jurisdiction of the Bishop of Winchester, outside the control of the London authorities and with rents and licence fees bringing in an income for the diocese – until they were finally closed down in 1546, when concerns about the spread of venereal diseases, especially syphilis, and yet another outbreak of plague finally tipped the balance against them. Later on, wealthy and powerful clients could offer a degree of protection to favoured brothels. Licensed premises catered primarily for the wealthier sections of society, providing an outlet for lawyers, gentlemen at court and a few clergy. The women who worked within them were generally well dressed and able to mimic the social niceties of the elite. An account recorded in the 1598 Bridewell court minute book describes a bawdy house run by Mistress Hibbens, who 'hath always lying in her house, ready of her owne, diverse suits of apparel for women, viz sylke gowns of several colours, as also silke rashe gownes and other stuff gownes, peticotes of durance with two or three yards of velvet as also smockes of holland'. When clients wished to have sex with a 'gentlewoman', she sent for one of her girls and completely redressed her to suit.

Elizabeth Kirkeman's description of her time at Gilbert East's brothel in the 1570s tells a similar tale of silk gowns and velvet gaskins kept on the premises for 'gentlemen and wealthy folk'. This was a brothel that accepted common men when the wealthy were not forthcoming ('when there was not other to serve, many prentices came thither', Kirkeman said), but significantly it was not while she worked in this establishment with its infrequent wealthy clients that she was arrested, but later, when she worked in a much humbler establishment whose clientele consisted of 'divers serving men, blackamores and other persons', without anyone who could have offered protection from the authorities. More exposed still were those who worked on the streets, where vagrancy was added to the list of crimes they were committing in the eyes of the law.

With all extramarital sex lumped together in one category called 'debauchery', the desire for one's own sex received little separate attention. There was no concept of homosexuality, only a division between the chaste and unchaste. It is clear from period sermons that the sins of Sodom and Gomorrah were frequently interpreted as general sexual laxity, incest, rape, bestiality, homosexuality, heterosexual anal sex and adultery, all wrapped up together. Thomas Becon's *Homilies against Whoredom*, for example, describes the sins of these two cities as 'whoredom and uncleaness', and the 1570 ballad 'The Horrible and Woeful Destruction of Sodome and Gomorra' highlights the sexual sins of the whole population: 'he did rebuke theer noughty lives, both yong and olde, both men and wives.' Only Lot and his family are to be saved because Lot is the one just man. Yet in the ballad even his daughters seek to tempt him with sexual sin:

> Loe wanton Girles which so doth burne,
> In venus pleasant games,
> If that they may content their turns,
> And eake the youthful flames,

They do desire their fathers bed,
The cankered flesh to please . . .

Here sodomy takes the form of incest. In 'Satire 4' (1597), John Donne's description of the debauched courtier 'who loves whores, . . . boys and . . . goats' is another example of this blended understanding of unchaste behaviour.

Aside from the moral and medical issues, the practical problems that could arise from illicit heterosexual transgression – namely pregnancy and financially unsupported children – tended to concentrate official attention primarily upon the behaviour of unmarried women. Of secondary interest to the authorities was the misbehaviour of married women, since the child of a married woman, howsoever conceived, was the responsibility of her husband, relieving the parish of the financial burden of the child's upbringing. Same-sex affairs, which carried far less potential for illegitimate children and marital breakdown, might have seemed to many to have been an even lesser social evil. Sex between two women does seem to have fallen into this category, receiving very little attention in either popular or elite writings and no attention at all from the courts. However, such a practical outlook has to be balanced against the universal expressions of abhorrence and disgust that erupted whenever male homosexual behaviour was discussed. Male homosexual behaviour seemed to threaten the natural order of society; it was something associated with a wide range of dangerous and anti-social activities, and it was believed that it could draw down the wrath of God upon the entire nation, just as it had for the biblical cities of Sodom and Gomorrah.

Sex between two men became illegal, rather than just being seen as immoral, when Henry VIII became head of the Church of England and Wales and began to see the law as a way of expressing his moral duty to lead his country to a more godly state. The penalty stated was death. Yet confusion abounded. There was no specific description of what sodomy was. People found it hard to know whether the specific activities taking place constituted an act of sodomy. On another level, the unde-fined nature of the sin led to an inflation of its evil in diatribes and sermons alike, associating it with heresy, popery and even werewolves. Such extremes were difficult to align with real-world actions by perfectly ordinary people. Those who took part in male homosexual behaviour, as well as their friends, colleagues and neighbours, could simply fail to see the connec-tion between that which was condemned and that which formed part of daily life. There is also the possibility that as the poten-tial consequences of an accusation were so severe, many who might have spoken out held their tongues.

Prosecutions were extremely rare, and even accusations are hard to find. The only case to arise at the University of Cam-bridge during the Tudor era, for example, was that of Robert Hutton, a Fellow of Trinity College, in 1589. Even after the Ref-ormation, scholars were required to remain celibate and lived in male-only institutions. Here, then, one might expect to find more references than usual to homosexual relations. Walter Las-sells, one of Hutton's students, alleged that Hutton had 'committed most unnaturall sinnes and abuses with and against the bodies of Martin Turner, Henry Wharton and my selfe'. Robert Hutton counter-sued for defamation of character and won considerable damages from all three students. The allega-tion had followed on from a previous one brought by Walter Lassells that Robert Hutton had been seen 'hard at yt' with his maid, Ann House. Whatever the truth about the protagonists' various sex lives, the reluctance of the authorities to take allega-tions of homosexual activity seriously is evident, as is Walter Lassells's belief that one sort of transgressive act of sex does not rule out another form. In 1541 the headmaster of Eton, Nicholas

Udall, was accused of having sex with a former pupil during an investigation into the theft of some silver. He was dismissed and imprisoned briefly for the theft, but there was no further action concerning the sex and Udall returned to teaching. Mr Cooke was also a schoolmaster in trouble in 1594 as 'a man of beastly behaviour amongst his scholars'. He failed to turn up when the case was heard at the ecclesiastical court and the matter was simply dropped. Meanwhile, both John Donne and John Marston refer to male prostitution in London in their writings. In 'Satire 1' Donne writes:

> But, in rank itchy lust, desire and love
> The nakedness and bareness to enjoy
> Of thy plump muddy whore or prostitute boy.

John Marston's *Scourge of Villanie* (1598) condemned 'male stews', meaning male brothels. Yet the courts are again largely silent on this matter. Men are prosecuted and punished for evil living, vagrancy, pimping and keeping bawdy houses but not for homosexuality. Even the slander cases reveal few accusations of it, and where slang is prolific in its descriptions of sex in general, there are few specific terms or phrases for same-sex activity. Homosexual behaviour, both male and especially female, barely makes it into the historical record.

The boundary between good sex (that within marriage) and bad sex (that outside of it) seems very clear-cut, but in practice there were several areas of uncertainty. As we have mentioned before, heterosexual anal sex was sometimes lumped in with other actions as sodomy, and this would have applied in some minds to anal sex within marriage. Oral sex, too, could provoke feelings of unease. The strict definition of sex within marriage as lawful and chaste required the act to be employed for procreation. Both oral and anal sex failed to meet this criterion. Moreover, anal sex for many mimicked animal sex: it was 'bestial', and the word 'bestiality' included this meaning along with sex between human and animal.

However, while couples may or may not have worried about such things in private, a much more public area of uncertainty arose from the question 'Are we married?' This was not always obvious. Even today we have two possible moments that could be taken as full marriage: at the end of the religious ceremony when the spiritual leader declares the marriage made, and the legal moment when the marriage register is signed and witnessed. Tudor marriage left much more room for doubt and question. The Church, having largely ignored marriage contracts in its early history, had been pressing from the late Middle Ages onwards for marriage to become the prerogative of the Church, but although by the Tudor period they had mostly brought people to the church door for a religious ceremony, they did not yet have a monopoly. A marriage was legal and binding if each partner said words to the effect of 'I marry you'. Witnesses to these words were helpful but not legally essential, and the union did have to be consummated if it was not to be annulled. If the words said amounted to 'I will marry you' in the future tense, then a betrothal had occurred rather than a marriage. Betrothals could be seen as conditional or, especially if sexual intercourse happened, as binding contracts. None of this had to take place in church or with any clerical involvement, and none of it needed any written record. The contracting of marriage could thus be open to a good deal of confusion, claim and counterclaim.

The case of Alice Cheeseman in 1570 shows some of this ambiguity and tension in action. Alice and Mr Cheeseman appear to have made a private promise to one another and to have had sexual intercourse before revealing their marriage to the wider community and attempting to arrange a formal marriage in church. Her friends and neighbours seem to have been horrified at the thought of the match. Richard Coste, a witness in the case, reported that:

> many of the cheefest of the parish councelled her to leave him because the parishioners mislyked of Cheeseman. The which they would not have done without goodwill borne to the woman for her good behaviour before that time . . . saith that although she did offend in carnallye knowing Cheeseman before marriage notwithstanding she made as he thinketh in recompence in that she being persuaded to forsake him bye her friends, she ever said that she should have him and in respecte also that she hath reconciled herself to god and the world by marrying her husband.

There are two competing visions of what constituted marriage evident here. As far as Alice is concerned she is already married, but the wider parish community feel that it is not yet certain until a public ceremony has occurred. To one group of people she and Cheeseman have sexually sinned, while they themselves believe that they have consummated a legitimate union, as can be seen in Alice's reported speech about 'marrying her husband'.

Most marriages at every level of society were preceded by a courtship phase with gifts exchanged and practical and financial details hammered out between the couple, their parents and wider networks of friends and family. Young men were the most prolific gift-givers, although young women also reciprocated to some degree. Presents of small sums of money were particularly common. In court cases they are described as 'tokens' of love rather than financial assistance. Gloves were also common gifts – they were given out at weddings and funerals as well as during courtship, and seem to have signified remembrance and affection. These, then, made good personal gifts but were suitable at the beginning of a relationship when relations were still a little tentative and more formal. The giving of a ring was a more intimate gesture. Rings, like gloves, had many gift-giving roles within society, but where a pair of gloves might be given to a wide circle of friends a ring was reserved only for those closest, whether they were memorial rings bequeathed to a particularly close friend or immediate family member or lovers' tokens. The giving and receiving of such gifts was often cited as proof of intent in contested marriage negotiations. Refusing or returning such gifts was a powerful statement that feelings or circumstances were unfavourable.

Practical considerations about setting up home and financing the household applied to every prospective union, often drawing in a wide network of parents, masters, friends and wider kin groups to the discussions. Agreements had to be reached; occasionally it was possible for those agreements to include only the couple themselves, but most people needed the support of those around them. At some point in this process promises were made in private, and then more publicly before witnesses. Ideally all of this culminated in a public ceremony at church, with consummation following on soon afterwards. It is clear, however, from the intervals between church ceremonies and the birth of a first child that many people considered sex to be permissible at earlier stages in the process. The custom in Yorkshire appears to have been particularly favourable towards couples who went ahead with sexual relations once a betrothal had been announced. Where a firm commitment to marry had been made and indeed went on to be contracted, considerable leeway could be afforded by many communities. As many as a third of Yorkshire brides were pregnant on the day of the church ceremony. Such custom made a promise of marriage tantamount to marriage itself. Broken promises could be a disaster, and people who tried to pull away could find themselves under severe social pressure.

The wills of the prosperous men of Monmouthshire in Wales

are distinctive when compared with those of English counties for their tolerance of certain types of heterosexual relationships outside of marriage. Among the vast collection of wills surviving from the county of Essex, for example, it is rare to find any reference to a bequest to an illegitimate child. Baptismal records show a small but steady trickle of such births, but by their very nature these children were ignored by their fathers. The public shame of bastardy created further pressure upon will writers to hide the existence of their illegitimate children from view, to turn their backs and pretend that such youthful indiscretions had never occurred. The will of Watkyn Thomas of Chepstow in Monmouthshire, however, who died in 1576, exhibits no such tendency: 'To John Watkyn my base son, son of Alice Philpott, my two tenements of land in Gotreye. To Anne Jones my wife £10. To William Watkyn my base son, son of Katherine Saunders, £10' (the word 'base' is used for illegitimate). The rest of his goods are split between maidservants, niece, brother and nephew. Watkyn Thomas's sex life was evidently not confined to the marriage bed, nor was he ashamed of openly acknowledging the fact. Both boys born out of wedlock carried his name. The family of Thomas Jones of Newport was similarly mixed: Thomas Morgan, his eldest son, appears to have been legitimate, but Amye, Erasmus and Thomas are all described as base born. At their father's death in 1577 Amye was already married with five children of her own, while all his boys were still underage, so again his children seem to be the result of a series of relationships over many years. He splits his inheritance between them and Amye's children. In 1594 John Morice of Keven Llitha had at least five illegitimate daughters – Elizabeth, Alice, Elenor, Katherine and Anne – all of whom he left in the care of his wife, Gwenllian Jankin. The wording of his will is a little unclear, but a sixth daughter, Marye, married to John Beane, may have completed the family. John Morice held his daughters in such high regard that it is to Elizabeth, 'my second reputed daughter', that he leaves the rest of his estate and the responsibility for discharging his debts and legacies. Sir Charles Somerset had married his base daughter Christian off to his godson Charles Vaughan and in 1598 left them a house and garden along with substantial cash legacies for their four children, alongside the even larger legacies to his legitimate children.

These were all wealthy men, confident and secure in their position, but so too were many of those will writers of Essex. What we are seeing are the traces of a different attitude to marriage, sex and family. Roughly one in ten of the Elizabethan Monmouthshire wills make provision for named illegitimate children. Welsh traditions are exerting an influence over the personal behaviour of this elite group. Welsh law upon both marriage and inheritance had differed from English in the past, and although the Tudor dynasty had by this point introduced English law, older attitudes remained. A Welsh mistress was not a wife, but nonetheless her position was one that accorded her a better social position than that of an English mistress. Elite men could carry on long-term committed relationships with women of a lower social ranking, maintaining them usually in separate households while marrying a woman of higher rank who presided over the main family residence. The Church did not approve, and more 'modern' attitudes would in time prevail, but there was a grudging tacit approval for a form of concubinage. Children born of such a union were generally acknowledged and financially supported by their fathers. It may well have been the change from Welsh to English inheritance law in 1536 that provoked many of Monmouthshire's will writers to put pen to paper. The Welsh legal code had allowed for any acknowledged child to inherit; the English system permitted only legitimate children inheritance rights. These wills document the attempts of men to hold by the old codes of behaviour, to honour promises made or implied to women like Alice Philpott and Katherine Saunders to whom they could or would not offer marriage.

Whichever bed you had ended up in, it was finally time to go to sleep – lying on your right side was considered healthiest!

Bibliography

Adams, Simon (ed.), *Household Accounts and Disbursement Books of Robert Dudley, Earl of Leicester* (London, Cambridge University Press, 1995)

Alcager, Juan de, *Libro de Geometria Practica y Tracia* (Madrid, 1589)

Alcock, N. W., *Warwickshire Grazier and London Skinner 1532–1555: The Account Book of Peter Temple and Thomas Heritage* (London, Oxford University Press, 1981)

Ambler, R. W., and B. & L. Watkinson (eds.), *Farmers and Fishermen: The Probate Inventories of the Ancient Parish of Clee, South Humberside 1536–1742* (Hull, University of Hull, 1987)

Ann F. Sutton, 'Two Dozen and More Silkwomen of Fifteenth-century London', in *The Ricardian*, vol. 16 (2006)

Anon., *A Boke of Cokerye* (London, 1500)

Anon., *A Boke of Prayers called ye Ordynary Fashyon of good Lyvyng* (London, 1546)

Anon., *The Deceyte of Women* (London, 1557)

Anon., *Groundeworke of Conny-catching* (London, 1592)

Anon., *Here Begynneth a Lytell Boke Called Good Maners* (London, 1498)

Anon., *Liber Cure Cocorum* (Sloane Manuscript, 1586; edited by Richard Morris, 1862)

Anon., *A Manifest Detection of the Most Vyle and Detestable Use of Dice-play* (London, 1552)

Anon., *A Merry Jest of John Jonson and Jakaman his wife, Whose Jealousie was Justly the Cause of all their Strife* (London, 1586)

Anon., *The Most Renowned Venture of our Brave and Valiant Earl of Essex in the Downe Fall of Cales* (London, 1596)

Anon., *A Proper Newe Booke of Cokerye* (London, 1557)

Anon., *Tales and Quick Answers, Very Mery, and Pleasant to Rede* (London, 1567)

Arbeau, Thoinot, *Orchesography* (Langres, 1589)

Arnold, Janet,'The "pair of straight bodies" and "a pair of drawers" dating from 1603 which Clothe the Effigy of Queen Elizabeth I in Westminster Abbey', in *Costume* vol. 41 (Wakefield, Maney Publishing, 2007)

—, *Patterns of Fashion: The Cut and Construction of Clothes for Men and Women c.1560–1620* (London, Macmillan, 1985)

—, *Patterns of Fashion: The Cut and Construction of Linen Shirts, Smocks, Neckwear, Headwear and Accessories for Men and Women c.1540–1660* (London, Macmillan, 2008)

—, *Queen Elizabeth's Wardrobe Unlock'd* (Leeds, Maney Publishing, 1988)

Arnold, Richard, *A Chronicle* (London, 1503)

Ascham, Roger, *Toxophilus* (London, 1545)

Aydelotte, Frank, *Elizabethan Rogues and Vagabonds* (London, Frank Cass & Co, 1967)

Bales, Peter, *The Writing Schoolemaster* (London, 1590)

Bath, Michael, *Renaissance Decorative Painting in Scotland* (Edinburgh, National Museums of Scotland, 2003)

Beauchesne, John de, *A Booke Containing Diverse Sorts of Hands* (London, 1570)

Becon, Thomas, *Homilies: Against Whoredom* (London, 1560)

Berger, Ronald M., *The Most Necessary Luxuries: The Mercers' Company of Coventry 1550–1680* (Philidelphia, Pennsylvania State University Press, 1993)

Beza, Theodore, *Household Prayers* (London, 1603)

Biringuccio, Vannoccio, *Pirotechnia* (Venice, 1540)

Boorde, Andrewe, *A Compendyous Regiment of Healthe* (London, 1540)

Braithwaite, Richard, *Some Rules and Orders for the Government of the House of an Earl* (1603)

Bray, Alan, *Homosexuality in Renaissance England* (London, Gay Men's Press, 1982)

Brayshay, Mark, *Land Travel and Communications in Tudor and Stuart England: Achieving a Joined-up Realm* (Liverpool, Liverpool University press, 2014)

Brunscheig, Hieronymous, *Vertuous Boke of Distyllation* (London, 1527)

Buck, Anne, 'The Clothes of Thomasine Petre 1555–1559', in *Costume* vol. 24 (Leeds, Maney Publishing, 1990)

Bullein, William, *The Government of Health* (London, 1558)

Burch, C. E. C., *Minstrels and Players in Southampton 1428–1635* (Southampton, City of Southampton, 1969)

Buttes, Henry, *Diets Drie Dinner* (London, 1599)

Capp, Bernard, *When Gossips Meet: Women, Family and Neighbourhood in Early Modern England* (Oxford, Oxford University Press, 2003)

Cardano, Girolamo, *Liber de Ludo Aleae* (1564; first published Lyons, 1663)

Caroso, Fabritio, *Nobiltà di Dame* (Venice, 1600)

Chandler, John (ed.), *John Leland's Itinerary: Travels in Tudor England* (Stroud, Sutton Publishing, 1993)

Clopper, Lawrence M. (ed.), *Records of Early English Drama: Chester* (Manchester, Manchester University Press, 1979)

Cogan, Thomas, *The Haven of Health* (London, 1584)

Collinson, Patrick, *The Elizabethan Puritan Movement* (Oxford, Clarendon Press, 1967)

Cooper, Tarnya, *Citizen Portrait: Portrait Painting and the Urban Elite of Tudor and Jacobean England and Wales* (New Haven and London, Yale University Press, 2012)

Coote, Edmunde, *The English Schoolmaster* (London, 1596)

Copeland, Robert, *The Manner of Dauncynge Bace Daunces* (London, 1521)

—, *The Seven Sorrows that Women have when their Husbandes be Deade* (London, 1526)

Davies, Kathryne, *Artisan Art: Vernacular Wall Painting in the Welsh Marches 1550–1650* (Little Logaston, Logaston Press, 2008)

Dawson, Mark, *Plenti and Grase: Food and Drink in a Sixteenth-century Household* (Totnes, Prospect Books, 2009)

Dawson, Thomas, *The Good Housewife's Jewel* (London, 1596)

Dickerman, Susan, *Painted Prints: The Revelation of Color* (Philadelphia, Pennsylvania State University Press, 2002)

Dietz, Brian (ed.) *The Port and Trade of Early Elizabethan London Documents* (London, London Record Society, 1972)

Duffy, Eamon, *Marking the Hours* (New Haven and London, Yale University Press, 2006)

—, *The Stripping of the Altars: Traditional Religion in England 1400–1580* (New Haven and London, Yale University Press, 1992)

Dugen, Holly, *The Ephemeral History of Perfume* (Baltimore, John Hopkins University Press, 2011)

Durston, Christopher, and Jacqueline Eales (eds.), *The Culture of English Puritanism 1560–1700* (London, Macmillan, 1996)

Eccles, Christine, *The Rose Theatre* (London, Walker Books, 1990)

Edwards, Peter, *The Horse Trade of Tudor and Stuart England* (Cambridge, Cambridge University Press, 1988)

Elyot, Sir Thomas, *The Banket of Sapience* (London, 1534)

—, *The Boke Named the Governour* (London, 1531)

—, *The Castel of Helth* (London, 1534)

Emmison, F. G. (ed.), *Essex Wills: The Archdeaconry Courts 1577–1584* (Chelmsford, Essex Record Office, 1987)

—, *Essex Wills: The Archdeaconry Courts 1583–1592* (Chelmsford, Essex Record Office, 1989)

—, *Essex Wills: The Archdeaconry Courts 1591–1597* (Chelmsford, Essex Record Office, 1991)

—, *Essex Wills: The Archdeaconry Courts 1597–1603* (Chelmsford, Essex Record Office, 1990)

—, *Essex Wills: The Commissary Court 1558–1569* (Chelmsford, Essex Record Office, 1993)

—, *Essex Wills: The Commissary Court 1569–1578* (Chelmsford, Essex Record Office, 1994)

—, *Essex Wills: The Commissary Court 1578–1588* (Chelmsford, Essex Record Office, 1995)

Englefield, W. A. D., *The History of the Painter-Stainers Company of London* (London, Hazell, Watson & Viney Ltd, 1923)

Erasmus, Desiderius, *The Civilitie of Childehode* (London, 1530)

Fissell, Mary E., *Vernacular Bodies: The Politics of Reproduction in Early Modern England* (Oxford, Oxford University Press, 2004)

Fitzherbert, John, *The Boke of Husbandry* (London, 1533)

Foakes, R. A. (ed.) *Henslowe's Diary* (Cambridge, Cambridge University Press, 1982)

Fox, Adam, *Oral and Literate Culture in England 1500–1700* (Oxford, Oxford University Press, 2000)

Gardiner, Julie, and Michael J. Allen, *Before the Mast: Life and Death Aboard the Mary Rose* (Portsmouth, Mary Rose Trust, 2005)

Gent, Lucy, and Nigel Llewellyn (eds.), *Renaissance Bodies: The Human Figure in English Culture c.1540–1660* (London, Reaktion Books, 1990)

Gesner, Konrad, *The Newe Jewell of Health* (1576)

—, *The Treasury of Euonymous* (1559)

Gibson, Gail McMurray, *The Theater of Devotion: East Anglian Drama and Society in the Late Middle Ages* (London, University of Chicago Press, 1989)

Gibson, J. S. W. (ed.), *Banbury Wills and Inventories: Part One 1591–1620* (Banbury, Banbury Historical Society, 1985)

Gosson, Stephen, *Schoole of Abuse* (London, 1579)

Gowing, Laura, *Common Bodies: Women, Touch and Power in Seventeenth-century England* (New Haven and London, Yale University Press, 2003)

—, *Domestic Dangers: Women Words and Sex in Early Modern London* (Oxford, Clarendon Press, 1996)

Greene, Robert, *A Notable Discovery of Cozenage* (London, 1592)

Griffiths, Paul, Adam Fox and Steve Hindle (eds.), *The Experience of Authority in Early Modern England* (London, Macmillan, 1996)

Hacket, Thomas, *A Dairie Booke for Good Huswives* (London, 1588)

Hailwood, Mark, *Alehouses and Good Fellowship in Early Modern England* (Woodbridge, Boydell Press, 2014)

Hamling, Tara, *Decorating the Godly Household: Religious Art in Post-Reformation Britain* (New Haven and London, Yale University Press, 2010)

Hanawalt, Barbara A., *The Ties that Bound: Peasant Families in Medieval England* (Oxford, Oxford University Press, 1986)

Harman, Thomas, *Caveat for Common Cursitors* (London, 1567)

Harrison, William, *The Description of England* (London, 1587)

Harvey, Barbara, *Living and Dying in England 1100–1540* (Oxford, Clarendon Press, 1993)

Hayward, Maria, *Rich Apparel: Clothing and the Law in Henry VIII's England* (Farnham, Ashgate, 2009)

Hayward, Maria, *Dress at the Court of King Henry VIII* (Leeds, Maney Publishing, 2007)

Heal, Felicity, and Clive Holmes, *The Gentry in England and Wales 1500–1700* (London, Macmillan Press, 1994)

Hecatonphila, Alberti Leon Battista, *The Arte of Love* (London, 1598)

Heresbach, Conrad, *Foure Books of Husbandry* (London, 1577)

Howard, Helen, *Pigments of English Medieval Wall Painting* (London, Archetype Publications, 2003)

Hubbard, Eleanor, *City Women: Money, Sex and the Social Order in Early Modern London* (Oxford, Oxford University Press, 2012)

Huggett, Jane, 'Rural Costume in Elizabethan Essex: A Study Based on the Evidence of Wills', *in Costume* vol. 33 (Leeds, Maney Publishing, 1999)

Hunnisett, R. F. (ed.), *Sussex Coroners' Inquests 1552–1603* (London, Public Records Office, 1996)

Hutton, Ronald, *The Rise and Fall of Merry England: The Ritual Year 1400–1700* (Oxford, Oxford University Press, 1996)

Isaac, Veronica, 'Presuming Too Far "above his very base and low degree"?: Thomas Cromwell's Use of Textiles in his Schemes for

Social and Political Success (1527–1540)', in *Costume* vol. 45 (Wakefield, Maney Publishing, 2011)

Jones, Ann Rosalind, and Peter Stallybrass, *Renaissance Clothing and the Materials of Memory* (Cambridge, Cambridge University Press, 2000)

Jones, J. Gwynfor, *Early Modern Wales c.1525–1640* (London, Palgrave Macmillan, 1994)

Jones, Jeanne (ed.), *Family Life in Shakespeare's England: Stratford-upon-Avon, 1570–1630* (Stroud, Sutton Publishing, 1996)

Jones, Judith (ed.), *Monmouthshire Wills: Proved in the Prerogative Court of Canterbury 1560–1601* (Cardiff, South Wales Record Society, 1997)

Jones, Malcolm, *The Print in Early Modern England: An Historical Oversight* (New Haven and London, Yale University Press, 2010)

Kempe, William, *The Education of Children in Learning* (London, 1583)

Kent, Ann and Paul, *Cherwell Thy Wyne* (Dolmetsch Historical Dance Society, 2013)

Kerridge, Eric, *Trade and Banking in Early Modern England* (Manchester, Manchester University Press, 1988)

Lanfranco, *A Moste Excellent and Learned Woorke of Chirurgerie* (London, 1565)

Langton, Christopher, *An Introduction to Physicke* (London, 1545)

Lauze, F. de, *Apologie de la Danse* (1623)

Levey, Santina, 'References to Dress in the Earliest Account Book of Bess of Hardwick', in *Costume* vol. 34 (Leeds, Maney Publishing, 2000)

Machyn, Henry, *Diary of Henry Machyn: Citizen of London, 1550–1563* (edited by John Gough Nichols, New York and London, AMS Press, 1968)

Maltby, Judith, *Prayer Book and People in Elizabethan and Early Stuart England* (Cambridge, Cambridge University Press, 1998)

Man, Thomas, *A Glasse for Gamesters* (London, 1581)

Markham, Gervase, *The English Husbandman* (London, 1613)

—, *The English Huswife* (London, 1615)

Marsh, Christopher, *Popular Religion in Sixteenth-century England* (London, Macmillan, 1998)

Marston, John, *The Scurge of Villanie* (London, 1598)

Mascall, Leonard, *The First Booke of Cattell* (London, 1591)

McGowan, Margaret M., *Dance in the Renaissance* (New Haven and London, Yale University Press, 2008)

Montague, Anthony Viscount *A Booke of orders and Rules* (1595)

Moore, John S. (ed.), *The Goods and Chattels of our Forefathers: Frampton Cotterell and District Probate Inventories, 1539–1804* (London and Chichester, Phillimore & Co., 1976)

Moore, Norman, *The History of St Bartholomew's Hospital* (London, 1918)

Moulton, Thomas, *This is the Myrrour or Glasse of Helth* (London, 1545)

Mulcaster, Richard, *The First Part of the Elementarie* (London, 1582)

Muldrew, Craig, *Food, Energy and the Creation of Industriousness: Work and Material Culture in Agrarian England 1500–1780* (Cambridge, Cambridge University Press, 2011)

Nashe, Thomas, *The Anatomy of Absurdity* (London, 1589)

Nevile, Jennifer, 'Dance Steps and Music in the Gresley Manuscript', in *Historical Dance* vol. 3, no. 6 (Dolmetsch Historical Dance Society, 1999)

O'Hara, Diana, *Courtship and Constraint: Rethinking the Making of Marriage in Tudor England* (Manchester, Manchester University Press, 2000)

Overton, Mark, *Agricultural Revolution in England: The Transformation of the Agrarian Economy 1500–1850* (Cambridge, Cambridge University Press, 1996)

Oxley, James E., *The Fletchers and Longbowstringmakers of London* (London, Worshipful Company of Fletchers, 1968)

Partridge, John, *The Treasurie or Closet of Hidden Secrets* (London, 1573)

Pelling, Margaret, *The Common Lot: Sickness, Medical Occupations and the Urban Poor in Early Modern England* (London, Longman, 1998)

Pietsche, Johannes, 'The Burial Clothes of Margaretha Franziska de Lobkowitz 1617', in *Costume* vol. 42 (Wakefield, Maney Publishing, 2008)

Plat, Sir Hugh, *Delightes for Ladies* (London, 1603)

—, *The Jewel House of Art and Nature* (London, 1595)

Pollock, Linda A., *Forgotten Children: Parent–Child Relations from 1500 to 1900* (Cambridge, Cambridge University Press, 1983)

Rangstrom, Lena, *Modeljon Manlight Mode* (Stockholm, Liverustkammaren Bokforlaget Atlantis, 2003)

Reed, Michael (ed.), *The Ipswich Probate Inventories 1583–1631* (Woodbridge, Boydell Press, 1981)

Rhodes, Hugh, *The Boke of Nurture* (London, 1577)

Rosewell, Roger, *Medieval Wall Paintings* (Woodbridge, Boydell Press, 2008)

Scot, Reginald, *The Discoverie of Witchcraft* (London, 1584)

—, *A Perfite Platforme of a Hoppe Garden* (London, 1576)

Seager, F., *The School of Virtue* (London, 1534)

Sharpe, J. A., *Crime in Early Modern England 1500–1750* (New York and London, Longman Press, 1984)

Shepard, Alexandra, *Meanings of Manhood in Early Modern England* (Oxford, Oxford University Press, 2003)

Shepard, Alexandra, and Phil Withington (eds.), *Communities in Early Modern England* (Manchester, Manchester University Press, 2000)

Shuger, Debora Kuller, *Habits of Thought in the English Renaissance* (Oakland, University of California Press, 1990)

Slack, Paul, *The Impact of the Plague in Tudor and Stuart England* (Oxford, Clarendon Press, 1985)

Slavin, Philip, *Bread and Ale for the Brethren: The Provisioning of Norwich Cathedral Priory 1260–1536* (Hatfield, University of Hertfordshire Press, 2012)

Spufford, Margaret, *Contrasting Communities: English Villagers in the Sixteenth and Seventeenth Centuries* (Cambridge, Cambridge University Press, 1974)

—, *The Great Reclothing of Rural England: Petty Chapmen and their Wares in the Seventeenth Century* (London, Hambledon Press, 1984)

—, *Small Books and Pleasant Histories: Popular Fiction and Its Readership in Seventeenth-century England* (Cambridge, Cambridge University Press, 1981)

Stern, Elizabeth, 'Peckover and Gallyard, Two Sixteenth-century Norfolk Tailors', in *Costume* vol. 15 (London, The Costume Society, 1981)

Stow, John, *A Survey of London* (London, 1598)

Stubbes, Philip, *The Anatomie of Abuses* (London, 1583)

Tasso, Torquato, *The Householders Philosophie* (London, 1588)

Taylor, John, *In Praise of Cleane Linen* (London, 1624)

Thirsk, Joan (ed.), *Agricultural Change: Policy and Practice 1500–1750* (Cambridge, Cambridge University Press, 1990)

—, *Food in Early Modern England* (London, Hambledon Continuum, 2007)

Thomas, Keith, *The Ends of Life: Roads to Fulfilment in Early Modern England* (Oxford, Oxford University Press, 2009)

Tilney, Edmund, *The Flower of Friendship* (London, 1568)

Tittler, Robert, *The Face of the City: Civic Portraiture and Civic Identity in Early Modern England* (Manchester, Manchester University Press, 2007)

—, *Portraits, Painters, and Publics in Provincial England 1540–1640* (Oxford, Oxford University Press, 2012)

—, *Townspeople and Nation: English Urban Experiences 1540–1640* (Stanford, Stanford University Press, 2001)

Tusser, Thomas, *Five Hundreth Pointes of Good Husbandrie* (London, 1573)

—, *A Hundreth Good Pointes of Husbandrie* (London, 1557)

Tymms, Samuel (ed.), *Wills and Inventories from the Registers of the Commissary of Bury St Edmunds and the Archdeacon of Sudbury* (New York and London, AMS Press, 1968)

Unger, Richard W., *Beer in the Middle Ages and the Renaissance* (Philadelphia, University of Pennsylvania, 2004)

Vanes, Jean (ed.), *The Overseas Trade of Bristol in the Sixteenth Century* (Bristol, Bristol Record Society, 1979)

Vanes, Jean, *Education and Apprenticeship in Sixteenth-century Bristol* (Bristol Branch of the Historical Association, Local History Pamphlets, 1981)

Vicary, Thomas, *The Englishman's Treasurie* (London, 1587)

Vincent, Susan, *Dressing the Elite: Clothes in Early Modern England* (Oxford, Berg, 2003)

Walsham, Alexandra, *Providence in Early Modern England* (Oxford, Oxford University Press, 1999)

Walter, John, and Roger Schofield (eds.), *Famine, Disease and the Social Order in Early Modern Society* (Cambridge, Cambridge University Press, 1989)

Watt, Tessa, *Cheap Print and Popular Piety 1550–1640* (Cambridge, Cambridge University Press, 1991)

Webb, John (ed.), *Poor Relief in Elizabethan Ipswich* (Ipswich, Suffolk Record Society, 1966)

—, *The Town Finances of Elizabethan Ipswich* (Woodbridge, Boydell Press, 1996)

Webbe, William, *Discourse of English Poetrie* (London, 1586)

Wheathill, Anne, *A Handfull of Holesome (Though Homelie) Hearbs* (London, 1584)

Wilson, D. R., 'Dancing in the Inns of Court', in *Historical Dance* vol. 2, no. 5 (Dolmetsch Historical Dance Society, 1986/7)

—, 'Performing Gresley Dances', in *Historical Dance* vol. 3, no. 6 (Dolmetsch Historical Dance Society, 1999)

Woodward, Donald, *Men at Work: Labourers and Building Craftsmen in the Towns of Northern England, 1450–1750* (Cambridge, Cambridge University Press, 1995)

Woorde, Wynken de, *Boke of Kervyng* (London, 1508)

Wurzbach, Natascha, *The Rise of the English Street Ballad 1550–1650* (Cambridge, Cambridge University Press, 1990)

Zell, Michael, *Industry in the Countryside: Wealden Society in the Sixteenth Century* (Cambridge, Cambridge University Press, 1994)

Illustration Credits

Acknowledgements

Exploring the Tudor world has not been a solo activity, but rather one shared with friends, colleagues and family, and I owe them an enormous debt. First and foremost my husband, who first introduced me to 'living history' and has journeyed with me in more depth ever since. Also my daughter, who was co-opted from five weeks of age before eventually spreading her wings and finding her own historical interests. I would also like to thank Andy Munro, Shona Rutherford and Joan Garlick for those first excursions into Tudor food and Tudor dance. Over the years Dr Eleanor Lowe, Jackie Warren, Karl Robinson, Natalie Stewart and Jon Emmett have been especially helpful, both intellectually and experimentally. Many of the thoughts, ideas and inspirations behind this book come from them. Hugh Beamish, Paul Hargreaves, Kath Adams, Sigrid Holmwood, Paul Binns, Cathy Flower-Bond, Hannah Miller, Sarah Juniper and Jennifer Worrall have all pointed me in new and interesting directions, for which they have my profound gratitude.

I should also like to extend my thanks to my colleagues within the television industry who have shared and sometimes endured Tudor experiences with me, particularly Peter Ginn, Stuart Elliott, Tim Hodge, Georgina Stewart, Giulia Clark, Tom Pilbeam, Sarah Laker, Felicia Gold, Tom Pinfold and Will Fewkes.

I owe another debt to Jenny Tiramani, Mark Rylance, all the wardrobe, props and other staff and the actors at the Globe Theatre who shared a passion for uncovering the practical realities of Elizabethan theatre and incidentally taught me to love both theatre and Shakespeare.

My thanks too to the staff at the V&A and the Museum of London for access to and discussion about their textile collections. The County Record Offices of Buckinghamshire, Essex, Cheshire and Devon have been generous with both their time and their expertise. Several museums have also allowed me to use their buildings, grounds and collections to experiment and practise different aspects of Tudor Life, adding their own thoughts and interpretations. My thanks extend to The Weald and Downland Museum in West Sussex, St Fagan's Museum of Welsh Folk Life in South Wales, Haddon Hall in Derby-shire, the Mary Rose Trust in Portsmouth, the Chiltern Open Air Museum in Buckinghamshire, the National Trust, English Heritage, and Rufford Country Park in Nottinghamshire.

I am indebted to my wonderful editors at Penguin, without whose work this book would be riddled with far more errors than it is (all of which of course are my own, not theirs).

Lastly, I would like to thank the myriad of historical re-enactors, museum staff, volunteers and students that I have worked alongside whose enthusiasm, willingness to get mucky and open-mindedness have made the last twenty-five years so much fun.

Index